Contents

Acknowledgements

I would like to thank all the many feminists whose activities meant that this book could be written. In particular, I thank those who have debated feminism with me, from the UK Women's Budget Group and End Violence Against Women campaign to the UNESCO gender experts.

The book took shape in the context of the EU Framework Programme, Quing – a context of analysing the quality of gender equality policies across the EU. I thank all Quingers for their contributions to my thinking.

I would like to thank the many people with whom I have discussed these ideas at various stages of their development, including Ulla Björnberg, Myra Marx Ferree, Anita Göransson, Heidi Gottfried, Karin Gottschall, Sue Himmelweit, Agnes Hubert, Liz Kelly, Andrea Krizsán, Ema Lombardo, Barbara Risman, Andrew Sayer, Karen Shire, Clare Short, Sofia Strid, Myria Vassiliadou, Janet Veitch and Linda Woodhead. I would especially like to thank Jo Armstrong, Sue Penna, John Urry and Mieke Verloo for their helpful detailed comments on the whole manuscript.

Finally I would like to thank the Polity team, especially Jonathan Skerrett and the copy-editor, Manuela Tecusan.

The Future of Feminism

The Future of Feminism

Sylvia Walby

polity

First published in 2011 by Polity Press

Polity Press
65 Bridge Street
Cambridge CB2 1UR, UK

Polity Press
350 Main Street
Malden, MA 02148, USA

ISBN-13: 978-0-7456-4756-2
ISBN-13: 978-0-7456-4757-9(pb)

A catalogue record for this book is available from the British Library.

Typeset in 10.5 on 12 pt Plantin
by Servis Filmsetting Ltd, Stockport, Cheshire
Printed and bound in Great Britain by MPG Books Group Limited, Bodmin, Cornwall

The publisher has used its best endeavours to ensure that the URLs for external websites referred to in this book are correct and active at the time of going to press. However, the publisher has no responsibility for the websites and can make no guarantee that a site will remain live or that the content is or will remain appropriate.

Every effort has been made to trace all copyright holders, but if any have been inadvertently overlooked the publisher will be pleased to include any necessary credits in any subsequent reprint or edition.

For further information on Polity, visit our website: www.politybooks.com

1
Introduction

Feminism is not dead. This is not a postfeminist era. Feminism is still vibrant, despite declarations that it is over. Feminism is a success, although many gender inequalities remain. Feminism is taking powerful new forms, which make it unrecognisable to some.

Feminism faces new challenges in new times. As a result of success, feminism now engages with power and with government; yet mainstreaming gender equality into governmental policy produces tensions for feminism. As a result of successful mobilisation, feminist projects intersect with others, creating dilemmas over priorities. The development of neoliberalism, together with increased economic inequalities, de-democratisation, and an environmental crisis, creates the biggest challenge for feminism.

The future of feminism depends on responses to these challenges. There are alternative strategies to address such challenges – with implications for feminism, gender relations and the wider society.

Why Is It Said That Feminism Is Dead?

There have been many attempts to declare that feminism is over; that we are living in the 'aftermath' of feminism (McRobbie 2008); that this is now a 'postfeminist' era (Tasker and Negra 2007); that feminism has been co-opted by neoliberalism (Bumiller 2008; Eisenstein 2009; Fraser 2009); or that feminism is in 'abeyance', surviving minimally in a hostile climate (Taylor 1989; Bagguley 2002; Grey and Sawer 2008).

Many reasons have been proposed as to why feminism should have ended. On one account, feminism would have been defeated by a hostile 'backlash' that opposes, caricatures, misrepresents and ridicules it (Faludi 1991, 1992). On another, feminism would have faded away, becoming irrelevant in a new, post-patriarchal era, since it would have met its goals, so there would no longer be any need for it. Feminism would have been replaced by new gender projects, by 'girl power' and the new raunch culture (McRobbie 2008) – and these alternative gender projects are labelled 'postfeminist' (Tasker and Negra 2007). The explanations for the purported demise of feminism range from hostile backlash to its incorporation into postfeminist or neoliberal projects.

Feminism Is Alive and Vibrant

But feminism is not dead; rather it is alive and vibrant. Today a very wide range of activities designed to reduce gender inequality exists. Projects for gender equality extend across the domains of economy, polity and violence, as well as across civil society. They are highly varied, depending on social location. Feminism is local, national, European and international, and influenced by the global horizon.

Feminism is, however, less visible than before. This is partly because projects to reduce gender inequality less often label themselves as 'feminist', and partly because the form that feminism takes has been changing beyond recognition. Projects for gender equality are less likely to call themselves feminist when they exist in alliance or coalition with other social forces; they adopt instead a more generic terminology concerning equality, justice and rights. There is also pressure not to use a term that has been criticised, even stigmatised. New forms of feminism have emerged that no longer take the form of a 'traditional' social movement, being institutionalised instead in civil society and in the state. These new institutionalised forms are less recognisable as feminist by those who are accustomed to thinking of feminism as merely visible protest.

What Is Feminism?

There are different ways of approaching a definition of feminism. These include the self-definition of individuals, groups or projects as feminist; treating 'reducing gender inequality' as equivalent to feminist; and treating 'promoting the interests of women' as equivalent to feminist.

Self-definition is perhaps the most common approach. A person or project is feminist if they say they are feminist. This approach is consistent with the traditions of the early second wave women's movement in that it is based on a person's own experience. However, there are some difficulties here. The term 'feminist' is contentious – indeed even stigmatised. 'Feminism' is a signifier of something very particular and comes with additional meanings attached, which many seek to avoid. It has acquired connotations of separatism, extremism, men-avoiding lesbianism. This narrowing of the term is partly a product of a hostile opposition, in which feminism is caricatured and ridiculed in segments of the media. The phenomenon is hardly new ('bra-burning' has long been used as an adjective linked to feminism in this way).

This stigmatising of the term 'feminism' had its effects. It has led to the development of the phenomenon of the person who states 'I'm not a feminist but . . .', where the 'but' is followed by an endorsement of goals that are usually thought of as feminist, such as equal pay for equal work and the elimination of male violence against women. As a consequence, other terminology has developed that can be used to signify 'feminist' without resorting to the 'f word' (Redfern and Aune 2010), such as 'gender equality', 'equality', 'equal opportunities' and 'diversity'. There is a further issue concerning the positioning of anti-sexist men in relation to feminism. Even if such men support, and contribute to, feminist goals and projects, there is a question as to whether or not they can be described as 'feminist' on the conventional approach, since men do not usually experience inequality as a result of their gender.

An alternative approach to the definition of feminism is to consider people and projects that pursue the goal of reducing gender inequality to be feminist. This does away with the need for self-definition and for direct experience of gender inequality. There are many people and projects which declare that they seek to reduce gender inequality but do not normally use the label 'feminist'. There are feminists who do not like the connotations that have been attached to the term, but actively support the goals. For example, women who state 'I am not a feminist but . . .' do support feminist goals that would be included by using this alternative approach to definition. Then there are men who actively support the goal of reducing gender inequality but hesitate at adopting the term, not least because they do not want to claim the status of victims of gender inequality. They, too, would be included under this wider definition. There are groups and projects at the intersection of multiple inequalities, and projects in which feminism and the reduction of gender inequality are just one strand, but not the primary one. It is not uncommon for projects and organisations that draw not only on feminism but also on other justice projects not to define themselves as feminist. Contemporary analysis and practice has promoted the development of intersectionality in practice and theory (see chapter 7). One of the consequences of such alliances and coalitions is that projects may not be named as feminist even when they have feminist goals. Coalitions of intersecting projects often use terms other than feminist, for example 'gender equality', or even just 'equality'. An example is that of trade unions that work towards equal pay, better promotion prospects, fair treatment, less harassment, and better regulation of working time – to be achieved for instance through maternity, paternity and parental leave – but for which feminism is not a primary purpose. Trade unions can contribute to the reduction of gender inequality; and, if they make this an important part of their activities, they would be included under the wider definition here. This second approach still requires a definition of gender inequality, which is itself subject to contesting approaches.

The goal of 'reducing gender inequality' offers a narrower definition of feminism than does a goal that extends to 'advancing the interests of women'. There are significant numbers of women's organisations which do not have the goal of 'reducing gender inequality', but rather of 'advancing the interests of women'. In any empirical study of feminism these groups are important, not least because they have so many members. The wider definition is particularly in use in the global South. In the global North, several national and international coalitions and umbrella groups include women's organisations that pursue the interests of women as they see them, but are not focused on reducing gender inequality. The approach to the domestic is often what underlies this distinction between women's organisations. In some forms of feminism, the emancipation of women from the domestic sphere, so that they can enter the public sphere and gain better access to education, employment and political representation, is a goal in itself. In other strategies to promote the interests of women, the protection and enhancement of their position in the domestic sphere, especially in domestic care work, is treated as an important objective. While some would not include this objective as feminist, others would. On the one hand, it can be considered to fall outside feminism because, even though it aims to improve the position of women, it also has a tendency to entrench existing gender divisions, which are unequal (Young 1990; Brown 1995). On the other hand, it can be considered feminist in at least two ways. One is to include, within the concept of equality, the notion of equal valuation of different contributions or the promotion of the value of domestic care work, regarded as part of a maternalist feminist strategy (Koven and Michel 1990). A second way is to see this objective as a stepping stone along a route designed to improve the condition of women's lives that is likely to lead eventually towards gender equality – that is, to see it as the beginning of a strategy of 'transformation' (Fraser 1997; Rees 1998), for example, as the beginning of a development of the welfare state that can ultimately lead to wide-ranging changes in the gender division of labour (Bock and Thane 1991; Skocpol 1995). The development of one form of political practice or another depends on the social context, in particular the form of the gender regime. Defence of women's space in the home is more likely to be a progressive force for women under a domestic gender regime than under a public gender regime when most women do not derive their livelihoods from unpaid domestic labour. In the contemporary UK, and in most of the EU and US, most, though not all, women of working age derive a significant part of their livelihood from waged labour, since the transformation from the domestic to public gender regime is significantly advanced. This is not the case in the global South, where the main type of gender regime in many (though not all) countries is domestic (see chapter 6).

The definition of feminism in this book is inclusive. It includes some projects that do not define themselves as feminist, but nonetheless share feminist goals. It is focused on the pursuit of the goal of gender equality by individuals, groups, projects and governmental programmes, but it expands so as to encompass the wider goal of the advancement of women, on the grounds that both these goals require the project of the transformation of gender relations before they can be achieved. Projects that potentially contribute to this transformation are included in this book as 'feminist', even if their immediate goals appear to be more limited.

Is Feminism Global, Transnational or National?

Feminism takes different forms in different places, with diverse priorities and strategies; but there are major commonalities despite the variations. There is a question as to whether the commonalities are sufficiently great for it to be appropriate to write of global feminism – or, more modestly, of 'transnational' feminism – or whether it is better to restrict the focus to nationally or locally specific forms.

Since feminism transcends national borders, not least by offering exchanges of ideas and practices across frontiers, the concept of 'transnational' feminism can be deployed (Sperling, Ferree and Risman 2001). Further, there are important forms of feminist interventions at the level of the European Union, feminism thus crossing conventional borders between states within this polity.

The disadvantage of the phrase 'global feminism' is that it can make less visible important distinctions, and in particular it may elevate inappropriately the practices of those in dominant countries. However, there are important forms of feminist intervention at the level of the UN, both in the inter-governmental forums of its various agencies and also in the NGO forums that are attached to major UN conferences – such as the 1995 UN conference on women in Beijing, which produced the Platform for Action and the five and ten yearly reviews of the Platform in New York. Insofar as the UN is an instance of a global phenomenon, some aspects of feminism are global; but otherwise the term 'global' is used only with caution. The phrase 'global feminism' is restricted to those projects that utilise the UN as a location, either within UN bodies or where there are coalitions of NGOs that engage in its varied institutions. In other instances, the qualifier 'transnational' is more appropriate; in others, there is more specific reference to EU, national or local forms.

Projects, Governmental Programmes and Social Formations

A distinction is made between 'projects', 'governmental programmes' and 'social formations'. While each is a set of ideas, practices and institutions, projects are the least institutionalised, social formations the most, and governmental programmes fall in between (for more details, see Walby 2009). The concept of 'project' is particularly important in understanding contemporary feminism.

A 'project' is a set of processes and practices in civil society that create new meanings and social goals, drawing on a range of rhetorical and material resources. Projects are typically fluid and dynamic, as they attempt social change. Civil society is an arena of contesting projects. The concept of 'civil society' (drawing on Gramsci) is preferred to that of 'culture', since it does not assume homogeneity, stability or consensus, in contrast to the concept of 'culture', which often does. 'Project' is a wider concept than 'social movement', since it can include groups and practices that are relatively stabilised and institutionalised, as well as ones that are more fluid and spontaneous. Feminism is more usually a project than a social movement in the UK, EU and US today. Many non-governmental organisations (NGOs) are active parts of civil society, but only a few would fall within the narrower concept of a social movement.

A 'governmental programme' is the set of policies that a government and its policy machineries pursue and that are institutionalised in governmental institutions, departments and ministries. In comparison with projects in civil society, governmental programmes are much better resourced; they have institutional, legal and material means to pursue their goals. Many, but far from all, projects aspire to become governmental programmes in order to be more deeply institutionalised in the social formation. While feminism is usually a project, it is coming to be increasingly embedded in governmental programmes.

The 'social formation' is constituted by the institutionalised practices in the four domains of economy, polity, violence and civil society. These institutional formations tend to be relatively stable over long periods of time, though there can be both gradual and sudden changes. In some writers, the concept of 'social formation' is replaced by that of 'society'. 'Social formation' is used in preference to 'society' because this concept does not assume that the boundaries of economy, polity, violence and civil society neatly map onto to each other in the same geographical space. Projects and governmental programmes usually seek to change the social formation. Long-lasting governmental programmes are often successful in this goal.

Gender Regimes

Gender regimes are systems of gender relations. The different aspects of gender relations are interconnected and form a system, named here a 'gender regime'. The forms of gender relations in the economy, polity, violence and civil society are interconnected in the sense that a change in gender relations in one of these institutional domains is likely to entail a change in gender relations in other domains. Gender regimes take different forms. The most important distinction is that between domestic and public forms of gender regime. Different varieties of the public gender regime can be found, including neoliberal and social democratic varieties (see chapter 6;

also Walby 2009). Struggles over the form of gender regime are an important aspect of feminist politics.

Neoliberalism and Social Democracy

Neoliberalism is characterised by attempts to limit the regulation of capital and markets in the economy, which thereby increase inequality and reduce the depth of democracy. Social democracy, by comparison, is characterised by attempts to deepen democracy so as to regulate capital, markets and violence in the interests of the majority of the population.

Neoliberalism and social democracy have been, variously, projects, governmental programmes and social formations at different times and in different places. There has often been a development from project to governmental programme to social formation, as the set of ideas, practices and institutions becomes more powerful and more deeply sedimented.

Neoliberalism and social democracy are two of the most important varieties of modernity: the contestation between them has marked the last hundred years of history in Europe and North America. There are other varieties, some of which were important historically while others appear to be of emerging significance – for example, fascism, state capitalism and communism (see chapter 6; also Walby 2009).

History of Feminist Waves

While this book focuses on contemporary and future feminism, there has been a long history of feminist activity, in a series of feminist waves. 'First-wave' feminism was a broad and deep project, extending from around 1850 to the winning of suffrage around 1920 in several countries in the 'West' (for example, 1918/1928 in the UK; 1920 in the US). While it is often remembered as winning the right to vote, this wave in fact addressed a wide range of issues, from employment and education to prostitution and married women's right to legal personhood (Strachey 1979; Banks 1981; Spender 1983; Drake 1984; Walby 1986, 1990; Skocpol 1995). Twentieth-century feminism was not only a western project; it was also part of nationalist campaigns for de-colonisation that often resulted in simultaneous suffrage for men and women at the moment of independence and in access to education for girls (Jayawardena 1986). There are important similarities in the development of first- and second-wave feminism, despite their different contexts. The issues addressed have striking similarities, including access to good jobs (removal of barriers to top jobs); access to governmental power via democratic processes (presence in parliament); reduction of violence against women (legal entitlements to leave violent husbands); decrease in the sexual exploitation of women (against coercive prostitution). Both waves of feminism had a transnational reach, making connections around the world. Both waves used a range of organisational forms, including grassroots mobilisations in demonstrations, and local and national voluntary associations; but only the second wave succeeded in establishing units that promoted feminist goals inside government.

New Challenges for Feminism

Although feminism has successfully achieved some, though not all, of its goals, new challenges have emerged. There are three in particular: mainstreaming, as feminism engages with government; the intersection with allies and competing forces; and the intensification of the neoliberal context.

Engagement with Power: Gender Mainstreaming

Feminism faces challenges as a result of its successes. Feminist projects are becoming embedded in institutions of civil society and of the state and are being placed on the mainstream agenda of government. This is no separatist embrace of victimhood, protest or opposition. The success raises dilemmas of choice among priorities, of how feminism engages with government, with the mainstream institutions of power. Significant parts of contemporary feminism have gone beyond protest, to engagement with and potential deployment of power.

Such mainstreaming of gender equality projects raises its own set of dilemmas. In the tension between feminism and the mainstream, does the feminist project become integrated in a way that assimilates it to the status quo, or does it colonise, hybridise or mutually adapt with and change the mainstream? This tension between feminism and the mainstream is potentially productive for both, although it can, in some circumstances, lead to the fading of feminism as a distinctive force.

The 'mainstream' with which feminism engages takes multiple forms itself. It includes governmental programmes rooted in different ministries and departments, for example programmes for economic growth, crime reduction and health promotion. It can include mainstream projects, for example to achieve sustainable relations with the environment, so as not to overheat the planet. At the points of overlap there are opportunities for the inclusion and promotion of feminist goals within these mainstream agendas. These programmes and projects may be modified by feminism; both feminist and mainstream projects may mutually adapt, though in an asymmetrical fashion.

While gender mainstreaming has often been presented as a choice between the maintenance of the purity of separatist feminist projects and integration into the mainstream with a loss of all that is distinctive, there is an alternative approach. The most successful approach to gender mainstreaming involves maintaining a core of distinctive expertise and specialist politics while simultaneously dispersing such feminist expertise into all policy areas and into the work of normal policy actors. This dual approach to gender mainstreaming does produce tensions, but these can be productive.

Engagement with Intersecting Projects

A further challenge consequent upon feminist success is how best to engage with diverse political projects. Feminism has many potential allies with perceived interests in overlapping projects, and it also faces enemies and hostile projects. There are choices as to alternatives in these alliances and coalitions, in their priorities and in the rhetorical framing through which they are organised. The intersection of feminist projects with other political projects may involve relations of alliance or coalition. It can lead to the revision of existing projects or to the creation of new hybrid ones. These intersections will often involve negotiation over the priorities of the project that constitutes the outcome.

Feminism intersects with the green or environmental agenda. There are points of overlap among feminist and green goals that, potentially, are mutually supportive. Like feminism, this is a project that was once considered to be outside the mainstream, but in recent years has become increasingly incorporated into government programmes, albeit usually at the margins.

Feminism intersects with the justice projects of 'human rights' and of 'social democracy'. Human rights have become more important as globalisation has proceeded, but they tend to form a relatively thin project of minimum standards. Social democracy offers a deeper analysis of the causes and remedies of global injustice, but has become weakened under globalisation and the neoliberal turn. Feminist goals have been expressed in terms of each of these justice frameworks, with different implications for how they are taken forward.

These projects have various degrees of success in engaging with the powerful forces of neoliberalism, financialisation, militarisation and fundamentalism. Feminism's engagement with these projects has implications not only for the form and success of feminist projects, but also for the potential success of these larger projects. Engagement with other projects involves not only a choice of alternatives, but also the potential synthesis of these projects into a new justice project, which should resonate even more widely. Feminism has much to offer to this potential synthesis. Future prospects are further discussed in chapter 7.

Neoliberalism and the Future

The intensification of neoliberalism over the last thirty years or so is a challenge for feminism. Neoliberalism entails increasing inequalities, especially in the economy, as well as processes of de-democratisation, as the democratic state is replaced by market principles in the organisation of major services. The neoliberal under-regulation of finance gives rise to periodic asset price bubbles, financial crises, and the expropriation of the taxpayer to bail out the banks and financial institutions that are 'too big to fail' (Krugman 2008; Stiglitz 2006; Walby 2009). The rise in inequalities and the shrinking of democratic spaces makes for a more difficult environment for the operation of feminism, which attempts to reduce inequalities and to deepen democratic governance.

It is possible that the financial crisis of 2008, with its ongoing repercussions on economies and societies, will lead to a tipping point away from neoliberalism. This might mean a turn towards social democracy and the democratic regulation of finance. However, it might also be a tipping point away from neoliberalism to fundamentalism, xenophobia and protectionism. Or the crisis may merely lead to the intensification of neoliberalism.

Feminist projects have an important contribution to make to the construction of alternative futures. They have significance not only for the form of gender regime, but also for the form of capitalism and of the environmental crisis.

Content of the Present Book

Chapter 2 explores and refutes the arguments that feminism is dead, has disappeared or has become irrelevant. It examines the backlash against feminism, attempts to incorporate feminism in postfeminist forms and men's projects that attack maternalist feminism. It introduces the challenges that the neoliberal turn raise for feminism.

Chapter 3 identifies the range of activities in which contemporary feminism is engaged. Current feminist issues include not only those related to culture, sexuality and recognition, but also those related to the economy, to redistribution, equality, power and violence. The vibrancy of engagement with issues of equality in the economy is too often ignored in the literature on feminism. While varying with location, many feminist issues cross national boundaries.

Chapter 4 examines the new organisational forms that contemporary feminism is taking. Feminism is not only a social movement, but is now also deeply institutionalised, both in civil society and in the state. It is a mistake to imagine that feminism is dead because women are not demonstrating in the streets. New forms of feminism may not be very visible, but they are at least as effective as the old ones. Women are now inside many major decision-making institutions, from parliament to the police, though not as frequently as men. New forms of feminist politics involve constant exchange between state and civil society, new forms of coalition and alliance.

Chapter 5 discusses the challenge for feminism of its relationship with mainstream power, as feminism moves beyond autonomous activities and institution building. It discusses the productive tensions generated as feminism is mainstreamed – no longer separatist, but not fully assimilated or integrated; changing the mainstream and becoming changed by it in the process.

Chapter 6 situates feminist projects within the context of systems of inequality – within the gender and class regimes that structure women's lives, and within the developing environmental catastrophe that affects everyone. The chapter clarifies the meaning of 'gender regime' and identifies the variety of forms that it can take, and thus the different opportunities that are open to women. By providing an account of the causes of gender inequality and of its changing forms, it offers the conceptual and theoretical tools to understand the issues of gender inequality that feminism addresses. It analyses the changing forms of capitalism, so as to demonstrate the ways in which feminism has potential implications for these wider social relations. It offers an account of the environmental crisis of global warming.

Chapter 7 explores the challenges faced by feminism as it interacts with other projects. It addresses in particular the projects of economic growth, environmentalism, human rights and social democracy. These intersections provide the context for the development of alliances and coalitions with other social forces, as well as for the production of newly emergent projects.

The conclusion, chapter 8, discusses the implications of the present analysis for the future of feminism. Feminism is not dead or in abeyance, but alive and engaged; its activities and projects address all major areas of social life; feminism is exploring its new position in relation to mainstream power, and is producing new tensions and solutions. There are potential syntheses of feminism with other projects, including those of economic growth, environmentalism, human rights and social democracy, with implications for these projects and for the wider society. However, there are major threats of neoliberalism, xenophobic protectionism, militarism and environmental catastrophe, which may mean that feminism has little effect. Alternative scenarios are described and their likelihood in the future is assessed.

2
Contesting Feminism

Introduction

Feminism is intrinsically controversial. Feminist contestation of established institutions and practices of power leads to critical responses. There are many ways in which the feminist project is itself contested in turn, both directly and indirectly. Some have argued that, as a consequence, feminism is dead – or at least transformed into something else, which is not really feminist. Here it is argued that feminism is alive and well.

It is possible to distinguish between various ways of contesting feminism. These include: 'backlash' that seeks to re-domesticate women; attacks on the gains of maternalist feminism; the prioritisation of diversity over inequality; co-option into postfeminism by transforming feminist demands for sexual liberation into raunch culture; incorporation by neoliberalism; a hostile de-democratising context. These forms of contestation vary according to whether they are direct attacks, more subtle contestations of specific kinds of feminist gains, or strategies of incorporation into some other phenomenon.

Backlash

There has been direct opposition to feminism and its successes, in a process known as 'backlash' (Faludi 1991, 1992; Walby 1988, 1993). Opposition to feminism is not new; it can be found in many historical instances. It may take the form of violence, as against the earlier suffragette movement (Morrell 1981), harassment against women who have entered jobs previously monopolised by men (Stanko 1988), or misrepresentation, caricature and ridicule in the press (Faludi 1991, 1992). Men are not the only actors, but they are engaged in opposition to feminism more often than women (Kimmel 1987). This can involve the promotion of projects that are constructed as if they were rivals and alternatives to feminism (whether or not this is actually the case) – for example, feminism is represented as if it were incompatible with a good upbringing for children (on the view that mothers need to stay at home) or with economic growth (on the view that equal opportunities procedures are expensive, time-consuming and detrimental to a firm's well-being).

Faludi's (1991, 1992) analysis of the backlash against feminism focuses on attempts to re-domesticate women, to turn back the clock to arrangements in which women focus on unpaid domestic care work and have a sexual partner for life. She recounts misleading stories in the press, which suggest that women with high levels of education will not be able to marry, that divorce has a very substantial negative impact on women's standard of living, that women who delay having children to pursue careers will not be able to have children later because they will have become infertile, and that women's mental health is worse among career women than among housewives; and she also points out that no corrections or retractions were made when evidence contesting these stories was made available.

Walter (2010) argues that one of the forms of contemporary opposition to feminism, 'the return of sexism', invokes biological determinism. This is a traditional form of opposition to feminism that resorts to biology, a revitalised version of biological determinism in which bodies and hormones are seen as more important than culture in the shaping of gender relations.

The response to feminism varies significantly according to location. Backlash takes different forms in different countries and at different times; that in the US is different from that in Europe, and again different from the diversity of responses in the global South. The varying form of the gender regime, the varying position in relation to the global core countries, and the varying post-colonial histories are important in generating these variations.

One of the fiercest forms of backlash against feminism is that of fundamentalism. In this cluster of phenomena, opposition to feminism usually takes the form of praising the domesticity of women and of locating it within some 'eternal truth' – often, but not always, religious, and often accompanied by notions of a 'natural' place for women. The domesticity of women is positioned as a form of purity that is of benefit not only to women but to the whole community to which they belong (for example nation, ethnicity or religion). Fundamentalist concerns for the purity of women are often bound up with parallel concerns for the purity of the group in relation to its collective identity as, for example a nation, ethnic group or religion (Marty and Scott 1993; Moghadam 1994).

A fundamentalist backlash against advances made by women towards gender equality has occurred in a wide variety of settings, though these often share the feature of rapid and uneven change. While much of the discussion of fundamentalism centres on particular variants of Islam – for example, the Taliban in Afghanistan – fundamentalism can be found in most of the major world religions in some part of the world today. For example, in the US, fundamentalist responses to feminism can be found in some Protestant sects and in some parts of the Republican Party. Key issues here are often focused on sexuality and reproduction, including opposition to abortion and homosexuality. Fundamentalism is less commonly found in contemporary Europe, though, of course, it has a historical presence there from the fascist period in the 1930s and, importantly, it can be found in some current versions of Catholicism such as the rejection of divorce, of non-marital sexuality, of contraception and of abortion.

The financial crisis generated by neoliberalism, which continues to generate economic instability and recession, has the potential to give rise to a protectionist and xenophobic response in some countries. This provides a context in which fundamentalism may become more widespread.

While direct opposition to feminism through the invocation of biological determinism and domesticity are important, there are other forms of opposition to feminism.

Attacks on the Gains of Maternalist Feminism

Another form of opposition to feminism draws on contemporary public feminism's claim for the equal treatment of men and women and turns it into an instrument of attack against maternalist feminism. Maternalist feminism is a form of feminism that focuses on improving the condition of women as mothers. This opposition project seeks to increase men's influence by way of contesting the privileging of women as mothers.

One example of this contestation is the demand for fathers to have equal legal rights with mothers over the care and custody of children after separation and divorce. This is a rejection of the previous assumption that mothers are the best carers and should be routinely awarded custody of children in these circumstances. Particular contestations have taken place where the father has been violent towards the mother, yet still demanded access to or custody of the children following divorce or separation (Hester and Radford 1996). The men's articulation of their concerns focuses here on children; the assertion of men's position in relation to their partner is expressed through a conflict over children (Eriksson and Hester 2001). This is a critique of the privileges that maternalist feminism has endorsed for women and a challenge to the entitlements of mothers – a challenge that utilises the public feminist discourse of 'equal treatment'. In a related manner, the discourse and practice of 'children's rights' have sometimes been used to contest women's rights, even though at other times they act in alignment with these rights (for example in combating child poverty).

This 'men's rights' project is not an attempt to re-domesticate women. In other words, this form of opposition to feminism does not involve a push back to a domestic gender regime, but rather challenges gender relations within the public gender regime. It involves an acceptance of the public gender regime, and an attempt to increase their own influence by using the discourse and practices of equal treatment, borrowed from public feminism, against maternalist feminism and against the privileging of women as mothers. It uses the success of contemporary feminism in establishing 'equal treatment' as an appropriate practice within the mainstream of public life against the older forms of success of maternalist feminism in establishing privileges for women as mothers. This contestation requires a new sophistication in determining just what would count as 'equal treatment' in a context where women are still – typically, but far from always – the main carer. Chapter 6 will provide a fuller discussion of the implications, for gender politics, of changes in the form of gender regime, from domestic to public.

Diversity rather than Equality

A further challenge to the feminist project arises from within the project itself. The source is the concern to ensure that the differences between women are adequately addressed within feminism. This issue has been formulated most sharply in relation to ethnicity, yet it is more general – it includes matters at the intersection of gender with age, disability, religion/faith, sexual orientation and social class; indeed there is a long-standing problem of the relation between gender and class. While this concern might be regarded as leading to the expansion of the feminist project so that it adequately engages with the additional issues that emerge at these intersections, it has in some instances led to divisions that have had destructive effects (Hartmann 1976; Crenshaw 1991; Phoenix and Pattynama 2006).

The concept of equality itself is subjected to critique from the perspective of diversity. There is a potential pluralisation of the competing standards against which equality may be assessed. The solution of proposing an equal valuation of different contributions is itself fraught with difficulties. One response to the alternative notions of equality as sameness and equality as the equal valuation of different contributions is that equality can only be achieved if there is a transformation, both of social practices and of the standards against which equality is assessed (Fraser 1997; Rees 1998).

The move towards the valorisation of difference has sometimes been made at the expense of the focus on equality. Most social divisions contain both inequality and difference, since there is usually some divergence in values between the dominant and the oppressed group. However, while some analysis engages appropriately with the duality of these complex inequalities, there is also sometimes a tendency towards the prioritisation of the analysis of difference over inequality. As Felski (1997) notes, this prioritisation can turn into the 'doxa of difference'. This occurs for example where there is a challenge to the standard against which equality is judged; rather than exploring and refining this standard, so that it may be relevant to a wider range of circumstances, there is instead a rejection of a single standard and its replacement with the vacuity of multiple standards. As the Office for National Statistics (2007) notes in its analysis of the statistics of equality and in its critique of the *Equalities Review* (2007) at the foundation of the Equality and Human Rights Commission, it is hard to measure equality if difference is prioritised.

There has been a tendency towards loss of confidence in the project of justice in the face of the ostensibly competing standards associated with the valorisation of difference at the expense of equality, with the drive to anti-essentialism, and with the loss of focus on systems of power. While the challenge to inappropriate abstractions and simplifications, and their replacement by others, constitute a useful analytic move, they have sometimes led to a challenge to abstractions and simplifications altogether, as in many of the critiques of 'essentialism' (Braidotti 1994). It is important to retain the practice of abstraction in order to place what is most significant at the centre of analytic attention (Sayer 1997; Conaghan 2000).

The intersection of gender inequality with other inequalities is a challenge for feminism that is currently being addressed. Various ways forward have been proposed. These will be discussed in chapter 7, which deals with intersections with feminism.

Postfeminism?

A further form of opposition to feminism is more indirect. Feminism can also be incorporated. The world is declared post-patriarchal and postfeminist. There is an attempt to transform the feminist challenge to inegalitarian forms of sexual practice into an embrace of commercialised forms of sexuality. This is the terrain of postfeminism. A key issue in the debates here is where to draw the boundary between a new form of feminism, a third wave feminism, and postfeminism (as opposed to feminism). The substantive focus is on sexuality and popular culture, in particular raunch culture. The question is whether these sexual and cultural practices are an extension of forms of feminism, or merely a variant of sexist culture. Is this a 'third-wave' feminism or postfeminism?

Third-wave feminism is a label attached to the contemporary feminism of young women, which defines itself as different from previous forms (Heywood 2005; Gillis, Howe and Munford 2007). The celebration of sexuality, of its explicit and free exploration, is considered by some to be central to this form of feminism (Shugart, Egley Waggoner and O'Brien Hallstein 2001; Kinser 2004; Gillis, Howe and Munford 2007). This feminism from a new young generation is considered to invoke 'girl power' or 'grrrl' style, as a positive and effective assertion of the self (Garrison 2000). It is positioned as a rejection of what is alleged to be the victim-centred feminism of the second wave (Henry 2004). This feminism comes in various forms, inflected by different cultures and circumstances (Springer 2002).

However, this celebration of individual agency in general and of raunch culture in particular has been contested (Kinser 2004). The individualism depoliticises, 'focusing on personal choices rather than political action' (Showden 2009: 172). Such understandings of the world can be a trap, merely recapitulating a denial of gender inequality and reifying dominant codes of meaning (Shugart, Egley Waggoner and O'Brien Hallstein 2001). This sexualisation of women in their reconstruction as 'babes', pole-dancers, lap-dancers and prostitutes can be seen as offering limited options rather than sexually liberating choices (Walter 2010). The preoccupation with beauty can be understood as a backlash against feminism: 'We are in the midst of a violent backlash against feminism that uses images of female beauty as a political weapon against women's advancement' (Wolf 1991: 10). The decrease in old forms of control over sexuality is replaced by new ones, through pornography (Dines 2010). Raunch culture, while purportedly offering sexual liberation, merely commercialises women as objects, denying them the full expression of sexuality through mutuality (Levy 2006). Feminism in all its waves has supported innovation and experimentation in forms of intimacy; this is not new or unique to contemporary feminism (Faderman 1981; Spender 1983; Rowbotham 1997).

This celebration of agency and raunch culture can be understood as an attempt to reincorporate feminism through the declaration of postfeminism. Here feminism is denied, in a complex manoeuvre that both recognises the history of feminism and declares it to be over, because it was successful and hence it is transmuted into new forms of activity – postfeminism. Postfeminism does not deny that there was once feminism, and indeed that it was once needed. However, it is a stance which assumes that the most important battles have been won and that it is time to celebrate, not contest, the new forms of gender relations. Postfeminism is seen as an ironic reincorporation of feminism in a postmodern moment (Tasker and Negra 2007; McRobbie 2008). It is understood as an anti-foundationalist move, which might have the potential to open up feminist debates (Brooks 1997; Dean 2010), but this, in its critical stance towards the concept of 'women', carries risks that undermine feminist projects, which require such a subject (Conaghan 2000).

But is 'postfeminism' the best concept for understanding young women's increased engagement in commercialised forms of sexuality? An alternative approach is to situate these engagements with feminism in the context of changes in the gender regime. It is more useful to see these developments as a new form of opposition to progressive gender relations. This is not an attempt to re-domesticate women (of the kind that occurs in 'backlash'), but rather a move within a public gender regime, the better to exploit women in the public gender regime, by supporting its exploitative neoliberal rather than its progressive social democratic form. It is important to avoid the simplicity of a binary division between domesticating women and celebrating any engagement in sexuality. Rather the mode of engagement in a non-domesticated sexuality is the issue. Raunch culture is bound up with the neoliberal turn, with its commercialised and competitive approach to intimacy. The alternative social democratic form is based on mutuality and equality. Hence a celebration of innovation and experimentation in intimacy and sexuality, in a context of mutualism and equality, is aligned with feminism, while competitive commercialised sex is not. It is important to understand the different forms of the public gender regime in order to understand the relationship between intimacy and feminism.

Feminism and the Neoliberal Turn

Current forms of feminism and of its opposition are affected by wider changes in the nature of social relations, including the development of neoliberalism. The neoliberal turn has potentially diverse implications for feminism. Some have argued that feminism is in danger of being incorporated by neoliberalism (Bumiller 2008; Eisenstein 2009; Fraser 2009). By contrast, it can be argued that neoliberalism produces a context that is hostile to feminism because of increases in economic inequality and in processes of de-democratisation.

Neoliberalism started as a project, which became a governmental programme, then an institutionalised social formation. It aims to reduce democratic state interventions in the economy and to achieve governance through market mechanisms. In practice, this usually entails an increase in economic inequality and a process of de-democratisation, as fewer aspects of social life are governed by the democratic state. The reduction in democratic state interventions often means greater power to capital, which is not the same as the market. The apparent desire for a small state is rarely achieved, since there is usually an increase in the deployment and regulation of violence by the state in the military, security and criminal justice systems (Harvey 2005; Wacquant 2009; Walby 2009). Despite its contradictions, the neoliberal project has become powerfully institutionalised in governmental programmes and, increasingly, in social formations.

Has neoliberalism incorporated feminism? Fraser argues that feminism is complicit with, and legitimating of, neoliberalism. She claims that neoliberalism has changed the meaning of feminism: 'neoliberalism resignified the feminist critique of androcentrism' (Fraser 2009: 109). On the basis of such claims made by neoliberals (who have resignified the meaning of feminism), Fraser argues that feminism legitimates neoliberalism. She states that 'feminism has unwittingly provided a key ingredient of the new spirit of neoliberalism' (110), in that 'utopian desires found a second life as feeling currents that legitimated the transition to a new form of capitalism: post-Fordist, transnational, neoliberal' (99). It seems rather odd to blame feminism for the representation of feminism that neoliberals seek to project. Fraser appears to be more interested in what non-feminists make out feminism to be than in what feminists actually do. She presents no evidence about any of the activities of contemporary feminists, let alone any evidence of any feminist group welcoming neoliberalism.

Eisenstein's (2009) argument about the link between feminism and neoliberalism has some similarities to that of Fraser.

> I want [. . .] to introduce the idea of feminist complicity (witting or unwitting), or perhaps a better word would be congruence: in what ways do aspects of the contemporary feminist project aid and abet the strength and power of neoliberalism, or free-market capitalism? To make this argument I want to show how the many varied feminist struggles of the 1970s have been selectively filtered into what I call hegemonic, mainstream feminism, of a kind that can be readily used by people whose motives are anything but woman-friendly. [. . .] In this welter of propaganda, one central claim is that the extension of capitalist democracy is the best hope for the world's women. (Eisenstein: 2009: viii–ix, x)

What is the evidence base for the claims? 'This is a synthetic work, not based on primary research' (xi), and 'many of my ideas were developed in the classroom' (xiv). Thus, as with Fraser, the core of her argument is that neoliberals have chosen to represent feminism as consistent with neoliberalism. No evidence is provided to show that any feminist group supports such a view.

The argument of Fraser (2009) and Eisenstein (2009) is that neoliberals have claimed that neoliberalism is good for women. Well they would, wouldn't they? They offer no evidence that any feminist group actually agrees with this view. The next chapter, on 'what feminism does', will give extensive evidence of the actual activities of feminist groups.

This is not an argument that neoliberalism is irrelevant for gender relations, but rather that it makes the achievement of feminist goals more difficult. The increase in economic inequality and the decrease in the legitimacy of state action alter the context in which feminism makes its demands. The decline of the trade unions (Visser 2006) changes the importance of the allies with which feminism can construct coalitions, so the traditional alliance of feminism with trade unions, within political parties constructed around social democracy (Huber and Stephens 2000), is reduced in power. The increased significance of business as a political force increases the salience of projects that are consistent with business interests. The cutting back of the welfare state affects women disproportionately (Hedlund 1998).

The neoliberal context affects both the form of contestation of feminism and the understanding of these processes in the academy. The neoliberal turn has inflected the opposition to feminism and the attempts to incorporate it through the notion of postfeminism. Feminism has been opposed and misrepresented within neoliberalism. The neoliberal turn in governmental programmes and in the social formation is echoed and reflected in academia, though with some distinctive twists. There has been a shift in the priorities, strategies, theories and epistemologies used in social science analysis. There has been a shift in interest from systems of power to that of agency. There has been a move towards relativism in the prioritisation of difference at the expense of equality. There has been a loss of confidence in the project of justice in the face of the ostensibly competing standards associated with the valorisation of difference at the expense of equality, with the drive to anti-essentialism, and with the loss of focus on systems of power.

There has been a shift in intellectual enquiry about systems of power towards the practice of agency. While this move is often represented as if it were a challenge to power (Pollert 1996), it functions in practice towards deflecting analytic interest away from the powerful and from systems of power and focusing it instead on the actions of the relatively powerless and on their twisting and turning in the face of power. A shift to agency instead of systems of power can lead to the blaming of the victim who has become the focus of attention, while the powerful and the systems of power escape the analytic gaze.

There is a crisis in the neoliberal project as a consequence of the near meltdown of the financial system and of the overheating of the planet (see chapter 6). This may contribute to a potential tipping point towards an alternative future. The renewed interest in the understanding of systems of economic power and the development of a democratic regulation of the economy in favour of the many, not of the few, create a different political environment within which feminism operates; this may lead to a tipping point to social democracy. However, the high levels of unemployment created by the economic recession do not make a context conducive to resurgence in the social democratic project (Bagguley 1991; Korpi 2002, 2003). Instead there is the possibility of a tipping point to xenophobic protectionism and, linked to that, of fundamentalism, including on gender issues. Alternative futures are possible (see chapter 8).

Is feminism dead?

The demise of feminism is greatly exaggerated. Feminism has been declared to be in abeyance (Taylor 1989; Bagguley 2002), since the traditional forms of protest of a social movement are less frequent and even less frequently reported. As Redfern and Aune (2010: 1) note, 'feminism is pronounced dead on a regular basis'. But a critical review of these arguments as marking the demise of feminism shows them to be unfounded.

Significant aspects of contemporary feminism are not noticed because they take new forms and are less visible (see chapters 3 and 4). This occurs when new forms of feminism exist within institutions of power and become less visible to the media. It occurs when feminism is understood as going beyond the politics of recognition, to include the less visible politics of redistribution. It also occurs when feminism acts in alliance or coalition with other forces and loses visibility when the project is no longer solely identified as feminist.

Feminism is no longer only a protest movement; it develops diverse forms and enters the institutions of power, contesting from within as well as from outside the state. Feminism is no longer an outsider protest movement, but is embedded in institutions of civil society and state. These institutionalised forms are often not recognised as feminist when the definition of feminism is narrowly limited to protest movements and popular culture. The wide range of organisational forms of contemporary feminism and the reasons for these changes are explored in chapter 4. Feminism is less visible when the strategy of gender mainstreaming is adopted and becomes entwined with the state (See chapter 5 on gender mainstreaming).

Feminism is sometimes understood as focused on the politics of recognition (Fraser 1997), with an emphasis on cultural challenges. Yet feminist politics more often takes the form of a politics of redistribution (Hobson 2000). The latter is less visible to analysts who focus on the politics of recognition, and thus it contributes to the false impression that feminism is weak (Walby 2001a).

Feminism can be less visible but no less significant when it forms coalitions with other social forces and joint projects, which are not explicitly labelled feminist. Projects that are feminist but are not visibly named as such are often ignored by those who declare feminism to be dead. When a broader definition of feminism is used, which includes projects based in institutions and projects pursuing feminist goals that are not self-styled as feminist, the vibrancy of contemporary feminism becomes more visible. Chapter 7 will discuss the implications of these intersections.

There are spiralling rounds of feminist and anti-feminist struggle. As soon as some feminist goals are achieved, then there is new opposition. Often this opposition takes new forms, which pay heed to these feminist advances rather than simply opposing them. Simplistic forms of backlash, pushing back to the previous form of gender relations, do exist, but are less common than the innovative forms of opposition to feminism and its successes. Thus concepts of rounds of struggle (Burawoy 1979) or of spirals of struggles (Boswell and Chase-Dunn 2000) are often more appropriate than that of 'backlash' (Faludi 1991, 1992).

The goals of feminism have not yet been achieved, even though there have been many partial successes. Many goals remain elusive, despite centuries of efforts. There are gender inequalities in the institutional domains of economy, polity, violence and civil society.

Conclusion

Opposition to feminism is not new, and it is not surprising. These contestations take a wide range of forms. There are some directly hostile attacks, which might be characterised as 'backlash' or 'rounds of struggle', but many of the contestations are more indirect and more subtle. There are attempts to mobilise public feminism's achievement of the legitimacy of the practice of equal treatment as an instrument to critique the privileges won for mothers by maternalist feminism. The development of anti-foundationalist epistemologies and ontologies has sometimes undermined projects that focus more simply on women. There are divisions as to how best to address intersecting inequalities, such as of class and ethnicity. There are attempts to incorporate feminist concerns within new projects, such as sexualisation and the development of raunch culture. Some new forms of activity embrace individualism rather than collective political projects. The intensification of neoliberalism makes for a hostile context for feminism. However, the claim that we are now in a post-feminist era is challenged. Evidence on the nature of contemporary feminism is detailed in the next chapter.

3

What Does Feminism Do?

Introduction

This chapter is focused on what feminist projects do. The focus is on the content of the feminist goals and on the nature of the collective activities undertaken in pursuit of them. The chapter provides an account of the goals, of the main actors, and of the processes and perspectives involved. It is not a survey of attitudes, of what people think; nor is it a survey of individuals, made in order to find out the activities in which they have engaged; nor is it a review of media representations of feminism. Rather it concentrates on the activities of projects, groups and organisations. Its purpose is to challenge many of the inaccurate representations of feminism that are in circulation, replacing them with an accurate account of the range of feminist activities.

The chapter begins by reviewing the main feminist goals that have been identified and promoted by major feminist bodies in the UK, EU, US and UN. For the sake of clarity of presentation, the discussion is then divided into sections concerning the economy, the polity, violence and civil society. In each section, different politico-spatial levels are addressed separately where necessary. These are: the global (UN, transnational) level; the European Union (EU) level; and the UK level – together with a few examples from other countries, especially the US. The chapter is focused on the UK, moving out to the EU, and out again to the UN. It provides information on the multiplicity of feminist goals in the domains of economy, polity, violence and civil society and at varied politico-spatial levels, and also a discussion of the strategies and perspectives on justice that are involved. It also provides information on feminist practices that will be revisited

in later chapters – on forms of feminist organisation, gender mainstreaming and intersectionality. The organisations addressed include
feminist NGOs and campaigns, NGOs that embrace feminist goals
alongside other goals, and governmental units that are focused on
gender equality issues.

Who Defines Feminist Goals?

The projects included here are those that pursue feminist goals.
Following the discussion in chapter 1, it is not considered necessary
for a project to define itself as feminist in order to be included. Thus
this chapter also concerns itself with projects and organisations which
have a feminist component but do not define themselves as feminist
(see chapter 7 for further discussion on intersections with feminism).
There are many reasons why groups might not wish to define themselves as feminist, either in general or in certain settings, even if they
understand their goals to comprise advancing the interests of women
in some way. Two of these reasons are the wish to have distance from
projects linked to perceived enemies, such as those with a colonial or
imperial past or current objective, and the wish to avoid a term that is
stigmatised as extremist. This broadens the range of entities subject
to analysis more than would be the case if self-definition as feminist
were necessary. The analysis encompasses not only civil societal
projects, but also institutions, including special governmental units,
which pursue feminist goals. The intersection of feminism with other
projects, oppositional and mainstream, in alliances and coalitions, is
an important part of the political process. This means that the kinds
of projects described here include not only those that stand alone and
are explicitly led by feminist goals, but also those that are embedded
in other entities and projects, which include the pursuit of feminist
goals but are not explicitly labelled as such.

Providing an account of the range of issues with which contemporary feminism engages requires a source of authority for a list
of such issues. This chapter draws on a range of sources, which
appear to command the greatest legitimacy and consensus within
contemporary feminism at UK, EU and UN levels. In each case the
list of issues is the outcome of a process of negotiation that involves
feminists in civil society, usually both grassroots and NGOs, and
gender equality bodies within government, which have themselves
been lobbied or been in negotiation with feminists in civil society.
The list of sources names documents and practices as well as the

originating body. The latter include the UK Fawcett Society, the UK National Alliance of Women's Organisations, the Seven Demands of the British Women's Liberation Movement, the European Women's Lobby and the UN Beijing Platform for Action.

It is useful to begin in the 1970s, when the British women's movement developed a list of Seven Demands. In 1970 a Women's Liberation Movement conference in Oxford agreed on four demands (Fairbairns, Graham, Neilson et al. 2002: 8):

1   equal pay for equal work;
2   equal education and equal opportunities;
3   free contraception and abortion on demand;
4   free 24-hour nurseries.

A longer list was finalised at the National Women's Liberation Conference in 1978 (see Women Demand 2006), and in this later form it included a preamble about sexuality – 'the women's liberation movement asserts a woman's right to define her own sexuality' – as well as three more demands:

5   legal and financial independence for women;
6   an end to discrimination against lesbians;
7   freedom for all women from intimidation by the threat or use of male violence; an end to the laws, assumptions and institutions which perpetuate male dominance and men's aggression towards women.

While these demands originated a long time ago, they nevertheless bear many similarities to continuing contemporary issues.

The UK currently has many feminist organisations, among which are two generic national ones: the National Alliance of Women's Organisations and the Fawcett Society. The National Alliance of Women's Organisations (2011) is an umbrella organisation of over 100 diverse groups in England. These include single issue and specialist organisations, faith groups, health centres, arts-based organisations and others, offering services and campaigning across a range of women's concerns. It was founded in 1989; it responds to government consultations; and it is a key link between British feminist organisations and ones in the EU and UN. Its aim is to seek women's human rights and equality between women and men. The Fawcett Society (2011) is the most important of the UK organisations that lead campaigns promoting the equality between women and men.

It is a campaigning rather than representative body; it engages with the media and with politicians, and it is funded by individuals and foundations. The Fawcett Society was founded in 1866 as part of the suffrage movement, so is one of the oldest and most long-lived feminist organisations in the UK. It is a feminist organisation, though the phrase 'equality between women and men' (rather than 'feminism') usually features in its work. Their campaigns in 2010 included women's representation in politics and public life; pay, pensions and poverty; valuing caring work; the treatment of women in the justice system; and opposing the disproportionate gender impact of the budget cuts.

In the UK there are also several networks of grassroots activists using new media – such as websites, blogs, Facebook and Twitter – to facilitate communication about a wide range of events and fast-changing campaigns. These networks include: 'The f word' (2011); London Feminist Network (2011); Feminism in London (2011); UK Feminista (2011); Carnival of Feminists (2011); and the Women's Resource Centre (2011).

The European Women's Lobby (2011) is the leading umbrella organisation for women's associations in the EU; it has representatives from the 'peak' women's organisations in the twenty-seven member states of the European Union and in three candidate countries, as well as from several pan-EU women's bodies. It promotes women's rights and gender equality across the EU, working with EU-level institutions and providing information to decision-makers so as to ensure that a gender equality perspective is taken into account, and it assists women's organisations with information designed to help towards their effective engagement with the EU. It was founded in 1990 and most of its funds come from the European Commission. Thus EU policy legislation and policy and legislation lie at the centre of the lobby's interventions. The lobby states that it carries out its work within a 'feminist analysis'. It encompasses a wide range of issues, including the economy, the polity, violence and civil society; but, because of the remit of the EU, it is especially important for economic issues. The priorities of the European Women's Lobby are in the following fields: women in decision-making and in parity democracy; social policy and employment; European gender equality policies and legislation; women's diversity and anti-discrimination; migration and asylum; fundamental rights within the European Union; the revision of European treaties; international action for women's rights, especially in relation to the UN; and ending violence against women.

The European Commission, both in its Women's Charter (European Commission 2010c) and in its Strategy for Equality between Women and Men 2010–2015 (European Commission 2010b), declares five key gender equality objectives, which are based on the Treaties of the EU: equal economic independence; equal pay for equal work and work of equal value; equality in decision-making; dignity, integrity and an end to gender-based violence; and gender equality in the external actions of the EU.

The US, likewise, has many feminist organisations. The largest generic national one is the National Organization for Women (NOW), which has 500,000 members and 550 local branches and is supported by an active website. NOW was founded in 1966, with the goal of securing equality for all women. Its objectives include eliminating discrimination and harassment in the workplace, schools, and the justice system; increasing access to abortion and reproductive rights; ending violence against women; and generally promoting equality and justice (National Organization for Women 2009).

The UN is the main arena in which the global is considered in this book; this involves not only the inter-governmental machinery of the various UN agencies, but also the feminist NGOs that utilise the spaces created and made available by the UN for civil societal engagement (United Nations 1995; Annan 1999). The transnational is a more modest concept than the global; it crosses over some state frontiers, though far from all (Sperling, Ferree and Risman 2001).

The most influential listing of feminist issues is that drawn up in the Beijing *Platform for Action* (United Nations 1995). This was constructed in 1995, at a global conference of governments that was subjected to intensive lobbying by many thousands of feminists from around the world who attended the event in Beijing. This listing has been accepted as a global standard by feminists around the world and has been the basis of reviews of progress and remaining challenges at five yearly intervals. The Platform is adopted by many other bodies and is accorded legitimacy by both governments and NGOs. It comprises aspirations for the advancement of women in twelve critical areas:

1 the persistent and increasing burden of poverty on women;
2 inequalities and inadequacies in, and unequal access to, education and training;
3 inequalities and inadequacies in, and unequal access to, health care and related services;

4 violence against women;
5 the effects of armed or other kinds of conflict on women, including those living under foreign occupation;
6 inequality in economic structures and policies, in all forms of productive activities and in access to resources;
7 inequality between men and women in the sharing of power and decision-making at all levels;
8 insufficient mechanisms, at all levels, to promote the advancement of women;
9 lack of respect for, and inadequate promotion and protection of, the human rights of women;
10 stereotyping of women and inequality in women's access to and participation in all communication systems, especially in the media;
11 gender inequalities in the management of natural resources and in the safeguarding of the environment;
12 persistent discrimination against, and violation of the rights of, the girl child.

The multiplicity of feminist projects reported through the Women's United Nations Report Network (WUNRN) (2011) is indicative of the range and dynamism of feminism worldwide. The UN Platform for Action constitutes an authoritative framing of feminist goals, which is widely accepted in many countries of the world.

In spite of differences in emphasis, there is remarkable consensus on the areas of concern to feminists, even at the ostensibly disparate locations of the UN, EU, UK and US. While the largest and most important feminist organisations engage with most, if not all, of these issues, many feminist projects have a more specific focus. In what follows, the account of these specific projects is divided into sections on the economy, the polity, violence and civil society, since these are the four major institutional domains.

Feminism in the Economy

Some feminist goals for changes in the economy are shared widely around the world. In the Beijing *Platform for Action* (United Nations 1995), two critical areas concern the economy. These are: (1) 'the persistent and increasing burden of poverty on women'; and (2) 'inequality in economic structures and policies, in all forms of productive activities and in access to resources'. Other goals are more specific to global region and country, for reasons related to the more public form of gender regime in the global North than in the global South and to different forms of governance and gendered political mobilisation. In the North there is greater focus on the paid economy, while in the South informal and domestic economies are more important for women's well-being. Issues of global governance concern both and are articulated in national, EU and global NGOs. While in some areas there is consensus as to what constitutes a feminist intervention, there are debates about the relationship between strategies for feminism and for economic growth.

In the EU, UK and US, feminist goals in the paid economy include both some that are general to women in the economy – such as narrowing the gender gaps in pay and in conditions of employment, reducing occupational segregation, facilitating the combination of caring with employment, reducing female poverty, reducing gender inequities in the tax-benefit system, and effectively regulating financial institutions (Armstrong, Walby and Strid 2009; European Women's Lobby 2011; European Commission 2006) – and access to basic rights and freedom from being subject to force or trafficking (International Labour Organisation 2005). There are also some goals that depend upon mechanisms more typically developed in the North – for instance fair recruitment and promotion processes, fair mechanisms for awarding and reviewing pay, the provision of paid maternity, paternity and parental leave, and flexibility of working hours (Trades Union Congress [TUC] 2011a, 2011b; European Trade Union Confederation [ETUC] 2011); quality childcare, available and affordable or free (Daycare Trust 2011); and a tax-benefit system that promotes rather than inhibits narrowing gender gaps in employment and equity in the household (WBG 2000, 2004). The interface between employment and care is gendered and has been subject to many feminist interventions, especially in the EU, because of its importance to both gendered employment and gendered care, allowing for the balance or reconciliation of the two. The achievement of this balance between employment and care requires the regulation of working time, the public provision of affordable childcare and care for the elderly, and an appropriate tax-benefit system. The processes designed to achieve these goals on a routine basis include the democratic regulation of the economy by the state, by using the law and the courts as well as collective bargaining between trade unions and employers; while strategic change involves a wider coalition of social forces (Fairbairns, Graham, Neilson et al. 2002; European Commission 2010b; European Women's Lobby

[EWL] 2011; Fawcett Society 2011; National Alliance of Women's Organisations [NAWO] 2011).

These goals are taken forward by feminist NGOs, other equality oriented NGOs, trade unions, and gender equality bodies within the state. There is a large range of non-governmental bodies that promote feminist goals in the economy, and these are often allied together in formal or informal coalitions and networks, especially for specific campaigns.

In the UK there are NGOs that are both explicitly and implicitly feminist. These include the Women's Budget Group (2011), the Daycare Trust (2011), the Child Poverty Action Group (2011), Women and Manual Trades (2011), and trade unions. In addition, there are local grassroots mobilisations from time to time, for example actions for equal pay and for nurseries.

The UK Women's Budget Group (2011) is an organisation based on a coalition of feminist researchers, policy analysts, other NGOs and trade unions. It produces annual analyses of the UK Budget, offering a critical feminist review of its priorities and a statement of its implications for gender equality. It engages with government departments on economic issues, especially the finance ministry, HM Treasury, and has participated in discussions on the reform of the tax-benefit system, the introduction of tax credits and the development of childcare. It uses the term 'feminist', though more usually it utilises a strategy of 'gender mainstreaming' (see chapter 5).

The Daycare Trust (2011) has been campaigning since 1986 for high quality affordable childcare. In addition, it provides research, expertise and advice about childcare options to parents, carers, childcare providers, employers, trade unions and policymakers. It has played a significant role in the development of a National Childcare Strategy. Although not labelling itself as a feminist organisation, it states that 'equalities, diversity and inclusion are central to our objectives'.

The Child Poverty Action Group (2011) campaigns for the abolition of child poverty in the UK and for improvement in state provision for low income families and children. Since the elimination of child poverty cannot be achieved without eliminating the poverty of the main carer, who is usually the child's mother, this action indirectly supports at least some aspects of gender equality. Campaigns have formulated demands for redistributive budgets, which increase tax credits to poor households with children – a measure that benefits women indirectly. This group is positioned at the intersection of gender and class inequality, even as its focus is on an age-specific group: children.

Trade unions are important actors pursuing feminist goals within the economy, but they are often neglected in analyses of feminist politics because only rarely do they overtly declare themselves led by feminist goals. Trade unions pursue the feminist goal of equality in employment, including equal pay for work of equal value and equal treatment in recruitment and promotion; they do it through collective bargaining, and also sometimes through political representation (Briskin 2006; Franzway and Fonow 2008). Apart from individual trade unions such as Unison and Unite, there is the Trades Union Congress (TUC 2011a), the peak association of trade unions in the UK, with around 6.5 million members. The TUC (2011b) announces that it campaigns for 'a fair deal at work and for social justice at home and abroad' as well as for 'women's equality in the workplace and in the wider community' – which includes not only equal pay, but also issues of childcare, poverty, abortion rights and violence against women. Individual trade unions rarely call themselves feminist, although today most of them declare a commitment to equality and diversity. They have changed significantly over time, moving away from patriarchal exclusionary practices, such as attempting to reserve the best jobs for men, towards promoting equality between women and men (Drake 1984; Walby 1986). Trade unions are more likely to engage with issues of concern to women workers than they used to be, constructing an agenda of equality issues (Colgan and Ledwith 2002). Most unions now make explicit commitments to pursuing equality for their members, often specifying the different equality strands such as gender, as does for example UNISON (2009), while UNITE (2011b) states: 'Equalities are a key priority for Unite and we are committed to promoting equality.' Women are increasingly mobilised within trade unions. However, overall unionisation rates have been declining. The proportion of employed men who are members of trade unions has typically been falling, while that of women, especially younger women, has not. Women are disproportionately employed in the public sector in Europe, where unionisation rates are higher than in the private sector.

In consequence, the gender composition of trade unions has gradually changed, so that now women make up, on average, half the membership. In the UK 30 per cent of the women in employment were members of trade unions, as compared with 27 per cent of men, while 59 per cent of workers in the public sector – as compared with

17 per cent of workers in the private sector – were members of trade unions in 2006 (Grainger and Crowther 2007). This re-gendering of trade unions is not unique to the UK but common across the West: in 2005 the proportion of women among trade union members was 51 per cent in the UK, 45 per cent in the US, 52 per cent in Sweden and 50 per cent in Ireland (Visser 2006). However, while women have been increasing their presence in trade unions, overall trade unions have become weaker over the last 30 years, as total membership has declined. The proportion of women in decision-making positions in unions has significantly increased, even though not yet reflecting the proportion of women who are members of unions (Colgan and Ledwith 2002). This combines with forms of internal organisation involving special committees, posts and conferences to support the representation of women and minorities (ethnic, religious, sexual) within the union. Today trade unions are among the most important of the mass organisations pursuing the feminist goal of equality in pay and conditions of employment. If the definition of 'feminist' is restricted to self-definition, then these mass organisations of women seeking to improve their pay and working conditions are not feminist. But, if the point of the analysis is to understand the forms and practices used in the pursuit of feminist goals, then it is better to treat as feminist such organisations, at least on the occasions when they pursue feminist goals.

The EU governs many matters concerning employment, especially equality issues, across all its twenty-seven member states. The EU produces Directives, based on Treaties, which are transposed by member states into the domestic law that governs the workplace; these concern, for example, the equal treatment of women and men in employment and in the sale and distribution of goods and services (European Commission 2007), the prevention of harassment (Zippel 2004), and maternity, paternity and parental leave. These Directives were passed as a result of pressure from the European Commission, feminists and trade unionists (Pillinger 1992; Hoskyns 1996; Rees 1998, 2005; Pascual and Behning 2001; European Gender Budget Network 2007; European Women's Lobby 2011). Such policies, especially for working time regulation, have been much slower to develop in the US than in the EU (O'Connor, Orloff and Shaver 1999; Kelly and Dobbin 1999; Gottfried and Reese 2003; Gottschall and Bird 2003; Walby 1999a, 1999b, 2004a).

There is a range of EU-level actors promoting the goal of gender equality. The largest feminist NGO is the European Women's Lobby (EWL 2011), which addresses these economic issues alongside other feminist goals. The EWL was discussed earlier in this chapter. The European Trade Union Confederation (2008) is a confederation of national peak associations of trade unions, founded in 1973, to promote an EU with a strong social dimension by building a unified European trade union movement and representing working people's interests in EU institutions. Its goals include equality, including for women. The EU has a range of governmental bodies that promote gender equality, especially the unit within the Commission (European Commission 2010d), the Women's Rights (FEMM) Committee of the European Parliament (European Parliament 2011) and the European Institute for Gender Equality (EIGE) (2011). The EU has an official strategy to promote equality between women and men, which is presented in the *Strategy for Equality between Women and Men 2010–2015* (European Commission 2010b).

The global level includes further bodies promoting feminist goals, which are positioned variously at global (UN), transnational and regional levels. The regulation of international finance and trade is a feminist issue because of the gendered composition of financial decision-making and its implications for the gendered economy, not only in the UK and EU, but also for the global South. The promotion of education for girls and women is a further issue, which, internationally, has linked gender equality to economic growth (UN 1995; Klasen 2002; European Women's Lobby 2011). Access to citizenship rights by those who have crossed national boundaries is a political issue in its own right, which is relevant for feminism – such is the problem of women's access to legal rights concerning employment conditions, for example in the case of migrant workers in global care chains (Ehrenreich and Hochschild 2003), and to asylum when they are subjected to gender-based violence for which no domestic legal remedy is available (Crawley 2001).

At the transnational level there are many NGOs concerned with feminist issues in economic development. Development Alternatives with Women for a New Era (DAWN) (2011) is a leading example of a feminist NGO based in the global South, which is working to improve the process and outcomes of economic development for women. The Association for Women's Rights in Development (AWID) (2008) is a further major international feminist NGO with bases around the world. Feminist goals have been inserted to some extent into the agendas of entities that are not dedicated to feminist ends, such as trade unions, where there have been significant developments in transnational feminist trade union organising (Franzway and Fonow 2008), and the International Labour Organisation (ILO), which was founded in 1919 to promote social justice and internationally recognised human and labour rights (ILO 2011), and which has concerns with 'decent work' and forced and trafficked labour (ILO 2005).

Environmental issues have been addressed as both global and gendered. 'Women for Climate Justice' (GenderCC 2011) is a network of women and gender activists and experts that acts as a platform for information, knowledge, and networking on gender and climate change. Its main goal is 'integrating gender justice into climate change policy'; it proclaims that 'GenderCC believes that in order to achieve women's rights, gender justice and climate justice, fundamental changes are necessary to overcome the existing systems of power, politics and economics' and proposes that 'linking women's rights, gender justice and climate justice is key to achieving these fundamental changes'.

The relationship between feminist and economic growth strategies has been subject to considerable debate. The issue is whether or not economic growth is good for women by reducing gender inequality. This tension between feminism and the mainstream goal of economic growth is typical of the tensions existing in gender mainstreaming. Can the achievement of feminist goals be assisted through engagement with the mainstream, because of overlaps between the projects, or does such integration lead to the loss of the feminist project (Moser 1993, 2005; Jahan 1995; Kabeer 2003; Walby 2005; Eisenstein 2009; Fraser 2009)?

On the one hand, economic growth is good for women. Economic growth and policies towards increasing it also increase women's employment, which is linked to reductions in unpaid domestic labour and vulnerable informal work; and it has the potential to increase women's economic autonomy and thereby to reduce gender inequalities, both in the economy and elsewhere. There are several components to this argument. Narrowing the gender gaps in employment by increasing women's employment develops the economy as well as contributing to gender equality. Thus removing discrimination against women and setting up policies that enable both employment and care work contribute both to economic growth and to gender equality (Walby and Olsen 2002; European Women's Lobby 2011; European Commission 2010b). Improving the education of girls, especially in the global South, where there is a gender educational gap to women's detriment, has the simultaneous effect of decreasing gender inequality and of stimulating economic growth (Klasen 2002). The goal of improving the education of girls was included within the UN Millennium Development Goals, partly because it contributed to both agendas at the same time (United Nations 2011).

On the other hand, some forms of economic growth can be to women's detriment. They can increase women's employment without any significant reduction in their unpaid and vulnerable labour and under conditions of such low wages and skills as not to contribute significantly to their economic autonomy, hence without any reduction in gender inequality. If the strategy for economic growth entails developing low wage jobs, with the effect of increasing women's employment only in poorly paid and low skilled jobs, then this is not a strategy for gender equality (Perrons 2005) but one that merely incorporates feminism into neoliberalism, especially in the US (Eisenstein 2009; Fraser 2009). It has been argued that this is the practical effect even in the EU (Young 2000; Wöhl 2008), for example with the loss of visibility of the goal of gender equality in the European Employment Strategy (Smith and Villa 2010) – even if this was not the original intention (Stratigaki 2004). But there are important differences in the situations of women workers in different countries; it is important not to generalise from US neoliberalism (Eisenstein 2009; Fraser 2009) to the situation in other parts of the world, where capitalism may take a different, perhaps more social democratic, form.

The conclusion on the implications of economic growth strategies for gender equality is that it depends on the nature of these strategies, in particular, whether they are for low wage, low skill jobs or for high wage, high skill jobs, and whether there is a specific set of gender equality policies within the policy package. The former is a neoliberal and the latter a social democratic economic growth strategy. Neoliberal strategies may be to the detriment of women, unlike social democratic growth strategies.

Polity

The feminist goal for the polity is to increase women's presence and power so that there is no gender inequality in political power any longer. The UN Platform for Action presents this goal as addressing 'inequality between men and women in the sharing of power and decision-making at all levels; [and] insufficient mechanisms at all levels to promote the advancement of women' (United Nations 1995).

In practice, this goal is often understood to mean increasing the percentage of women in decision-making bodies, so that a gender balance may be achieved; and creating policy institutions, machinery or 'gender architecture' within government that supports the promotion of feminist issues. The point of these procedural changes is to allow for the effective democratic voice of women to be equal to that of men. The highest profile bodies where this is discussed are the conventional democratic venues of parliament, cabinet, and local councils. However, a wider range of decisional bodies has been addressed, including public bodies such as the boards of directors of top companies, banks and major financial institutions, peace keepers, and churches (Lovenduski 2005; Squires 2007; European Women's Lobby 2011).

Within the UN there has been significant development of the policy machinery that addresses gender inequality. There has been a long campaign to reform the UN so as to strengthen this machinery, for instance by integrating the relevant agencies into a single entity. The Gender Equality Architecture Reform (2011) was a campaigning network of over 300 women's groups, human rights groups and social justice groups around the world, which achieved its objective when the UN General Assembly voted on 2 July 2010 to create 'UN Women' – that is, a UN Entity for Gender Equality and the Empowerment of Women.

There is a range of global NGOs and institutions promoting gender-equal democracy. The Inter-Parliamentary Union (1995, 2010) supports such a change, providing data on the development of parliamentary democracy and on the presence of women and information on the electoral systems under which this is most likely to occur.

A wide range of women's organisations and sections within political parties have campaigned for a series of reforms of democratic procedures so as to increase the proportion of women. The actors pushing for these changes include the full spectrum of feminist organisations at local, national, EU, international (e.g. Inter-Parliamentary Union 1995) and UN levels, and especially feminist lobbies within political parties. These bodies promote arguments for replacing electoral systems based on 'first past the post' by 'proportional representation', quotas in the selection mechanisms for parliamentary candidates by political parties, and quotas in parliaments and in executives (Lovenduski 2005; Squires 2007; Women into Politics 2011). These campaigns have often focused on moments of change in political systems, for example the campaigns following the decision to create the Scottish Parliament and Welsh Assembly in 1997 led to new electoral systems that elected far higher proportions of women to these institutions than to the older Westminster Parliament (Squires and Wickham-Jones 2001).

There have been campaigns to develop new governmental institutions, centred on gender equality (Squires 2007; Walby, Armstrong and Strid 2010b). In most member states of the EU this has led to the development of policy units in central government and of implementation agencies (Walby 2004a), though some of these are under pressure during recent cutbacks on expenditure. There has been pressure to develop agencies for gender equality within the EU institutions, building on the equality unit within the Commission and on the FEMM Committee of the European Parliament to establish the European Institute for Gender Equality, created in 2010 (European Institute for Gender Equality 2011).

Women have also successfully entered a range of other public bodies that are concerned with governance, often, although not always, taking a feminist agenda with them. For example, there have been major struggles for women to enter into senior positions in the religious rituals and decision-making in the Anglican and Catholic Christian churches – efforts which have led to some partial successes; at the same time there have been feminist attempts to redefine Christian positions on intimacy, including sexuality, divorce and abortion (Christians for Biblical Equality 2011). Resistance to the admission of women to these positions and to the re-gendering of religious doctrines on intimacy has been very strong and globally varied, with serious threats of schism in the churches. There has also been a development of new religious and spiritual practices – such as those known as 'new age', which have differently gendered composition and leadership practices (Heelas, Woodhead, Seel et al. 2004).

These developments embed feminism within the state and institutionalised public bodies (Mazur 2002; Squires 2007). They are a challenge to older notions of feminism as a protest movement situated outside of political institutions. Today feminist projects are being conducted inside these state institutions as well as outside them. These new forms of feminist organisation will be further discussed in chapter 4.

Violence

A major feminist goal is to reduce and eliminate gender-based violence against women. In the twelve critical areas of the UN Platform for Action, this kind of violence is named as 'violence against women' and 'the effects of armed or other kinds of conflict on women' (United Nations 1995).

The political activity aimed at stopping violence against women has developed steadily over the last forty years or so. A multiplicity of policies and practices have been developed, all designed to move towards this goal. These include: providing shelters, refuges and specialised advice; increasing police action (Kelly, Bindel, Burton et al. 1999); improving civil legal instruments and criminal laws (Edwards 1996); collecting information and changing public awareness (Zero Tolerance 2011); changing policies towards women and increasing the percentage of women in peace-keeping forces in conflict zones (Shepherd 2008). The feminist demands include: changing the priorities of the criminal justice system so that police resources may be used to protect women and to arrest and prosecute violent men; and supporting challenges to the status quo (Rights of Women 2011). Following a period of autonomous feminist organisations setting up new institutions, resources have been demanded from the state to support refuges to help women who have been abused by men (Dobash and Dobash 1992; Hague and Malos 1993; Taylor-Browne 2001; Westmarland 2004; Kelly, Lovett and Regan 2005) and rape crisis and other specialised centres for women who have been sexually assaulted (Lovett, Regan and Kelly 2004). Some aspects of these policies are now mainstream, with consequent tensions as to whether all interventions are now feminist (Bumiller 2008) – for example when the police rather than the abused women make key decisions about the prosecution process.

One of the basic goals has been to name this violence and make it visible. The United Nations Secretary-General's (2006: 15) definition is widely cited in diverse circumstances: Gender-based violence against women is 'violence that is directed against a woman because she is a woman, or violence that affects women disproportionately. It includes acts that inflict physical, mental or sexual harm or suffering, threats of such acts, coercion and other deprivations of liberty.'

The UN and its various agencies now engage in activities to prevent and eliminate violence against women. This work is supported by strong NGO lobby groups that have learnt to work effectively at a transnational level, within the spaces created by UN institutions and conferences. The framing of violence against women as a human rights issue facilitated its inclusion among UN activities. In 1993, under the influence of feminist activists, a conference on human rights in Vienna adopted a resolution stating that women's rights were human rights and included the right to be free from male violence (Bunch 1995; Kelly 2005). In 2006, the Secretary-General presented to the UN General Assembly a major in-depth report on violence against women, which was based on work by the UN Division for the Advancement of Women (United Nations Secretary General 2006). In 2008, the UN Secretary-General launched a campaign called UNiTE, which was designed to end violence against women. Its goal is to achieve in all countries, by 2015, national laws for addressing and punishing all forms of violence against women and girls; national action plans; stronger data collection; increased public awareness and social mobilisation; and to address sexual violence in conflict (UNiTE 2011a). The United Nations, Division for the Advancement of Women (UNDAW) (2009) published a handbook on guidelines for legislation on violence against women. These UN initiatives build on feminist work in other UN agencies, including UNIFEM (2000), which has long taken a lead on violence against women, the World Health Organization (WHO) (Krug, Dahlberg, Mercy et al. 2002) and the UN Security Council (Shepherd 2008).

There are transnational feminist organisations and campaigns to combat both war and the particular abuse of women in conflict zones. The Women's International League for Peace and Freedom (2011) has long engaged in these actions. The position of women as victims of violence after war and as peace keepers has been made the focus of UN Security Council resolutions, as part of the campaign to address these issues (Shepherd 2008).There is a large, vibrant, diverse and well-networked NGO sector in the UK, in the EU and internationally. In addition, there are several bodies within the state, from cross-departmental committees on violence against women to expert police groups and specialist prosecutors. There are feminist projects to reduce and eliminate violence against women in many countries around the world, including in all the global regions (Counts, Brown, and Campbell 1992; Davies 1993; Nelson and Chowdhury 1994; Ariffin 1997; Keck and Sikkink 1998; Crawley 2001; Weldon 2002). The goals of these projects vary slightly according to local and national circumstances, but there is much common ground between them. Violence against women is perhaps the feminist issue on which there is greatest global agreement.

In the UK there is a wide range of NGOs, many of which work together in a major coalition called 'End Violence against Women' (EVAW) (2011). EVAW is a coalition of individuals and organisations, activists, survivors, academics and feminist service providers that calls on the government, public bodies and others to take action to end violence against women. They declare their vision to be a society where women and girls can live their lives free from violence and from the threat of violence; and they have four campaign goals: (1) to make violence against women be understood as a cause and consequence of women's inequality; (2) to raise awareness about the nature, extent and impact of violence against women in the UK and about how it can be prevented; (3) to make the UK Government and devolved administrations develop integrated and strategic approaches to ending violence against women; (4) to share good practice across the UK and learn from the experience of Scotland, where a framework is being developed. The members of EVAW see themselves as linked both to equality projects and to human rights projects. A wide range of organisations are part of this coalition: Bristol Feminist Network, Nia Project, Agency for Culture and Change Management, Amnesty International UK, National Council for Voluntary Youth Services, Refugee Council, BAWSO, Central Scotland Racial Equality Council, YWCA, Eaves Housing for Women, Eva Project, Scottish Women against Pornography, Fawcett Society, FORWARD, Greater London Domestic Violence Project, Ethnic Minority Foundation, The Havens, Oasis Domestic Abuse Service, The Women's Centre Sutton, Open Clasp, Imkaan, Lilith Project, Midlothian Women's Aid, London Centre for Personal Safety, London Feminist Network, National Federation of Women's Institute, One Voice 4 Travellers, Peace Child International, Newham Asian Women's Project, Object, POPPY, Rape Crisis England and Wales, Refuge, Refugee Women's Resource Project at Asylum Aid Respect, Roehampton University, Scottish Women's Aid, Soroptomist International UKPAC, South Essex Rape and Incest Crisis Centre, Southall Black Sisters, SWELL, Centre for Safety and Well Being, University of Warwick, TUC, UK Joint Committee on Women, Womankind Worldwide, Welsh Women's Aid, Women's Aid Federation England, Women's Aid Northern Ireland, Women's Design Service, Women's National Commission, Women's Resource Centre, Women's Resource Development Agency, Wales Women's Voice, Zero Tolerance. In 2009, the UK government announced a national strategy to end violence against women and girls; this strategy was revised in 2010 (HM Government 2010).

In addition to organised NGOs there are repeated grassroots mobilisations. In the UK they include the Million Women Rise (2011), annual march on International Women's Day, 8 March, against violence against women, as well as events publicised by feminist websites such as UK Feminista (2011) – which, for example, supported a campaign to stop the UK opting out from the new (2010) EU law on anti-trafficking measures.

The EU has limited competence in areas of violence against women. Violence against women may be considered an EU-level matter insofar as it is a public health issue, a cross-border issue of crime, an employment issue of harassment at work, or an issue of fundamental rights. It is included as a matter of EU strategy for equality between women and men (European Commission 2010b). However, across the EU there is a network of NGOs (WAVE) partially funded by the EU to develop and exchange best practice (the Daphne Programme), which is supported under the EU jurisdiction for public health (European Commission 2011a). Trafficking is an area where the EU has some competence due to trafficking's intrinsic cross-border nature, appointing an Anti-Trafficking Coordinator in 2010 (European Commission 2010e); but, as a crime, it falls within the field of justice and home affairs, which is subject to a UK 'opt-out', negotiated in order to retain national sovereignty. Anti-Slavery (2011), in association with 38 Degrees and ECPAT UK, led a campaign, disseminated by the UK Women's National Commission Violence against Women Working Party, to persuade the UK government to opt into the EU Anti-Trafficking Directive. This is an example where a coalition that involves groups not focused on feminist goals actively supports an issue seen by others as a feminist goal. It is also an example of the intricacy of the intersection of UK and EU politics.

While the goal of ending violence against women has not yet been achieved, there have been major, if highly uneven, policy developments using a range of approaches. There have been legislative developments concerning all the main forms of violence against women, including domestic violence, rape and sexual assault, stalking and harassment, female genital mutilation, forced marriage and trafficking. There have been developments in civil legal instruments, so that it is easier for women to eject violent men from their homes. There have been changes in associated policies, such as giving priority access to public housing to those made homeless through domestic violence. There has been a major growth in specialist agencies dedicated to assisting women who have suffered this violence – with refuge, specialist advisers and telephone help lines. These services had been receiving increasing funding up until 2010, when cuts have been proposed as part of the attempts by governments to reduce their budget deficits in the wake of the financial crisis. The feminist projects to end violence against women utilise a multiplicity of perspectives to articulate their concern; such perspectives range from regarding men as the enemy in early US writings (Brownmiller 1976; Daly 1978) to invoking gender inequality in EU institutions and in the Daphne programme (European Commission 2011a), violation of women's human rights in the UN and its agencies (Bunch 1995; United Nations Secretary-General 2006), the detriment to health (Hindin, Kishor, Ansara and Macro International 2008) and serious crime (Home Office). In addition, there are also mainstream interventions against violence against women, for example by the police, which raise questions as to their implications for feminism.

Civil Society

Feminist projects in the sphere of civil society address issues concerning the media, sexual autonomy and sexual objectification, pornography, lap dancing, sex work, sexual orientation, intimacy, marriage and divorce, abortion, contraception, reproductive health, eating disorders, sport and leisure, and the knowledge industry, including universities. This is an area of very considerable variation between countries, although there are nevertheless several common themes. There are differences linked to whether the form of the gender regime is domestic or public, and to its intersection with different national, ethnic and religious systems. A key issue in countries with a public gender regime is whether intimacy is organised along principles of mutualism rather than of commercialism and inequality.

At the global level, one of the most contested sets of issues in the UN, in its conferences and declarations, is that of sexual and reproductive rights, as to whether the principle of individual autonomy that underlies human rights applies to women's decision-making in relation to abortion, contraception, sexuality and reproductive health. Here the EU takes a more progressive stance than the US and the organised religions of Catholicism and Islam (Moghadam 1996a). On other issues there is greater global consensus. For example, there are shared concerns about the representation of women in the media and in culture. The Global Media Monitoring Project (2010) surveys global media to discover the extent to which women are underrepresented, especially in the category of 'expert', and presented through blatant or subtle stereotypes, in order to encourage changes in media reporting.

The EU has a limited remit to address issues pertaining to civil society, since most of these are the responsibility of member states under the subsidiarity principle. One way in which the EU does have implications is through its incorporation of the European Convention of Human Rights into EU law, and thereby into national or domestic law (e.g. the UK 1998 Human Rights Act), which opens a route to feminist lobbying using human rights principles.

Turning to the UK, there is a multiplicity of feminist projects in civil society. These concern the media, sexual autonomy, pornography, sex work, new forms of intimacy, access to abortion, women's bodies and the knowledge industries.

The multiple and contradictory representation of gender in the media (Gill 2006) offers many sites for feminist interventions. There have been campaigns for special prizes for women in the arts (e.g. Orange); protests to television companies when older women were taken off screen; and concern over the gender composition of decision-making bodies of media, including the editors and boards of governors for newspapers and television.

In British feminism, sexual autonomy is considered to be a goal in itself. This issue is raised in many different projects, by NGOs and campaigns opposed to the sexual objectification of women in its many forms. For example, Object (2011a), founded in 2003, is a campaigning organisation 'dedicated to challenging the sexual objectification of women in the media and popular culture'; it targets the growth and mainstreaming of 'Lads' mags', internet porn and lap dancing clubs, indeed the 'pornification' of society. The mainstreaming of lap dancing clubs, which until 2010 needed no more restrictive license than cafés, was challenged by a coalition of feminist organisations which included Fawcett, Object and UK Feminista. This move won a change in the law in 2010; as a result, such clubs faced more restrictive local licensing by virtue of being sex establishments, and there was a shift in campaign tactics towards using the new powers to enforce tighter local licensing laws on lap dancing clubs (Fawcett 2011; Object 2011a; UK Feminista 2011). The mainstreaming of sex work in lap dancing clubs and escort agencies through its inclusion in Job Centres Plus adverts was opposed by Object (2011a) and other organisations, and this led to the Department of Work and Pensions stopping the practice in 2010. In 2010, the 'Demand Change' campaign – including Object and a petition signed by 67 women's and human rights organisations – succeeded in its attempt to criminalise men who bought sex from women coerced into prostitution; this was part of a general project to criminalise men who bought sex, while protecting sex workers from additional abuse (Object 2011b).

As well as projects to limit the commercialisation or porno-graphication of sexuality, there are projects to explore and develop the expression of sexuality and intimacy. Experimentation and the development of new cultural forms and ways of living has been a long-standing part of the feminist project.

This feminist project sometimes intersects with gay, lesbian, queer and trans-gender projects (Weeks 2007). There are regular gay pride marches, which have become so mainstream that even the Tory mayor of London joined in the march to show his support of them in 2010. Stonewall (2011), founded in 1989, is an organisation for lesbians, gay men and bisexuals that engages in lobbying and campaigning as well as in providing an information and resource centre. Its projects have included equalising the age of consent for gay men to that of heterosexuals, lifting the ban on lesbians and gay men serving in the military, securing legislation that allows same-sex couples to adopt, repealing Section 28, which prohibited teaching about gay and lesbian practices, helping to secure civil partnerships and ensuring the Equality Act 2010 extended protection for lesbians and gay men in relation to the sale and distribution of goods and services. In addition to Stonewall, there are organisations concerned with gender identity (Press for Change 2011).

Solidarity with those resisting, and attempting to reform, restrictive regulation on marriage and divorce and sexuality abroad as well as in the UK includes groups such as Women Living under Muslim Laws (2011) and Women against Fundamentalism (2011), which was set up in 1989 to oppose all forms of fundamentalism.

While access to abortion is largely a settled issue in the UK, at least in comparison with the US (Ferree, Gamson, Gerhards and Rucht 2002b), there are from time to time attempts to place limits on it, for example over the time period in which it is legal. Abortion Rights (2011) is the main UK pro-choice campaign to defend and extend women's rights and access to safe, legal abortion. It opposes restrictions in women's rights and access to abortion and seeks to make abortion available on request as well as to improve abortion services. It was formed in 2003, from the merger of the National Abortion Campaign and Abortion Law Reform Association.

Women's bodies are another site of feminist activity. This includes addressing obsessions with body size and food, which are manifest for instance in super-thin or 'zero size' models and in eating disorders. Beat (2011) is an eating disorders campaign founded in 1989 that, although not centred on a feminist analysis and inclusive of men's eating disorders, is informed and inflected by feminist insights and goals. The concern for bodies also encompasses women's equal access to sport, as reflected in the work of the Women's Sports Foundation (2011).

The knowledge industries are themselves sites of feminist activities. Within these spaces there is engagement within universities, developing women's/gender studies, and mainstreaming gender analysis into both teaching and research – as in the activities of the Feminist and Women's Studies Association (2011) and Feminist Library (2011).

Tensions between Visions of Gender Equality

There is a long-standing tension between a vision of gender equality in which the same standard applies both to women and to men, and a vision of gender equality in which standards are different for women and men but there is equal valuation of different contributions. An important attempt to resolve this tension lies in the construction of a vision of equality being achieved through the transformation both of the standards of equality and of the practices of women and men (Scott 1988; Fraser 1997; Holli 1997; Rees 1998, 2005; Freedman 2001).

Maternalism, or the protection of the status and conditions of motherhood, has been a long-standing political project; it is supported by a range of institutions, including many organised religions. Since it is an attempt to improve the status of women, it may be regarded as a form of feminism. However, the promotion of domesticated motherhood may sometimes come at the expense of other activities for women and thereby be in tension with varieties of feminism that focus on the equal treatment of women and men. The tension finds expression especially, but not exclusively, in the approach to the performance of domestic care work by women. On the one hand, the performance of domestic care work by women is considered to be a significant part of the construction and perpetuation of gender inequality, not least because it reduces women's access to power in the public sphere, so that gender equality requires either its replacement with public care work, for example nurseries, or its equal sharing by men and women (Bergmann 1986). On the other hand, care work is considered to be an important value in itself, so that the equality issue resides in its adequate recognition and reward, not in its replacement (Tronto 1993). This tension can be seen in the historical disagreements over whether the 'protective legislation' that restricted night work among women was in their interest or not (Banks 1981; Walby 1986; Jenson 1989).

There is a concern that using existing gender categories as the basis of claims-making by women can, perversely, act so as to entrench existing gender inequalities. For example, Brown (1995) considers that this is a problem in forms of feminism built around notions of 'injury'. However, while this may be a problem in theory, in practice many of those making claims for women take steps in the direction of transformation rather than entrenchment of gender inequality. Even maternalism can have this effect. For example, the combination of maternalism with other social forces played an important role in the development of the public services of the welfare state during the nineteenth and twentieth centuries in North America and Europe (Koven and Michel 1990; Bock and Thane 1991; Skocpol 1995). In this way maternalism can be part of a broader transformative feminist project, with potential to reorganise the form and variety of the gender regime.

In practice, the priority given to the use of the same standard or different standards for equality can vary by institutional domain, even for the same group or project. In the sphere of paid employment, equal pay for work of equal value is now widely accepted; similarly, equal treatment in education and in the sale and distribution of goods and services, equal access to political representation, and equal rights to protection from violence by the law are the norm. However, in the domain of domestic care work, there remains controversy as to whether this is a protected sphere for women or not. One example of such controversy is whether mothers should have a presumptive entitlement to the custody of their children after separation/divorce, or whether fathers should have equal rights; another example concerns the use of the individual or of the household as the unit in tax and benefit systems, the former presuming the financial autonomy that follows upon the equal participation of women and men in employment, while the latter does not (Bergmann 1986; Himmelweit 2002; Women's Budget Group 2004; Verloo 2005b).

Equality can only be obtained when there is transformation, both of gendered standards of equality and of gendered practices. While the gender regime is still undergoing its transformation from domestic to public form, there will be tension between the visions that rest on shared standards and those that rest on the valorisation of domestic care work by women. In practice, feminists with different visions will sometimes oppose each other, while at other times they will find a way to reach a compromise (Banks 1981; Women's Budget Group 2004).

Conclusions

Feminism is vibrant and effective in the contemporary UK, EU and many countries around the world, as well as in the UN. This can be seen when the lens through which feminism is viewed is broadened from culture to the entire range of human social life, when the definition of feminism focuses on the pursuit of feminist goals rather than on self-identification, and when institutionalised practices are included alongside the more fluid social movement forms of feminism. When these clarifications to the definition to feminism are made, then the argument that this is a postfeminist era, in a sense that implies the end of feminism, is contradicted.

There is a multiplicity of diverse feminist projects. There are many feminist goals that engage with all major institutional domains. Feminist projects can be found in all such domains: in the economy, in the polity, in violence – as well as in civil society. They are not restricted to the arenas of culture and sexuality. There are many different ways in which the subject of feminism is constituted, including promoting womanhood, claiming the equal treatment of women with men, and imagining the transformation of gender relations. There is not a single approach, but rather a mix. A range of frameworks are invoked to support these projects, including justice frameworks of equality and human rights and mainstream frameworks of economic development and crime reduction. The claims-making includes both the universal and the particular. There are both shared common goals and diverse projects. There are specificities due to the nature of the gender regime and intersections with other regimes of inequality. But there are also similarities, partly due to exchanges associated with globalisation and partly due to common processes of gender inequality. There are multiple forms of organising of this activity, including near-spontaneous grassroots events, NGOs, as well as specialised governmental bodies. While the more formal bodies are relatively new, they are additional to the range of feminist activities rather than an alternative to it. This is further discussed in chapter 4.

Feminist demands may be explicit or embedded, found in projects that are mainstreamed or not, intersecting with other projects or not. Feminism continues in new forms and new coalitions, even when it does not name itself 'feminist'. The consequential variation in the visibility of feminist goals has had serious implications for the analysis of the strength of feminism. The tensions involved in gender mainstreaming are addressed further in chapter 5, while those concerning intersecting projects are addressed in chapter 7. This account of the strength of feminism is not an argument that all feminist goals have been achieved – far from it. Chapter 6 analyses the remaining and emerging challenges of the structural and systemic context.

4

New Forms of Feminist Organisation

Introduction

Feminism is taking new organisational forms. Not only are there local autonomous groups, but there are also national and transnational non-governmental organisations (NGOs), as well as feminist bodies within states. The fluidity of the grassroots and the vibrant and spontaneous events and campaigns continue, but some feminist initiatives have become formally coordinated and institutionalised. Within the state itself, there are now feminist entities, variously known as women's policy agencies and as the gender equality architecture. There is an increasing use of coalitions and alliances and networks as modes of organising, which engage with difference in a more nuanced way than either the earlier, tightly knit groups based on 'identity', or the more traditional democratic and bureaucratic centralist forms. There has been an increase in the significance of the global level, partly in the sense that communications among feminist networks have increased, but more importantly in the sense that new political spaces are being used, which have been developed within, and by, emergent forms of global and regional institutions (such as the UN and the European Union, respectively).

These changes mean that feminist activity is often less visible than before. Protest movements intrinsically seek to be noticed by the public, while engagement with the state involves lobbying activities that are less frequently reported in the press. The term 'feminist' is used less often to describe projects which are working with allies or with the mainstream, even if feminist goals are sought. Hence, while these new organisational forms add to the power of feminism, they make it less visible, feeding the false impression that feminism has faded away.

The present chapter first describes the range of forms of feminist organisation and analyses their increasing power; then it turns to an account of why the changes involved have been happening. These changes are linked to the ongoing transformation of the gender regime (see chapter 6), which has implications for the economic resources, political opportunities, rhetorical possibilities and epistemic devices available for taking forward feminist projects.

Waves of Feminism

Feminism develops in waves. 'First-wave' feminism, from the mid-nineteenth century to the 1920s, presents many similarities to 'second-wave' feminism, which has been developing since the late 1960s. The concept of 'wave' is deployed in order to capture the non-linear way in which such civil societal and political projects can develop. A wave starts in one location, builds rapidly through endogenous processes, and then spreads out through time and space, to affect social relations in other locations. The concept of wave captures the sudden transfer of social practices from one social system to another (Walby 2009).

First-wave feminism, like second-wave feminism, started out from local groups on specific issues, and then additionally developed national associations and coalitions that directed attention to key shared goals. Women organised into local, then national, suffragist and suffragette organisations; into women's trade unions and mixed sex trade unions; into a co-operative party and an independent labour party; and they developed specialised organisations for each of their many goals. Suffrage was a key shared goal. However, first-wave feminism was not restricted to suffrage, but addressed a wide range of goals. These included access to good employment; equal pay; access to education, for instance universities and medical training; the rejection of prostitution and sex trafficking; legal personhood, especially for married women; married women's property rights; a stance on the problem of violence against wives, and the right to legal separation; divorce; reduced penalties for infanticide; and the right to sit on juries. First-wave feminism started in the UK and in the US; then it spread to most countries of the West, a situation which promoted suffrage in many of them around 1920, and it also became an integral part of nationalist movements seeking de-colonisation.

After the victory of the achievement of suffrage in the more economically developed countries around the North Atlantic rim, feminism
lost its visibly unifying goal. There were divisions, for example, over
'protective' legislation restricting women's hours of work in factories,
which exacerbated other divisions related to war (1914–18) and to
the priority accorded to suffrage for men and racialised minorities.
There were changes in organisational form – for example, some
women's trade unions merged with men's unions, which eroded even
further a distinctive feminist agenda (Strachey 1979; Banks 1981;
Drake 1984; Spender 1983; Lewenhak 1977; Liddington and Norris
1978; Middleton 1977; Jayawardena 1986; Walby 1986, 1990;
Rowbotham 1997; Joannou and Purvis 2009).

Second-Wave Feminism: Grassroots and NGOs

Second-wave feminism emerged in the late 1960s in the global
North, especially in the US and in the UK. The most visible new
organisational forms were grassroots mobilisations and consciousness raising groups, although there was also the development of
more formally organised NGOs. The groups were typically small,
independent feminist bases, separate from mainstream political fora
such as the state, and engaged in public protests and campaigns on
specific issues.

   An example of such projects can be found amidst the development
of 'violence against women' projects in the 1970s. In the UK and
elsewhere, these projects included the establishment of refuges for
battered women and rape crisis centres run by women for women
(Dobash and Dobash 1992; Hague and Malos 1993; Harwin 1997).
Indeed the state was often seen to be a part of the problem as
much as a source of the solution (Hanmer 1978). Funding from the
state was minimal and marginal, more often at a local rather than
national level (Pahl 1985). There was wariness about taking money
from the state if this was thought to compromise the ideals of those
involved.

   The same period saw the development and flourishing of new
independent sites of cultural activity, which supported the possibility
of alternative lifestyles. These sites were feminist bookshops, music
events, self-help health groups, and small collectives for many lifestyle
activities. There was a politicisation of sexuality and the development
of lesbian feminism, which was regarded as a radical separatist way
of life. Significant feminist interventions took the form of street and

media oriented protests. There were demonstrations, for example, aiming to 'take back the night' and to demand 'a woman's right to choose' whether or not she required an abortion. There were women-only protest camps, such as Greenham Common, for protests against US nuclear missiles (Roseneil 1995; Bell and Klein 1996).

In most cases these early activities of the 'second-wave' feminist movement took a rather fluid form, sometimes spontaneous, often with relatively little formal organisation. It is this form of feminism that is best captured by the concept of 'wave'. This wave spread rapidly around the world, building on itself, in an endogenous manner, and surging with enthusiastic growth.

More formal organisations developed along with this wave of feminism. However, the fluid grassroots side of the movement never went away. As shown in chapter 3, grassroots mobilisations are still ongoing. Today they often use new media forms, such as websites, Facebook and Twitter, to aid coordination, but the fluidity and innovation of such organisational forms are alive and well.

Institutionalisation of Feminism and Engagement with the State

From the 1980s on, the second wave of feminism became embedded in institutions, taking more stable and rooted forms in civil society as NGOs. This institutionalisation of feminism in civil society sometimes involved the creation of entirely new organisations (e.g. End Violence against Women 2011), at other times it entailed the revitalisation and expansion of old feminist organisations (e.g. Fawcett Society 2011), while in other instances the new inclusion of women in already existing organisations (for instance trade unions) led to the adoption of new feminist goals on the agendas of these entities (Gagnon and Ledwith 2000). In the case of trade unions, there has been a steady increase in the proportion of female trade unionists, which reached around 50 per cent in most European and North American countries by 2005 (Visser 2006).

Following the sedimentation of feminism in institutions, the way in which feminist projects engaged with the state shifted. By the 1990s, feminist organisations in the US and UK were routinely making demands on and engaging with the state as part of their core activities. This involved lobbying and working with councillors, MPs and civil servants in local and national government. In response, small changes were made to policies, laws were reformed, and grants were awarded. These small positive responses encouraged the further engagement of feminist organisations with the state.

Changes in feminist approaches to the elimination of violence against women are one example of how the form itself of feminism has changed. The state responded to demands to address violence against women (Grace 1995), though not to a degree that the feminist community generally understood to be adequate, since it did not substantially address issues of gendered power in the home and in the state (Hester, Kelly and Radford 1996). By 2000, a wide range of feminist networks and service providers, such as the Women's Aid Federation of England, women legal professionals, feminist academics, and senior women police officers came to be in a more systematic dialogue with the state, at local and at national level, over improving the policy in relation to violence against women (Labour Party 1995). This process was aided by the significant increase, over the last thirty years, in the proportion of women at senior levels in professions relevant to criminal justice policy. This lobbying happened not only at local and national level, but also involved regional and global institutions, including the European Union and the Council of Europe (Kelly 1999). The Home Office began to address violence against women more systematically and to fund and support a wider range of policy developments, while simultaneously seeking to shape the agenda on its own terms (Taylor-Browne 2001). However, there remain ongoing demands – for instance demands for a more substantial central support for the network of refuges and rape crisis lines, and for improved court procedures to deal with the exceptionally high rate of attrition in rape cases and with the consequent low conviction rate for rapists (Kelly 1999; Lees 1996). Since 2010, the reduction in government resources to the sector, resulting from wider budget cuts, has raised the issue of the under-funding of these services yet more acutely. Nevertheless, the shift in strategy from relying primarily on the women's own resources in civil society towards engaging with the formal political sphere has been consolidated. In their engagement with the British state, UK feminists have drawn on the resources of a transnational movement aiming to reduce and eliminate violence against women.

A further example of the institutionalisation of feminism and of its engagement with the state is to be found in the economy. Economic issues are also being mainstreamed, with increasing emphasis on the state (Walby 2001b). This development is in contrast with the situation of the 1970s, when feminist strategies more often involved the building of separate women's committees in trade unions and professions, in order to give women an independent voice. By 2010, such basic capacity building for the articulation of women's voices was more developed, even if it is rarely regarded as sufficient. Over the last thirty years there has been a considerable increase in the proportion of women in senior positions in trade unions, in the academy, in management and in government, which has facilitated the articulation of a variety of women's perspectives on economic and redistributive issues (Gagnon and Ledwith 1996; Ledwith and Colgan 1996; Colgan and Ledwith 2002; Shaw and Perrons 1995). Feminist strategies in relation to economics build on the already existing institutionalisation of women's voices as part of the agenda of gender mainstreaming, that is, the incorporation of a gender perspective on all economic matters (Rees 1998). Examples include the Treasury engaging in dialogue with the Women's Budget Group (an informal think tank of NGOs, feminist academics in the field of the economy and social policy, and trade unions) over the gender implications of the budget (Himmelweit 2000; Women's Budget Group 2000). Of course, the process of gender mainstreaming is far from complete (Gregory 1999); nonetheless, the mainstreaming of gender in the economic domain, integrating feminist concerns into state policy and into the policy machinery, is proceeding.

This change in the form of feminism, from protest to engagement, has implications for the effectiveness of feminist projects (Nelson and Chowdhury 1994; Stetson and Mazur 1995; Silliman 1999). Some of these issues are common to social movements (Snow, Rochford, Worden and Benford 1986; McAdam, Tarrow and Tilly 2001), not only to specifically feminist varieties of such movements. There is ambivalence in the feminist analysis as to whether or not the institutionalisation of fluid grassroots feminism is likely to advance the position of women. There is concern that such institutionalisation may lead to the emergent NGOs becoming drawn into dominant perspectives and abandoning their original radical ideas and demands, as they are funded by corporations, foundations and states with mainstream agendas and they engage in international fora that are geographically and politically far from their local origins (Silliman 1999). However, increased influence does usually accrue to activities that are more rather than less coordinated. For instance, strongly coordinated trade unions have greater impact on the regulation of working conditions than those that are not (Visser 2006). A stronger coordination of feminist activities – in organisations, and at national, European and international rather than local levels – increases rather than reduces their influence. The evaluation of the compromises that ensue is further discussed in the following chapter, which will address gender mainstreaming.

Feminism within the State

Not only are the new forms of feminist practice oriented towards the state, but some forms of feminism have entered the state. There has been a significant increase in the proportion of women who are Members of Parliament (or legislature) and government ministers (Lovenduski 2005; Inter-Parliamentary Union 2010). In addition, there has been a development of new forms of state machinery, oriented towards gendered goals and variously conceptualised as 'women's policy agencies' (Stetson and Mazur 1995), 'gender machinery' (Rai 2003), the 'gender architecture' (Gender Equality Architecture Reform Campaign [GEAR] 2009, 2011), and as constituting a form of 'state feminism' (Stetson and Mazur 1995; Mazur 2002; Outshoorn and Kantola 2007).

The proportion of female Members of Parliament has been increasing in most countries around the world, rising from an average of 11 per cent in 1995 to 19 per cent in 2010. However, the figure has varied between countries; for example, in the UK it increased from 4 per cent in 1960 to 6 per cent in 1990 and to 22 per cent in 2010; in the USA it increased from 4 per cent in 1960 to 6 per cent in 1990 and to 17 per cent in 2010; while in Sweden, it increased from 14 per cent in 1960 to 38 per cent in 1990 and to 46 per cent in 2010 (Inter-Parliamentary Union 2010). The proportion of government ministers who are women has also been increasing, and, again, it varies between countries, reaching 23 per cent in 2008 in the UK, 24 per cent in the US and 48 per cent in Sweden (United Nations Development Programme [UNDP] 2009).

In the UK, the 2010 elections returned a Parliament in which women held 22 per cent of the seats, the highest proportion ever (Inter-Parliamentary Union 2010). The increase is higher in those parties or countries where feminists have been successful in gaining some kind of quotas inserted into the party or parliamentary procedures and where the electoral system is based on proportional representation, as well as on the nature of the gender regime. For example, the largest increase in female MPs in the UK occurred in 1997, because the Labour Party introduced women-only shortlists in some constituencies in order to ensure this outcome. Within the UK the effects of changes in the electoral system can be seen: there are much higher proportions of women in the newly established Scottish Parliament and Welsh Assembly than in the UK Parliament in Westminster (Squires and Wickham-Jones 2001).

Within political parties, historically there have been more women in parties of the left or social democracy, and feminist issues have been more frequently raised by these parties than by those on the right. However, the articulation of feminist issues in party politics is not always so confined. Sometimes there are cross-party alliances among female MPs on issues concerning women, especially if there are 'free votes'. More importantly, some feminist issues have become sufficiently part of the mainstream for them to be adopted by centrist and centre-right parties. For example, in Germany the centre-right Christian Democrat Party led by Merkel introduced policies to develop public childcare policies and to reduce gender-based violence against women. In European centrist and centre-right parties it is not unusual to see social democratic policies on gender-led issues (e.g. public childcare, reduction of gender-based violence) being combined with more neoliberal policies on class-led issues (e.g. reduction of welfare benefits, reduction of trade union bargaining powers), though the latter also have detrimental consequences for women, especially poor ones.

Important developments in the equality architecture have been part of the institutionalisation of feminist projects within the state, which in turn have been important in the pursuit of feminist goals in the economy. These developments include, in the UK, the establishment in 1975 of the Equal Opportunities Commission, which was replaced by the Equality and Human Rights Commission in 2007; and the establishment of the governmental policy unit, successively called the Women's Unit, the Women and Equality Unit and the Government Equalities Office, though this latter unit was integrated into the Home Office in 2010 (Squires and Wickham-Jones 2004; Squires 2007; Walby, Armstrong and Strid 2010b). In the EU, which is important for the regulation of the UK economy, these developments in the equality architecture include the European Women's Lobby (2011), the European Parliament's Women's Rights and Gender Equality Committee, the European Union Commission's Directorate on Equality between Men and Women and the European Institute for Gender Equality (Squires 2007; European Commission 2010a, 2010b, 2010c, 2011b; European Institute for Gender Equality 2011; European Parliament 2011; Walby, Armstrong and Strid 2010b).

The European Union has internal bodies that promote gender

equality, as well as bodies focused on other forms of inequality and discrimination – including Directorate G on 'Equality between women and men and action against discrimination' within the European Commission Directorate-General on Employment, Social Affairs and Equal Opportunities (European Commission 2011b). This body produced a Strategy, adopted by the European Commission (European Commission 2010b), which works towards the achievement of equality between women and men and identifies progress towards this goal by using indicators in the following areas: equal economic independence; narrowing gender gaps in employment; unemployment and pay (with specific reference to gaps within immigrant and ethnic minorities); reducing occupational and industrial segregation; ensuring that women are no more likely than men to be reduced to poverty; equality of healthy life years; flexible working arrangements for both women and men; increased provision of care services for children and the elderly; the development of parental leave; equal participation of women in political and economic decision-making, including in science and technology; eradication of gender-based violence; elimination of gender stereotypes in education, training, culture, the labour market and the media; and promotion of gender equality outside the EU.

The establishment of national machineries for the advancement of women is a global development; such machinery has been created in over 100 countries between 1995 and 1997 (True and Mintrom 2001), following the Beijing *Platform for Action* in 1995 (United Nations 1995). However, the form and resources of these national gender machineries are highly uneven, as can be seen in the country reports on these matters to the 2005 review of the UN Platform for Action, Beijing+10 (Theisen, Spoden, Verloo and Walby 2005). They vary in the positioning of these machineries in relation to other government departments – for example in whether the machinery is attached to the prime minister's office or to some other ministry, in whether there are dedicated ministers for gender equality or not, in whether there are established consultative relations with civil society organisations, in whether tools such as gender impact assessment and gender budgeting are developed and routinely in use, and in the extent to which they have specially trained personnel and resources of their own (O'Cinneide 2002; Theisen, Spoden, Verloo and Walby 2005; Veitch 2005). There are also variations in the extent to which there are bodies dedicated to gender equality, or bodies which encompass a wider range of inequalities issues (Verloo 2006; Ben-Galim, Campbell and Lewis

2007; Kantola and Nouisainen 2009; Squires 2007, 2009; Walby, Armstrong and Strid 2010b).

The organisational history of the relationship of feminist projects to the state differs around the world. In the West, civil societal projects typically started before feminist agencies were developed within the state (Stetson and Mazur 1995). In communist states, including those of eastern Europe, Russia and China, certain forms of gender equality, for example quotas for women in parliament, were part of official practice (Inter-Parliamentary Union 1995). In the global South state feminism often developed before or alongside civil society-based projects, partly as a consequence of engagement with transnational feminism (Valiente 2007).

Within the UN, there has been considerable development of the gender architecture. There have been specialised units promoting gender equality, the advancement of women and the protection of the human rights of women in UNIFEM the UN Division for the Advancement of Women (DAW), the Office of the Special Adviser on Gender Issues (OSAGI) and the Advancement of Women, and the UN International Research and Training Institute for the Advancement of Women (INSTRAW). Following a long campaign by the Gender Equality Architecture Reform coalition, in July 2010 these were merged into a single more powerful unit: UN Women, the UN Entity for Gender Equality and the Empowerment of Women (GEAR 2011).

These developments embed feminism within the state and institutionalised public bodies. They are an outcome of, and at the same time a challenge to, older notions of feminism as a protest movement situated outside of political institutions. Today feminist projects are being conducted inside these state institutions as well as outside them.

Coalitions and Networks rather than Identity Politics

Some early forms of feminism in the 1960s and 1970s drew on the strength of a belief in a common identity of women as women, which can be illustrated by the notion that 'sisterhood is powerful' (Morgan 1970). However, this was often an aspiration or an invented tradition that was only partially achieved or constructed, given the long-standing recognition of the significance of differences and inequalities between women (Jakobsen 1998; Walby 2000). Later forms of feminism addressed these differences more directly and through new organisational forms. Thus 'identity politics' was increasingly replaced by the overt politics of alliances and coalitions (Ferree and Hess 1995).

Diversity has rightly been a major theme of social analysis in recent years (Calhoun 1995; Mohanty 1991; Taylor 1994; Young 1990). One of the major issues for contemporary feminist theory and practice is how to address differences between women simultaneously with commonalities (Felski 1997). There is a need to capture the multiple and overlapping nature of social differences, the way in which individuals are simultaneously located within several different social groupings, which have varying significance and priority according to time and place. The complexity and the partially overlapping and cross-cutting nature of social divisions, rather than that of reified differences, is the central issue for feminist politics (Jakobsen 1998).

The discussion of the concept and practice of 'intersectionality' (Crenshaw 1991) represents a further attempt to engage with the difficulties that lie at the point of intersection of different forms of inequality, especially when the underlying social relations are changed at this point of intersection (McCall 2005; Hancock 2007).

It is important to address the concepts and practices of networks and coalitions in order to avoid being consumed by the 'doxa of difference' (Felski 1997). Such concepts and practices include those of alliance (Jakobsen 1998), coalition (Ferree and Hess 1995), network (Keck and Sikkink 1998; Moghadam 2005) and, more specifically, 'velvet triangle' (Halsaa 1998; Vargas and Wieringa 1998; Woodward 2004). Concepts of networks, alliances and coalitions are more helpful in an analysis of feminist politics than concepts of identity or difference, because they foreground the practice of recognising differences and commonalities simultaneously. They point up the social and political work that is done when engaging across difference. They are suggestive of the contingency and of the combined potential for fragility and resilience of the grouping of those supporting a political project, especially over time and space.

The concept of 'velvet triangle' (Halsaa 1998; Vargas and Wieringa 1998; Woodward 2004) refers to the alliances that develop between various feminist groups inside and outside the state. This can be the relationship between three gendered constituencies of elected representatives, women's units in government and women's groups in civil society (Halsaa 1998; Vargas and Wieringa 1998). In some circumstances feminist academics can be significant, as in the 'velvet triangle' of feminist bureaucrats, academics and activists analysed by Woodward (2004). Other sets of alliances can be identified, including that of gender machinery (or architecture), Members of Parliament and academics (Veitch 2005).

While there is a whole range of ways of conceptualising alliances and coalitions, the important point here is that there has been a move away from simple forms of identity politics.

Argumentation and Epistemic Communities

Some new political forms draw especially on evidence-based argumentation and make coalitions that include both political and scientific communities. The concept of 'epistemic community' has been developed to capture these new political forms. They can be found in the articulation of feminist advocacy networks with state authorities.

The notion of epistemic community is embedded in an awareness of the importance of argument (Haas 1992). As articulated by Haas,

An epistemic community is a network of professionals with recognized expertise and competence in a particular domain and an authoritative claim to policy-relevant knowledge within that domain or issue-area [. . .] they have (1) a shared set of normative and principled beliefs [. . .] (2) shared causal beliefs, which are derived from their analysis of practices leading or contributing to a central set of problems in their domain [. . .] (3) shared notions of validity [. . .] (4) a common policy enterprise. (Haas 1992: 3)

This concept is used in order to get a grip on the role of knowledge and information. Epistemic communities are increasingly important because of the increasing significance of scientific knowledge in modernity.

The analysis of epistemic communities is inspired by the Habermasian tradition (Habermas 1987, 1991), which argues that power and norms are not sufficient to explain changes in political processes, but that processes of argumentation can be significant in some circumstances (Risse 1999). While processes of political change are about power, there is also a space where argumentation plays a part. The principles of human rights are diffusing internationally, involving a process of socialisation of states. Some aspects of feminist projects have become embedded in a variety of international regimes and organisations, thus forming part of the normative setting of international society, increasingly defining what constitutes a 'civilised state' as a member of the international community in 'good standing' (Risse, 1999: 529–30). The process of argumentation potentially unsettles fixed identities and perceived interests, which become subject to discursive challenges. Thus moral persuasion can prompt a redefinition of interest and of identity, potentially leading to argumentative 'self-entrapment' and change (531). The concept of epistemic community presents some parallels with the concept of 'communities of practice' (Wenger 1998), in which social rather than individual processes are seen as central.

Contemporary feminism has increasingly included epistemic communities. These have increasingly made claims to expertise and increasingly argued with key holders of institutional power. There has been a proliferation of expert feminist networks that engage on the basis of argumentation. However, feminism is not exclusively an epistemic community; the basis of the claims for justice remains varied.

Transnational and Global Feminism

Feminism is now a transnational, sometimes global, practice (Moghadam 2005). Feminist projects were rapidly developed in many countries around the world. Indigenous feminist groups picked up ideas and practices, absorbing them into their existing practices, creating new versions of feminist projects so as to suit themselves (Davis 2007). In turn, the new versions spread around the world, modifying earlier ideas and practices. These developments were facilitated by feminist networking, travelling, global media, development aid, the global publishing industry, and the spaces created by the UN and other transnational bodies. These feminist projects can take the form of global waves (Walby 2009). There is much exchange of information, ideas and practices about feminist projects around the world. This takes place not only at conferences, but through the internet, letters, phone calls, books, journals, magazines and other publications (Counts, Brown and Campbell 1992; Keck and Sikkink, 1998; Moghadam 2005). Then there is the use of modern technologies, such as the internet sites and video-conferences. A global feminist civil society is now effectively in existence. The discussion of difference is a constant feature of this politics. The policies and practices used in response are reflexively monitored and adapted to particular circumstances. The use of coalitions as a method of organising feminism across difference is now taken for granted. Such transnational feminist coalitions have worked hard to engage constructively with issues of difference within the overall project (Ferree and Hess 1995; Friedman 1995; Mayer 1995; Rao 1995).

There were, of course, many precursors to contemporary international feminism (Banks 1981). They have included not only the well-known campaigns for the vote for women, but also demands for education and employment. The International Labour Organization (ILO) has attempted to set standards for employment since its inception in 1919; one set of standards – Convention 100, adopted in 1951 – was for equal pay for equal work by men and women (Valticos 1969). This decision has been ratified by most of the many states that are members of the ILO. The UN adopted a Convention on the Elimination of All Forms of Discrimination against Women at the General Assembly in 1979, which has been ratified by most members of the UN (Nelson and Chowdhury 1994). While in itself this Convention has little binding force, it was, nonetheless, important as a form of legitimation of this demand, when it was made by local activists in particular countries. For example it was important in the campaign by Japanese women, who were demanding equal opportunities legislation. They successfully used this convention by threatening to embarrass their government if it had not passed suitable legislation before an international meeting (Yoko, Mitsuko and Kimiko 1994).

The attempt to stop violence against women involved the development of political networks at local, national and global levels. There has been a globalisation of demands to restrict men's violence against women through the use of legal regulation and to provide resources to women who have suffered such violence. Like economic equality, the demand to reduce and stop men's violence against women has a long history. Campaigns to protect women from domestic violence and sexual assault can be found at the end of the nineteenth century. During the 1960s and 1970s, feminist activists in the US and UK were prominent in the development of national, yet mutually informed, movements around domestic violence and rape (Dobash and Dobash 1992). Local campaigns to address violence against women have been established both in western nations (Hanmer, Radford and Stanko 1989) and in the developing world (Counts, Brown and Campbell 1992; Davies 1993), from Canada (Johnson 1996) to Malaysia (Ariffin 1997) and India (Sen 1998).

The European Union facilitated the spread of feminist practice on violence against women within the EU by funding a series of networks and projects with the explicit intent of sharing knowledge and stimulating developments in further countries. Support was particularly strong in the European Parliament, which voted three times for Daphne initiatives to fund the development of a large number of innovatory measures, and also of networks of NGOs working in this area. The movement into this policy area goes beyond the earlier restrictions of EU interventions to economic matters; it necessitated discussions as to the legal basis of these developments. In April 1999 the European Parliament decided that it had legal authority for these actions under Article 152 of the Treaty of Amsterdam, which referred to human health, including respect for physical integrity (Women of Europe Newsletter, 1999) – a broadening of remit from that in earlier treaties. Reference to cross-border issues, which fall clearly into the jurisdiction of the EU, have further extended the EU remit in relation to violence against women in areas such as trafficking (European Commission 2010e).

By the early 1990s the demand to stop men's violence against women was articulated in international fora, including those of the UN (Friedman 1995). The demand was translated into language and concepts more appropriate for the predominantly male forum of the UN: the language of human rights rather than that of men's oppression of women. The argument was that women's rights were human rights, hence violence against women constituted a violation of human rights. This was a call for the transformation of the existing agenda of human rights and for a new interpretation, which placed women's issues at the heart of the mainstream (Bunch 1995; Stamatopolou 1995). In 1993 a UN conference in Vienna made the following declaration, endorsed later by the United Nations General Assembly:

Violence against women constitutes a violation of the rights and fundamental freedoms of women [. . .] there is a need for a [. . .] clear statement of the rights to be applied to ensure the elimination of violence against women in all its forms, a commitment by States [. . .] and a commitment by the international community at large to the elimination of violence against women. (United Nations General Assembly 1993)

This outcome was the result of actions by a set of alliances, networks and coalitions at both grassroots and international levels (Toro 1995). While this declaration was not legally binding on member states, nonetheless it recommended a series of specific legislative, educational and administrative measures to be taken by states, and, further, it has provided an important source of legitimation to feminist activists by putting pressure on their states. The declaration was used as a resource in arguments advanced by feminist expert networks. These actions were reiterated and developed in the Beijing *Platform for Action* (United Nations 1995). In 1996 the UN established a trust fund in support of actions to eliminate violence against women; the fund was administered by UNIFEM. UN agencies have encouraged the sharing of knowledge about the effects of violence and effective means of combating it, both for non-governmental organisations and for states. Further developments have taken place during recent years, as discussed in chapter 3, so that the UN is now a significant force in policy developments to reduce and eliminate violence against women.

This conceptualisation within the discourse of universal human rights has facilitated the spread and legitimation of the campaign combating violence against women (Bunch 1995). This feminist practice has transcended the 'doxa of difference' in feminist philosophy (Felski 1997). Rather, feminists have learnt here to work with and across difference (Friedman 1995). However, the rhetoric of 'cultural difference' was used by some states in order to resist this expansion of women's human rights (Mayer 1995; Rao 1995). Nevertheless, the 1993 UN declaration directed states not to 'invoke any custom, tradition or religious consideration to avoid their obligations' regarding violence against women (United Nations General Assembly 1993). Important to the feminist success here was the constant engagement with the issue of diversity through the breadth of a variety of grassroots organisations, together with the use of networks and coalitions rather than monolithic organisational forms. This engagement enabled fluid and flexible political responses, which were sensitive to context within the framework of a shared desire to end male violence against women and a willingness to utilise the rhetoric of rights that resonated both with the grassroots and with the administrators of international organisations. The development of communication technologies facilitated the rapid transfers of knowledge and practice between grassroots and international organisations. In this way globalisation facilitated the development of feminist campaigns around violence against women.

Explaining Changes in the Forms of Feminism

The explanation of these developments in feminism involves a multi-layered approach to changes in social structure, in political opportunity structures, in economic and political resources, in the framing of the issue, and in the development of feminist epistemic communities.

These are interrelated levels of explanation rather than competing ones.

Social Structural Changes

There have been important changes in the form of the gender regime affecting many dimensions of women's lives, thereby creating new possibilities for feminist politics (see chapter 6 and Walby 2009 for more details of changes in the gender regime). During processes of gendered social change, the category 'woman' is not a stable one. As the gender regime changes, so do the constitution of masculinity and femininity, and the interests and priorities of 'women'. The political priorities of different groups of women may change along with changes in their economic and domestic situations. As certain types of material situation become more prevalent, so too may the political priorities associated with those situations. As social situations change, so too may the economic and organisational resources and political opportunities available to some women. The issues addressed below are debates about the specific changes that might be leading to the developments in feminism noted above, and about the linkages between them.

Macro-social change associated with industrialisation has often been implicated in the rise of feminist politics, though the way in which this takes effect is understood through quite different mechanisms, ranging from modernisation (Chafetz and Dworkin 1986) to postmaterialist values (Inglehart 1997; Inglehart and Norris 2000), and women's employment (Manza and Brooks 1998). Chafetz and Dworkin (1986) found that industrialisation, urbanisation and the growth of the middle classes (proxied by education) were the most important factors explaining variations in the strength of feminist movements. Inglehart (1997) and Inglehart and Norris (2000) argue that the link between industrialisation and new forms of feminist politics in advanced industrialised countries is a result of the development of postmaterialist values. Those who have the most postmaterialist values are the well-educated and young. This is a development not only of feminism and of postmaterialism, but one in which women are increasingly moving leftwards in their political priorities. Norris (1999b) finds a gender-generation gap in voting in the UK since 1992, in which women under 30 are more likely to vote left than men of their own age or older women. Manza and Brooks (1998) attribute the increase in left voting among women in the USA to the increase in the proportion of women in employment, since the policy priorities of employed women include the provision of public services. Their sophisticated statistical modelling shows that this shift in political priorities relative to the average is not found among all women, but specifically among employed women. The growth in the number of employed women is fuelling the gender gap in voting and increasing women's demands on the state for intervention in institutions perceived as relevant to gender inequalities. Huber and Stephens (2000) find that women's labour force participation, as well as social democratic governance and state structure, are important correlates of the expansion of public social welfare services in an analysis of sixteen advanced industrial countries.

Thus economic development is part of the explanation of the increased feminist mobilisation of women and of their leftwards political movement, which involves increasing demands for state services. The improvements in women's employment and education are part of the mechanism by which this shift occurs. These changes are part of the transition in the gender regime from a more domestic to a more public form (Walby 1990, 1997). However, questions remain as to the exact nature of the link between structural change and changes in women's politics, which are addressed below. One of the links is the relationship between social change and the resources available to projects.

Economic and Organisational Resources

Economic and political resources are key components in changes in political mobilisation (McCarthy and Zald 1977). Increases in women's employment and education and in women's presence in a variety of civil society institutions, from trade unions to feminist advocacy networks, constitute increases in the resources available to feminism. As women's employment has grown, so have not only the economic resources of many women, but also women's presence in organisations which make demands on employers and government (Ferree 1980; Gagnon and Ledwith 2000). This happened despite the ongoing gender gaps in wages and conditions of work. There has been a significant increase in the proportional presence of women in trade unions (Grainger and Crowther 2007) and in the growth of expert feminist advocacy networks, both in the UK (Himmelweit 2000) and at the international and transnational level (Keck and Sikkink 1998; Moghadam 2000).

Political Opportunity Structures

The form that political action takes depends to some extent on the nature of political opportunities (Eisinger 1973). There has been a very significant change in the political opportunities facing feminism as a consequence of the transition in the gender regime, in which women have come to have considerably greater, though still less than equal, participation in the state. The implications for feminism of this partial opening of the state to women are subject to debate, not least because the conceptualisation and location of the state in feminist politics have long been subject to controversy and development. The rejection of the significance of the state for gender politics by some radical feminists (Millett 1977), its dispersal in feminist Foucauldian analysis (Smart 1989) and its micro-level conceptualisations of gov-ernance (Haney 1996) have recently been critiqued as a result of the analysis of the significance of the welfare state for gender relations (Orloff 1993), of new configurations of feminist practice through the discourse of human rights (Peters and Wolper 1995), of the increased representation of women in parliaments and cabinets around the world (Githens, Norris and Lovenduski 1995; Walby 2000), and of increased theoretical interest in conceptualising the complexities of the issue of representation and the state (Squires 1999; Kymlicka 1991, 1995; Phillips 1995; Young 1990, 1997).

There has been a significant change in the political opportunity structures as a result of the slow opening of positions in parliament to women. The shift in the opportunity structure is implicated in the shift of emphasis in feminist politics, from radical separatist autonomous political developments towards mainstream politics, focused on the amelioration of the position of women through a reform of state actions. In the 1980s, the contrast in political opportunity structures between the US, the UK and Sweden led Gelb (1989) to conclude that such structures were a major deter-minant of whether feminist politics took an autonomous or a state oriented form. At a local level, within a rape crisis movement, there has been a trajectory of development in the history of several organisations, from radical autonomous groups to engagement with the state (Matthews 1994) almost everywhere. However, this does not necessarily mean that the separatist groups have entirely disap-peared; in many places some remain and coexist with those engaged with the state.

There has been an increase in the proportion of women involved in elected national parliaments (Inter-Parliamentary Union 1995;

2010; Walby 2000). This has occurred in most, though not in all the countries around the world (Inter-Parliamentary Union 1995, 2000). The increase in women elected to parliament represents a shift in the political opportunity structure. Part of this increase is linked to the rapid spread of the practice of quotas around the world (Dahlerup 2006). There is a debate as to whether, and if so how, the increased physical presence of 'women' in parliamentary (or other decision-making) bodies causes an increase in the representation of 'women's interests' (Squires 1999; Norris 1996a; Lovenduski 2005; Childs, Webb and Marthaler 2010), though the balance of judgement is that it does (Mansbridge 2005). However, the relationship between the 'descriptive' and the 'substantive' representation of women in politics can only be understood by taking into account not just the role of gender regimes in constituting the description of who women are, but also the role of gendered and feminist projects in constructing the perception of the interests of women that might be substantively represented. Different forms of gender regimes not only produce differently situated women, who are likely to perceive their interests in different ways, but also varied resources with which they may develop their projects.

There is evidence of a correlation between the women's presence and pro-woman policies in parliaments, but nonetheless there are significant exceptions. This increase in the number of women in parliament is often associated with a change of attitude and a change of policies towards attitudes and policies which women prioritise – according to studies on the UK (Norris 1996a), US (Thomas 1991), Sweden (Wängnerud 2000) and Norway (Skjeie 1991). In the UK, prospective female parliamentary candidates for the 1992 election were more likely than male candidates to support women's equal opportunities and their rights in abortion, in marital rape and in domestic violence, as well as to adopt positions more typical of women in a range of other matters, including nationalisation/ privatisation, nuclear weapons and the death penalty (Norris 1996a). In the US, women in the state legislatures with the highest proportion of female representation introduced and passed more priority bills dealing with issues of women, children and families than men in their states did, and more than female representatives did in states where women were low in number (Thomas 1991). However, a simple correlation between the presence of women and feminist policies is not always found (Dahlerup 2006). It is important to consider the background and experience of the women who are entering parliament, as well as the organisational forms they utilise in parliament. Women's policy priorities appear to be diffused through a high percentage of women in office or through the presence of a formal women's legislative caucus; that is, both numbers and organisation made a difference (Thomas 1991).

The change in the gender composition of parliaments is a significant shift in the political opportunity structure, which contributes to the change of form in politics by opening new possible lines of political engagement. When these state institutions were *de facto* closed to women, feminist politics engaged in more radical, separatist and autonomous, forms of politics. As these institutions have slowly admitted more women, there has been a growth in the kinds of politics that are oriented to the state. The development of feminist bodies within the state, as governmental policy units, implementation commissions, and consultation bodies, itself helps to increase the political opportunities open to feminists. There are more locations within the state that are interested in engagement and more potential allies with whom to build coalitions. The increase in opportunities for feminists to engage with mainstream politics strengthens the likelihood that feminists will choose to develop organisational forms that further facilitate this engagement. This creates a pull towards stably organised groups and away from separatist and more spontaneous types of political activity.

However, the simplicity of the concept of 'woman' has become part of the problem, since it encourages reductionist and essentialist ways of thinking about gender relations. It is better to acknowledge that the concept of 'woman' is differentiated, that the presence of different types of women makes a difference, and that the concept of 'women's interests' is likewise differentiated, so that such interests are not always obvious to identify among competing alternatives. In the analysis offered here, which draws on work to be presented in chapter 6, the concept of 'woman' is replaced by 'gender as constituted by varieties of gender regime', and the concept of 'women's interests' is replaced by 'multiple alternative feminist projects'. This approach offers a way forward beyond overly stable gender categories, by providing more fluid gendered categories for investigation, which nonetheless offer sufficient purchase for empirical as well as theoretical analysis. This discussion of the changing relationship between multiple feminist projects and varieties of gender regimes is an alternative resolution of the dilemmas in the long-running discussion of the relationship between the descriptive and the substantive representation of women in feminist political science.

Framing

While these changes in social structure and institutions, and in the associated political resources and opportunities which follow from them, are important in explaining variations in the extent and nature of feminist politics, they are by themselves insufficient. Symbolic resources and the ability to challenge existing notions of social order are an important part of the repertoire of a social movement (Eyerman and Jamieson 1991). The ideas held by a movement may be very important to participants, and not merely instrumental to more material goals (Melucci 1989). It is useful to ask why certain kinds of framings of politics were used, and to find the links between the economic, political and institutional level of analysis and that of the individual actors (della Porta and Diani 1999; Diani 1996; McAdam, Tarrow and Tilly 2001). Frame theory offers such a linkage (Snow, Rochford, Worden and Benford 1986). 'Frame alignment' occurs when an individual's (including the movement entrepreneurs') interests, values and beliefs become congruent and complementary with those of a social movement organisation. Frames organise experiences and events, making them meaningful. Frame alignment is necessary for movement participation (ibid.). Diani reinterprets Snow and his collaborators' (1986) concept of frame alignment to make it refer to the process of 'the integration of mobilising messages with dominant representations of the political environment' (Diani 1996: 1058), rather than to the connection between the values and goals of the movement entrepreneurs and those of their potential constituents.

Frame theory can be fruitfully applied to changes in feminist politics – for example to investigating the development of the meaning of gender equality at different times and in different places (Ferree, Gamson, Gerhards and Rucht 2002b; Verloo 2005a), or to investigating the extent to which this concept can be stretched without losing its meaning (Lombardo, Meier and Verloo 2009).

Frame alignment analysis, the process of 'the integration of mobilising messages with dominant representations of the political environment', is a useful addition to the layers of analysis. The extent to which feminists have sought to reshape conceptions of gender justice radically, or to work within a dominant frame, depends on specific sets of social circumstances and has potentially tremendous consequences for their impact. The relative shift in the framing of feminist analysis from one which is autonomous, radical, oppositional and anti-system to one which is inclusionary and mainstream is significant and, while the selection of the frame is affected by the social context, it has nonetheless important consequences for the reception of feminist ideas.

Frame theory may be deployed so as to reinterpret changes in feminism. For example, rather than the feminist movement being seen to be in abeyance (Bagguley 2002; Sawyers and Meyer 1999), changes in feminist activity should be understood as a re-framing of feminism into an inclusionary discourse (as opposed to an anti-system discourse). This strategy involves the loss of a media profile, as there is a shift away from being simply oppositional and towards more involvement with the government. While the consequence may be loss of visibility as an oppositional, protest oriented social move-ment, this is not the same as a decrease in feminist political activity. The development of an inclusionary strategy instead of an anti-system strategy for feminism is an act of re-framing in the context of wider changes. If the political situation continues to re-polarise, for example as a result of the detrimental impact on women's well-being of the large cuts in government welfare expenditure planned in the UK in 2010, then anti-system strategies and public protests are likely to become more common again.

Attempts to mainstream feminist goals in government have invoked the use of multiple frameworks. One illustration of this multiplicity is the range of government departments to which gender equality units have been attached in the UK. Here gender equality has been the focus of a separate unit within the govern-ment departments of employment, within the Cabinet Office, and within the Department for Trade and Industry, within a separate Government Equalities Office, then within the Home Office. In the commissions designed to implement equality, gender started with its own commission in 1975 – the Equal Opportunities Commission; but since 2007 it has been taken alongside other inequalities and human rights, in the Equality and Human Rights Commission (Squires 2009; Government Equalities Office [GEO] 2009, 2011; Walby, Armstrong and Strid 2010b). However, in the context of the spending cuts to all public services in 2010, there was a significant reduction in the budgets of these equality bodies.

The development of a governmental policy focus on 'violence against women' provides another example of the range of framings that are possible to use. In the UK, this issue has long been led by the Home Office, thereby giving the issue a 'crime' framing. However, there have been persistent attempts to get the issue treated as one of gender equality (and hence as one based in the government gender equality unit, or EHRC (Kelly 2005, 2007), or as one in which several ministries needed to be involved in cross-governmental responsibility, with the development of special inter-departmental and inter-ministerial groups to address the issue. This did emerge as a cross-government strategy in 2009/2010 (HM Government 2010). Within the EU there is weak legal competence to address the issue: within the Commission the topic is addressed marginally in relation to health and increasingly in the Directorate General for Fundamental Rights and Justice, but it remains marginal to the main gender equality unit, which is rooted in employment issues. The European Parliament, especially its Women's Rights and Gender Equality Committee, has consistently pushed forward on violence against women with a series of initiatives, using a framing of equality and rights. An EU survey on violence against women is planned by the European Union Fundamental Rights Agency (EU FRA) (2011) – a human rights framing; while the planned Observatory on Violence against Women is to be located in the new European Institute for Gender Equality – a gender equality framing.

Within the various agencies of the UN, violence against women is consistently framed as a human rights issue. Globalisation constitutes a new framing, actively invoked by those feminists who use a discourse of human rights. It is a major dominant framing of social relations. Its juxtaposition to human rights knowingly elides the distinction between the global and the universal (Walby 2001a).

Globalisation

Important global processes are involved in the transfer of politics and policies from one location to another. The conventional notion that new ideas and political practices usually develop first in the West, especially the US, then are transferred from there to the rest of the world has been heavily criticised and other directions of movement have been suggested (Chabot and Duyvendak 2002; Snyder 2003). The process of policy and politics transfer has sometimes been described as a process of diffusion, but the concept of diffusion has limiting connotations. In particular, some processes involve unequal power, so that the changes may involve degrees of coercion or compulsion. The development of gender equality policies is not a simple process of diffusion from core countries to the periphery (Chabot and Duyvendak 2002), but rather one in which there is complex hybridisation and development of variations of form in different locations.

A range of processes are involved, including advocacy by civil society groups and movements within a country; transnational advocacy networks (Keck and Sikkink 1998; True and Mintrom 2001; Zippel 2004), epistemic communities and expert networks (Hoskyns 1996), perhaps drawing on the legitimation of universal human rights (Peters and Wolper 1995; Kelly 2005); isomorphic development within the European organisational field (Wobbe 2003); legal compulsion from a transnational polity such as the EU (Pillinger 1992); a mix of pressure from societal actors and ideological issues of prestige in the EU setting (van der Vleuten 2005); a mix of forms of soft law and targets, as in the EU open method of policy coordination (Behning and Pascual 2001; Mósesdóttir 2011; Rubery, Smith and Fagan 1999). The process may involve a mix of processes, for example pressure from national civil society groups in dialogue with transnational experts (Women's Budget Group 2004; Pillinger 2005; Veitch 2005).

Feminist political activists have been important players in the construction of a newly globalising world (Ramirez, Soysal and Shanahan 1997; Waylen 1996). New kinds of alliances, political forms, political strategies and substantive fields have been involved (Marchand 1996; Peterson and Runyan 1999) in the context of changing gendered global power relations (Mies 1986; Mitter 1986). There have been knowledge transfers around the world, with lessons passed along transnational networks (Keck and Sikkink 1998). Feminists are increasingly using transnational networks to pressure 'national' parliaments (Keck and Sikkink 1998). Emergent parts of the international level are conducive to the articulation of new political agendas and new political constituencies, because they are more recently institutionalised. Those political institutions, which were created later in the development of women's political organisations, typically have more women-friendly practices. For example developments in electoral procedures – such as quotas and proportional representation, which tend to increase the proportion of women in parliament – are more often applied to new parliaments and assemblies than to those that were established hundreds of years ago. This is illustrated by the proportion of women elected to the new Welsh and Scottish assemblies and in the European Parliament by using proportional representation in the voting system – which was higher than the proportion of women elected to the old House of Commons in the UK under the first-past-the-post system.

Within the increasingly global framing of political discourse, feminists have been adept at utilising the discourse and constitutionalised practice of equal human rights, drawing down on its universalistic logic to legitimate and concretise their claims (Peters and Wolper 1995). While the rights discourse has many well-rehearsed limitations, it has nonetheless provided a potent source of legitimation for those feminist demands that are articulated through this perspective. This cuts across the contemporary privileging of difference in feminist philosophy (Braidotti 1994; Felski 1997). But many of those who practise feminist politics have found a way of working across difference while utilising the powerful discourse of universal human rights.

The global is often mediated by institutions that are situated between the local and the global in scope (Hettne, Inotai and Sunkel 1999). In the context of the UK, an important body here is that of the European Union. The understanding of politics in the UK requires an understanding of the EU, since this body crucially mediates the relationship of the UK to the global. In particular, the EU is now responsible for key aspects of economic policy, such as the regulation of labour markets (Weiler 1997).

Campaigns and leverage have increasingly utilised the transnational levels. The nation-state has been the subject of a successful pincer movement by feminists, organised both at grassroots and at transnational level (Keck and Sikkink 1998). The nation-state is still important as the location of state apparatus, in particular of the implementation of the law. My argument here is that the state is no longer the origin or main focus of political activity; rather it is an object or a prize along the way. Key debates, the formation of strategic political alignments, do not take place principally inside national parliaments, but rather at a range of levels. Political actors engage with states merely as one node in a wider network of relevant political fora. States matter; but they are no longer quite so uniquely important as sites of politics, as transnational processes have developed.

There is a variety of relationships among transnational gendered actors, ranging from mutualism to dominance and leading to outcomes that vary from increased hostilities to hybridisation. Networks may be of mutual benefit, with relatively equitable relations within them (Keck and Sikkink 1998). Or they may involve relations of compulsion, as when the EU has legal dominance over member states in its arenas of competence (Hoskyns 1996). Further, there may be a relationship of conditionality, such as when financial aid is tied to the meeting of certain conditions, for instance human rights, or to the curtailment of government expenditure, which the recipient may not have otherwise prioritised (Moser 1993). The interventions of western or global institutions may purport to be in the recipients' best interests, but prior historical relations of colonialism call this principle into question (Mohanty 1991). The actual nature of specific international feminist political relations is a question for empirical analysis. The outcome of increased communications may range from increased self-definition and hostility between cultural groups, as in some fundamentalist reactions to the West (Marty and Scott 1993; Moghadam 1994), to the borrowing of cultural and political forms and hybridisation (Jayawardena 1986; Ramirez, Soysal and Shanahan 1997).

While many differences and divergent priorities associated with local circumstances remain, globalisation has now developed so much that feminist projects in different parts of the work will often share links and common engagements with an emerging global feminist civil society. The emergent forms of feminism share similarities as well as differences.

Conclusions

Feminism has changed its form in recent years. There has been a significant broadening of its organisational forms, so that, in addition to autonomous separatist groups and grassroots protest movement tactics, there is now engagement with the state; indeed there is entry into the state itself. There has been a move away from identity politics towards alliances, coalitions and networks. There has been a move towards a transnational politics, near-global rather than national in reach. These processes vary significantly between countries.

There have been feminist attempts to develop political interventions in both civil society and state. These are part of a set of global feminist politics, which, while tailored to local circumstances, draws profoundly upon a common web. In each case these are political issues of long standing, which were articulated during first-wave feminism at the end of the nineteenth century, as well as today. But their current form is new, drawing upon the political capacities of women that are newly available as a consequence of the transformation of the gender regime and of the development of the global linkages.

In order to explain these political developments, a broad conception of politics is required, together with a multi-level analysis of the determinants of political engagement. These draw on, but go beyond, the analysis of feminism as a social movement. Many aspects of feminist politics have shifted from autonomous forms of organisation to increased engagement with the state and, further still, to locations within the state. The consequence of these changes is that feminist politics and activities are not best captured by the traditional notion of a 'social movement' of outsiders, in mediatised protests against the institutionalised holders of power. Feminist politics now encompass most of the range of the political repertoire. Feminists are within the institutions of power as well as outside them. This is not the end of feminism; it is rather a new set of forms of its practice.

Changes in the gender regime have involved increases in economic and organisational resources as a result of increased paid employment and education for women, an increase in their organisational capacity, including increasing involvement with a variety of organisations. These developments have changed the political opportunity structure and have contributed to the presence of women in formal political arenas, such as the parliament and the state. Groups of feminists have re-framed key feminist projects within the powerful legitimation of the discourse of universal human rights and have reoriented political claims-making towards the state. Globalisation has facilitated the development of feminist transnational networks, along which ideas and political practices can spread. Rather than regarding feminism as a social movement entering abeyance, it is more appropriate to conclude instead that feminism has changed its repertoire and form.

5
Gender Mainstreaming

Introduction

Gender mainstreaming is a new form of feminist strategy, which engages with existing configurations of power institutionalised in the state. As a consequence of changes in the gender regime and in the political environment, there is greater potential than previously to engage effectively with this power. However, there are also dangers in such a strategy, in that the feminist component can be weakened, dispersed and made to disappear. Doing gender mainstreaming in a way that is successful is a major challenge for feminism.

Gender mainstreaming is an essentially contested concept and practice. It involves the re-invention, restructuring, and re-branding of a key part of feminism in the contemporary era. It is both a new form of gendered political and policy practice and a new gendered strategy for theory development. As a practice, gender mainstreaming is a process to promote gender equality. It is also intended to improve the effectiveness of mainline policies by making visible the gendered nature of assumptions, processes and outcomes. However, there are many different definitions of gender mainstreaming, as well as considerable variations in practice. As a form of theory, gender mainstreaming is a process of revision of key concepts, undertaken in order to grasp more adequately a world that is gendered, rather than the establishment of a separatist gender theory. Gender mainstreaming encapsulates many of the tensions and dilemmas in feminist theory and practice over the last decade and provides a new focus for debates on how to move them on (Daly 2005; Beveridge, Nott and Stephen 2000; Behning and Pascual 2001; Mazey 2000; Moser 2005; Squires 2005; Veitch 2005; Verloo 2001, 2005b; Walby 2001a; Woodward 2003).

There are at least six major issues in the analysis of gender main-streaming. First is how to address the tension between 'gender equality' and the 'mainstream', and attempts to re-position these two configurations. Second comes the issue of whether the vision of gender equality invoked by the mainstreaming process draws on notions of 'sameness', 'difference' or 'transformation'. Third is the issue of whether the vision of gender equality can be distinguished from the strategy employed to get there, or is merely a different dimension of the same process. This question is linked to the sig-nificance of the distinction between specifically focused actions for gender equality and widespread mainstreaming of gender equality. Fourth comes the problem of the relationship of gender mainstream-ing with other complex inequalities, especially those associated with ethnicity and class, but also with disability, faith, sexual orientation and age. Fifth is the issue of the relationship between 'expertise' and 'democracy', and the re-thinking of the concept and practice of democracy so as to include gender relations. Sixth is the issue of the implications of the transnational nature of the development of gender mainstreaming, including the influence of international regimes, the development of human rights discourse, and the development of the European Union in the context of global processes.

'Gender Equality' and the 'Mainstream'

Gender mainstreaming involves at least two different frames of ref-erence: 'gender equality' and the 'mainstream'. Thus gender main-streaming is inevitably and essentially a contested process. While there are attempts to bridge the gap between these two frames, it is important to note the frequent opposition to gender mainstream-ing in order to understand the dualism between gender equality and mainstream agendas. Elgström (2000) argues that new gender norms have to 'fight their way into institutional thinking', in com-petition with traditional norms, since established goals may compete with the prioritisation of gender equality even if they are not directly opposed to it. This means that the process is contested and can involve 'negotiation' rather than simple adoption of new policies. Perrons (2005) provides a different perspective on the origin and nature of opposition to gender mainstreaming. She argues that, at least in the UK and perhaps more widely, the goal of the competi-tiveness of the economy takes precedence over equality considera-tions, leading to the increase of rather than challenge to the low paid work, so frequently found among women. These other goals, such as competitiveness of the economy, are not necessarily articulated as opposition to the goal of gender equality, but nonetheless receive priority. In this instance, policies to improve the competitiveness of the UK's economy are seen to have indirectly detrimental consequences for gender equality.

The conceptualisation of this dualism between gender equality and the mainstream is central to many of the debates about gender mainstreaming. There is a variety of ways in which this mix of contestation and compromise can be analysed and outcomes assessed, in multiple registers, in several different theoretical vocabularies. This variety of registers and vocabularies includes the 'frames' of social movement theory (Ferree 2009; Verloo 2005a); the 'discourses' of cultural studies/poststructuralism/Foucauldian analysis; the 'epistemologies' of Harding (1986); and the paradigms of Kuhn (1979). The postulated end point of the process of mainstreaming can also be described using different theoretical vocabularies. One vision of gender mainstreaming is that it offers 'transformation' (Rees 1998), that is, neither the assimilation of women into men's ways, nor the maintenance of a dualism between women and men, but rather something new, a positive form of melding, in which feminists – the outsiders – changed the mainstream. There are other ways to characterise the outcome. Jahan (1995) contrasts two possible outcomes as either 'agenda setting' or 'integration', as do also Lombardo (2005) and Squires (2005), while Shaw (2002) makes a similar contrast between 'embedded' and 'marginalised'. There are concepts of 'frame extension' or 'frame bridging' (Verloo 2005a; Ferree 2009) and of 'stretching and bending' (Lombardo, Meier and Verloo 2009). There are further parallel concepts in the field of ethnic politics, where some concepts represent asymmetrical processes, such as 'assimilation', while others imply a more mutual accommodation, such as 'hybridisation' (Gilroy 1993). These analogies may be illuminating for the gender context.

Jahan (1995) contrasts 'agenda setting' and 'integrationist' approaches to gender mainstreaming. This distinction is applied and developed further by several writers (Daly 2005; Lombardo 2005; Shaw 2002; Squires 2005). Agenda setting implies the transformation and reorientation of existing policy paradigms, changing decision-making processes, prioritising gender equality objectives and re-thinking policy ends. In this approach, it is the mainstream that changes. Integrationist approaches are those that introduce a gender perspective without challenging the existing policy paradigm, 'selling' instead gender mainstreaming as a way of achieving more effectively existing policy goals. While this approach means that gender mainstreaming is less likely to be rejected, its impact is likely to be less substantial. Lombardo (2005) applies this distinction between agenda setting and integration to events in the European Convention aimed at developing a European Constitution. While most of the feminists who sought to adopt a gender mainstreaming strategy preferred to be 'agenda setting', there was a drift towards one that was merely 'integrationist'. The strategic framing of gender mainstreaming is an ongoing dilemma. Shaw (2002) addresses the relationship between gender equality and the mainstream around the proposed new EU Constitution by asking, in a parallel manner, whether gender mainstreaming is 'constitutionally embedded' or 'comprehensively marginalised'. She finds that, while gender concerns are embedded in the Treaty framework, especially that of the Treaty of Amsterdam, they are less prominent in the politics of the Convention, which was established to develop the Constitution (for example there were few women present in senior positions), and in its ensuing white paper.

Frame theory has been developed to capture variations in the relationship between gender equality projects and the mainstream (Verloo 2005a; Ferree 2009; Lombardo, Meier and Verloo 2009). Originating in the work of Goffman, and influentially articulated by Snow, Rochford, Worden and Benford (1986), frame theory has become a key influence in the theorisation of social movements in general (della Porta and Diani 1999; Diani 1996) and of gender mainstreaming in particular (Pollack and Hafner-Burton 2000). Frame theory provides a fluid vocabulary to engage with the contestations and shifts in meaning that are important in understanding social movements and related civil society activities. The concepts of 'frame extension' and 'frame bridging' have been developed in order to capture some of the ways in which social movements either modify and extend the dominant frame so as to include their own projects or find a way to link or bridge these projects to the dominant frame. The concept of 'stretching and bending' (Lombardo, Meier and Verloo 2009) takes this plan further. Ferree (2009) and Verloo (2005a) are critical of some features of frame theory – in particular, that it does not distinguish carefully enough among the available discursive structures and resources, the actors' strategic choices in this context, and the outcomes attained. As they develop frame theory in their work, they include national structures of opportunity as well as the voices and activities of a range of actors, as they re-work frames in complex ways. For example, Ferree (2009) links frame theory with comparative institutional histories, so as to provide greater depth to the account of the resources on which feminist social movements draw.

An issue in assessing the outcomes of gender mainstreaming is how 'success' is to be defined (Gamson 1975; Mazur 2002; Stetson and Mazur 1995). The definition of success is complicated by the possible change in the nature of the goal during the process of negotiation (Elgström 2000), since such processes are social constructions which go on in a context where what is perceived to be possible is changing. The implementation of the policy can be open to varying interpretations, and these have different implications. For example, policies designed to support the reconciliation of work and family life have the potential to produce a transformation of gender relations, generating equality in the domains of both care and employment, but some interpretations of these policies may merely integrate women into the paid economy, without bringing many changes elsewhere. Indeed, Stratigaki (2004) argues that this policy has come to be less about the sharing of family responsibilities between women and men and more about encouraging flexible forms of employment.

The outcome of the negotiation of feminism and the mainstream may not be as simple as either 'agenda setting' or 'integration'. Instead there may be asymmetrical resolutions of these negotiations, depending on the environment and on the historical strength of the varying forces (see chapter 6). There are diverse mainstreams into which gender equality goals can be included. There are multiple relevant governmental programmes, from economic growth to crime reduction. Even international corporate bodies have begun to mainstream gender, as can be seen in the efforts of the World Economic Forum (2009) to measure global gender gaps.

During the contestation and negotiation between 'gender equality' and the 'mainstream(s)', both are likely to change simultaneously, in response to each other as well as to other changes. It is important to be able to capture the continuously evolving nature of the interaction between feminist and mainstream conceptions. The conceptualisation developed by complexity theorists, according to whom such processes happen between 'complex adaptive systems', which are 'co-evolving' within 'changing fitness landscapes' (environments that privilege some groups and systems over others), captures these dynamics more adequately than one-way conceptions of 'impact' (Kauffman 1995; Mitleton-Kelly 2003; Walby 2007, 2009). The approach thus informed by complexity theory goes beyond the concepts of 'agenda setting' and 'integration', which tend to imply that there is more stability in the alternative projects of gender equality and of the mainstream than might be warranted (Walby 2007, 2009).

While the analysis has so far considered a single version of feminism and a single version of the mainstream, there are several versions of each. The engagement between multiple feminisms and multiple mainstreams produces additional complexity, as will be discussed in chapter 7 on intersections with feminism.

Contested Visions of and Routes to Gender Equality

Underlying the variety of definitions of gender mainstreaming are different models of gender equality (Eveline and Bacchi 2005; Squires 2005), three major types of which are usually distinguished. These models of gender equality include some elements that incorporate visions of the nature of a gender-equal world, as well as elements that concern the strategies and tactics for getting there. Often the visions and the strategies are conflated, but it may be more appropriate to treat them as analytically separable. A key typology of models of gender equality distinguishes between models based on sameness (equal opportunities or equal treatment), models based on difference (special programmes) and models based on transformation (Rees 1998, 2005). Embedded within these debates are implicit theories of gender relations and of their connections within a gender regime – in particular, the extent to which the different policy domains are seen as being closely interconnected or relatively independent, since this affects the extent to which 'sameness' may be held as a standard in one domain simultaneously with 'difference' in another (Walby 2004a). These models (Rees 1998, 2005) contain elements of both vision and strategy. An alternative approach separates the elements of vision and strategy (Booth and Bennett 2002). These authors interpret the components of the trilogy formed by models of 'equal treatment perspective', the 'women's perspective' and the 'gender perspective' as strategies rather than as end visions. They argue that, when vision and strategy are separated, then the three components are complementary rather than mutually exclusive, thereby challenging the compartmentalisation of different types of equality strategies. They suggest that the models are better conceptualised as components of a 'three-legged stool', in that they are interconnected and that each one needs the other. Such a separation of vision from strategy enables a variety of strategies to be seen as potentially complementary rather than necessarily as alternatives.

These discussions contain important aspects of the 'sameness/difference' debate that has taken place in contemporary feminism. This key analytic distinction, indeed often dichotomy, has been subject to much debate within feminist theory (Felski 1997; Folbre 2001; Fraser 1997; Holli 1997; Lorber 2000; Nussbaum 2000a; Scott 1988). This is a multi-faceted debate, which is simultaneously normative, philosophical, theoretical, substantive, empirical and policy-relevant. Thus an analysis of gender mainstreaming contains the classical arguments within feminist theory about difference, universalism and particularism. Gender can be an example of difference, which is a major issue in social theory (Calhoun 1995; Felski 1997). In particular, there are the dilemmas of how to recognise difference while avoiding the trap of essentialism (Ferree and Gamson 2003, Fraser 1997) and paying heed to the global horizon (Benhabib 1999). Postmodern ambivalence and the prioritisation of situatedness and fluidity (Braidotti 1994) may be contrasted with a new assertion of universal standards (Nussbaum 2000a; Sen 2009). Running through this analysis is the issue of whose standards are to be used, and from which or for which constituency are they developed (Squires 1999).

It has often been argued that traditional equal opportunities policies are inherently limited because they mean that women can only gain equality with men if they are able to perform to the standards set by men (Guerrina 2002; Rossilli 1997; Rees 1998). Can there be an effective route to gender justice in which existing separate gender norms/standards are retained and become equally valued, or is it never really possible to be 'different but equal', because the differences are too entwined with power and resources? Some standards, such as equal pay for women and men, may already be held by women as well as by men. Some policy interventions, such as legislation on equal pay and government policy to improve child care, may be better conceived of as contributions to gender mainstreaming rather than as mere equal treatment or special programmes, since they have the potential to transform women's association with domesticated care. Is gender mainstreaming introducing new hybrid standards of gender justice for human beings – replacing the ostensibly more male oriented standard of the old equal opportunities policies, for instance, by beginning to transform the workplace so as to organise it around standards suitable for those who combine care work and paid work? While the elimination of gender inequality is the goal of the gender mainstreaming strategy, the extent to which this can mean accepting and valuing existing gendered differences is a key source of disagreement within gender mainstreaming theory and practice. The relationship between equality and difference in each of various institutional domains has been a major debate within gender theory. While all the definitions of gender equality include equality within each social domain, they vary as to whether a change in the balance of the domains, and the equalisation of any differential representation of women and men in each domain, constitute legitimate areas for intervention or not.

A leading definition of gender mainstreaming is that of the European Union Commission Directorate on Employment, Social Affairs and Equal Opportunities:

> Gender mainstreaming is the integration of the gender perspective into every stage of policy processes – design, implementation, monitoring and evaluation – with a view to promoting equality between women and men. It means assessing how policies impact on the life and position of both women and men – and taking responsibility to re-address them if necessary. (European Commission 2010a)

A further definition of gender mainstreaming is the one devised by Mieke Verloo as Chair of the Council of Europe Group of Experts on Gender Mainstreaming:

> Gender mainstreaming is the (re)organization, improvement, development and evaluation of policy processes, so that a gender equality perspective is incorporated in all policies at all levels at all stages, by the actors normally involved in policy making. (Council of Europe 1998: 15)

In contrast to Rees (1998), the Council of Europe definition of gender equality implies that differences between women and men are not an essential obstacle to equality:

> Gender equality means an equal visibility, empowerment and participation of both sexes in all spheres of public and private life. [. . .] Gender equality is not synonymous with sameness, with establishing men, their life style and conditions as the norm. [. . .] Gender equality means accepting and valuing equally the differences between women and men and the diverse roles they play in society. (Council of Europe, 1998: 7–8)

The Council of Europe (1998) specifies the need for the 'equal participation of women and men in political and public life' and the need for 'the individual's economic independence', and that 'education is a key target for gender equality'. It defines equal participation in political and public life, education and the achievement of economic independence as universal goals, while other spheres (notably the family and care work) remain sites of difference. An underlying question here is that of the assumed degree of connection among gender practices in different domains. The Council of Europe (1998) text suggests that it is possible for a model of gender equality to be based on sameness in some domains and at the same time on the equal valuation of different activities in other domains. However, if domains are coupled tightly, it may not be possible to have equality through sameness in one domain and equality with difference in another. It is only if the links are looser that such a combination may be theoretically and practically possible. This debate depends on an implicit theory of gender relations that needs to be made explicit in order for us to understand the nature and degree of the postulated connections between different gendered domains and the implications of changes in one of them for the others (Walby 1997, 2004a, 2006).

Employment is perhaps the field where the development of similar standards, such as equal pay, is the most developed, while other areas, such as the care of children, are more likely to contain at least some elements that value differences between average men and women. Rather than generalising across all gendered domains within a country, it is important to consider the specificities of each domain and the nature of its links to other domains in order to understand the development of gender mainstreaming. Each domain is likely to have its own institutional history and to have been subject to different types of gender equality policy and politics. It is important both to distinguish between different domains and to examine the nature of the connections between them, so as to be able to understand whether, ultimately, changes in one domain are likely to have implications for other domains.

Booth and Bennett (2002) suggest that the three models of equal treatment, women's perspective and gender perspective can coexist. Their interpretation of these models prioritises the strategy used to reach gender equality rather than the end vision of the type of gender equality. Is this an appropriate interpretation? An examination of documents from the European Commission about gender equality finds that the European Commission recommends the use of all three gender equality strategies simultaneously. First, it posits a single standard of equality for women and men in employment, which is based on minimising gaps – that is, on achieving the same level of participation in employment, the same level of unemployment, and the same level of pay (European Commission 2010b).

This approach would appear to have significant similarities to the 'sameness' approach to gender equality. Second, there is reference to 'specific policy actions' and to the naming of policy domains that are focused on women's activities, an approach which emphasises difference. These actions and domains include targets for increased childcare agreed at the Barcelona European Council, according to which childcare is available to at least 90 per cent of children between 3 years and school age and to at least 33 per cent of children under 3 years of age. Third, this is combined with a vision of transformed relations between care and employment:

> particular attention will be given to reconciling work and family life, notably through the provision of care services for children and other dependants, encouraging the sharing of family and professional responsibilities and facilitating return to work after a period of leave. (European Commission 2003)

At least in the programmes of the EU, the three visions of gender equality coexist: the utilisation of the same standard for women and men in policies of 'equal treatment'; policy actions to support women's distinctive activities, such as childcare; and transformation, as in the reconciliation of work and family life. It is thus useful to make a distinction between the vision of what is meant by gender equality and the strategy of moving towards gender equality. The EU strategy for reaching gender equality involves two components: specific actions and gender mainstreaming. 'Community strategy on gender equality' states that the 'principle of equal treatment for women and men' is a fundamental principle of European Community law, while it notes that action should be continued 'combining integration of the gender dimension with specific action' (European Commission 2000: 5). The use of both components simultaneously is important for effective gender mainstreaming.

Diverse Inequalities

The category 'woman' is internally divided by many other forms of difference and inequality, with which there are complex intersections. Gender mainstreaming takes place in a context of multiple and diverse forms of social inequality. Within the EU there has been a recent increase in the number of grounds on which it is possible to make legal complaints on discrimination; so these are no longer confined to gender, ethnicity and disability, but additionally they include religion/faith, sexual orientation and age. This is a result of the slow implementation of Article 13 of the 1997 Treaty of Amsterdam in the Employment Directive, which only came into force in 2006, and it has raised the question of the practical intersection of diverse forms of equality politics in relation to gender mainstreaming in an increasingly insistent manner (Department of Trade and Industry [DTI] 2004; Walby 2004a; Woodward 2008).

The diverse forms of inequality and their intersection have implications for the theory and practice of gender mainstreaming (Ferree 2009; Hankivsky 2005; Squires 2009; Woodward 2003, 2008). A range of strengths and weaknesses has been identified with the re-positioning of gender equality projects within a framing that is centred on diversity (Barmes and Ashtiany 2003; Squires 2005; Woodward 2008). On the one hand, attention to other inequalities may dilute the effort spent on gender mainstreaming, if resources are allocated elsewhere, if there is loss of focus, if there is loss of appreciation of the specific structural causes of inequality, or if there is competition over the priority accorded to different forms of inequalities (Woodward 2008). On the other hand, the outcome of gender mainstreaming may be strengthened if there were concerted actions of previously separate communities and initiatives on agreed priorities for intervention, and if such outcome were to lead to a strengthening of procedures for deliberative democracy (Department of Trade and Industry 2004; Hankivsky 2005; Squires 2005).

Underlying the issues raised by the practical interconnection of gender mainstreaming with other forms of equality and diversity policies and politics is the question of the theorisation of difference and complex inequalities. Much debate in social theory has concerned these issues (Anthias and Yuval-Davis 1992; Braidotti 1994; Felski 1997; Kymlicka 1995; Nussbaum 2000a; Scott 1988; Walby 2001a). While early concerns focused on the cross-cutting of gender inequalities by ethnicity and class, the inequalities and differences now considered extend at least so as to include sexuality, disability, religion/faith, and age. However, class is now more often treated implicitly, being embedded within concepts of 'poverty' (Kabeer 2003), 'social exclusion' and 'pay', more than as a focus of theoretical debate. Much current interest lies in understanding the intersectionality of the various forms of inequality rather than treating them as merely additive (Collins 1998; Crenshaw 1991).

There are at least two major analytic strategies for addressing the concept of gender within debates on difference (Holmwood 2001;

Sayer 2000). The first has been to disperse gender as a category, so that it can only be understood together with other complex inequalities rather than as a category in its own right – because gender is always embedded within other social forms (Holmwood 2000). Intersectionality with other complex inequalities is always present. In this approach, the utilisation of the category of 'woman' is criticised as problematically essentialising and homogenising. The second approach is to retain the concept of gender, while always noting that this is an abstraction, since any practical category is always socially constructed. This approach has been supported by the revitalisation of realism as an approach in social theory – an approach that argues for greater depth in ontology, which can be better achieved through the abstraction of specific categories than through their dispersal (Sayer 2000).

Squires (2005) suggests that, in constructively addressing the diversity agenda, groups that are currently isolated from each other should be brought into dialogue. Such dialogue could help to resolve the tension between individual egalitarianism and the politics of group recognition, which holds back the development of gender mainstreaming. Potentially, the discussions could lead to new ways of thinking about old problems, ways that combine elements in innovative ways. Such dialogue could be understood to be a form of deliberative democracy, which could develop new political projects that transcend old barriers.

There is a variety of ways in which the intersection of feminism with other inequalities and other political projects occurs and can be understood. These are discussed further in chapter 7 (on intersections with feminism).

'Expertise' or 'Democratisation'?

Expertise and democracy are often treated as rival forms of governance. Democracy is usually contrasted favourably with expertise, which is regarded as being associated with, and contaminated by, the dominant order. However, a different kind of contrast draws on the connotation that expertise is scientific, and thereby politically neutral and above mere sectional interest. Gender mainstreaming sits in the middle of such debates. Sometimes it is represented as if it were primarily a technical process, and at other times it is represented as a primarily political process. On the one hand, this process has been understood as one of developing a more inclusive democracy, by improving gendered democratic practices. On the other hand, the process is represented as one of efficiency and expertise, which is carried out by the normal policy actors with a specially developed toolkit. This issue raises larger questions – about the changing nature of democracy in a gender unequal context, and about the positioning of 'expertise' in debates on democracy. There is a question as to whether it is appropriate to polarise 'expertise' and 'democracy' as alternative models or interpretations of gender mainstreaming.

Beveridge, Nott and Stephen (2000) make a distinction between the 'expert–bureaucratic' model, which involves primarily experts and specialists, and the 'participatory–democratic' model, which involves a range of individuals and organisations. They suggest that these constitute real differences in the ways in which gender mainstreaming is implemented – and not just perceptions of such processes. They consider that only the participatory–democratic process can accomplish gender mainstreaming as agenda setting rather than integration (see Jahan 1995).

Rai (2003) conceptualises gender mainstreaming as a process of gender democratisation, of including women and their own perceptions of their political interests and political projects into policy-making processes. A range of different processes and practices are identified as being involved, with a particular focus on the national gender machineries in the state and on their relationship with civil society women's groups. The accountability of the national machineries to a wider context, which includes NGOs and women's groups, is seen as essential to their effective operation. Gender mainstreaming is seen as a process by which various actors, previously outside the privileged policy arenas, get to have voice within them. This view runs counter to the view that gender mainstreaming is done by the 'normal policy actors' (e.g. Council of Europe 1998).

In the Council of Europe (1998) text, the definition of gender mainstreaming incorporates the notion that the process is implemented 'by the actors normally involved in policy making'. This might be understood to imply that, once the political goal of mainstreaming gender equality has been set, the process itself can be effectively implemented by technocrats and bureaucrats within the policy and state machinery. This approach is further exemplified by that part of the discourse that prioritises the use of 'tools', such as those of gender disaggregated statistics, gender budgeting and gender impact assessments (Rees 2005). Here the issue under discussion is focused on how, not whether, to mainstream gender equality. The focus is then on the resources – such as expertise – that the technical experts have in order to do their jobs. This approach depends upon the prior incorporation of gender equality goals into the mainstream.

The relative significance of expertise or democracy may be an issue of context or one of interpretation (Verloo 2001; Woodward 2003). Woodward (2003) argues for the importance of contextual factors in determining the success or otherwise of gender mainstreaming initiatives. In particular, the level of sophistication of the gender equality awareness within the political environment affects whether state functionaries can effectively implement gender mainstreaming. Where this level is high, as has been the case in the Netherlands at certain times, the normal policy actors may be effective in implementing gender mainstreaming (Verloo 2001; Roggeband and Verloo 2006). Where the level is low, as is the case in Flanders in Belgium, the normal policy actors are unlikely to carry out this process effectively. Woodward also draws attention to significance of experts who are outside of government. Verloo (2005b) makes clear that the political context – that is, whether there are political opportunities, strong mobilising networks within and outside the bureaucracy, and appropriate 'frames' available – makes a difference to the process and outcome of gender mainstreaming.

An alternative to polarising 'expertise' and 'democracy' is to see them as entwined in contemporary practice in a complex way. An example of such entwining can be found in gender budgeting. This is conventionally represented as a process invoking 'expertise' rather than one of 'gendering democracy' (Budlender, Elson, Hewitt and Mukhopadhyay 2002), but in practice the process usually involves both. Gender budgeting requires a specialised toolkit, which includes gender disaggregated statistics, equality indicators and gender impact assessments. The use of statistics and economic data involves an authoritative technical and abstracted mode of expressing the expertise. It is often presented as the efficient and neutral application of techniques to an already agreed agenda and set of policy goals. However, gender budgeting is often more complex that this presentation suggests (Sharp and Broomhill 2002; Women's Budget Group 2004). First, it usually includes explicit statements about the importance of improving women's lives, that is, it situates the analysis within a wider framework, which is not politically neutral. Second, to represent the intervention as one based on expertise is often itself a political strategy. For example, the UK Women's Budget Group held meetings with elected politicians (both ministers and backbench MPs), civil servants (both within and outside the specialised gender machinery of government), and wider civil society (both other non-governmental organisations and individuals), and knowingly positions itself as an expert and technical group, even as it uses democratic accountability to create pressure for change. There is a duality of expertise and participatory democratic working in this gender mainstreaming in which the components are complementary rather than in contradiction with each other.

These topics insistently raise the issue of the nature of democracy, in particular of the inclusiveness of formal elected representation and of the processes by which political projects are developed and support is mustered. The traditional view of liberal democracy has centred on the formal election of representatives to national parliaments, so the narrow and conventional definition of democracy focuses on free elections and free political parties in the context of a free civil society (Potter, Goldblatt, Kiloh and Lewis 1997). However, recent debates highlight the nature and meaning of representation as well as the relevance of participation in deliberation about political projects (Held 1996). Conventional liberal practices of electoral representation have not delivered equal numbers of women and men in elected positions, or proportionate members of minority communities. There has been much discussion of the role of different kinds of political mechanisms (e.g. quotas, different voting systems) in explaining variations in the representation of women (Lovenduski and Norris 1993). These discussions have given rise to a deeper consideration of what is meant by the 'representation' of women, both in parliament and in other political arenas (Squires 1999). Is the presence of women (their substantive representation) essential to their democratic representation (Childs 2002; Phillips 1995)? Do women have collective political interests that might be represented electorally, or are these interests either too individual or too diverse for such representation to be appropriate (Young 2000)? Does 'identity' politics essentialise and stabilise the group at stake and underestimate the significance of differences within that 'group' in a politically problematic way? Does the concept of women's interests too readily assume that political interests can be read off from social structural location?

The investigations of associations between political preferences and location with the gender regime have found positive correlations, although these do not add up to a complete explanation of differences in political preferences (Huber and Stephens 2000; Manza and Brooks 1998). The development of feminist theories of the state and democratic representation drew attention to the plurality of arenas that are relevant to the representation of voices and political projects associated with perceived women's (or gendered) interests

(O'Connor, Orloff and Shaver 1999; Hobson 2000). These arenas include not only the traditional focus on the elected representatives in parliaments and similar institutions, but also the consideration of the development of gender machinery and women's bureaux within the state, and the articulation of political projects by social movements and other civil society actors (Stetson and Mazur 1995; Mazur 2002). The relationship between these three gendered constituencies – elected representatives, women's units in government and civil society – has been shown to be important in explaining variations in the impact of feminist projects (Halsaa 1998; Vargas and Wieringa 1998). There are further sites where women's voices are being newly articulated, for instance corporate social responsibility agendas (Grosser and Moon 2005), or academia.

Woodward (2004), as noted earlier, demonstrates the importance of the 'velvet triangle' linking feminist bureaucrats, trusted academics and organised voices in the women's movement for the development of gender mainstreaming in the EU. This trio of relevant female players is slightly different from the relevant players proposed by Vargas and Wieringa (1998), but the conception of alliances between differently positioned individuals and groups is common to both. In Woodward's trio of allies there are academics rather than elected representatives, which suggests the importance of expertise as a key component in these EU gender networks. The development of the analysis of gendered democracy has led to a consideration of the significance of alliances between those who find themselves in different political arenas but are engaged in complementary projects. The analysis of gender mainstreaming includes, as a key element, expertise in the form of academic knowledge.

The importance of expertise in the context of the gender machinery, elected politicians and academics for gender mainstreaming is argued by Veitch (2005) in relation to the UK. The absence of information, knowledge and resources holds back gender mainstreaming by government officials. The acquisition and utilisation of expertise is situated within the processes linking different parts of the gender machinery, other government departments, ministers, MPs, academic researchers and the legal framework. In a related way, Zippel (2004) shows how governing bodies may have an interest in developing such expertise and in working with such non-electoral networks, using the development of sexual harassment policy in the EU as her example.

'Accountability' is a concept within the repertoire of democratic practices, but it is slightly off-centre. It has been used in several ways in relation to gender mainstreaming. Rai (2003) argues that national gender machineries should be accountable to civil society NGOs and women's groups. It is used by Grosser and Moon (2005) in their argument about the need for corporations to be accountable, beyond their shareholders, to a wider range of stakeholders, including women as employees, customers, community members and investors, if they are to deliver value and genuine corporate social responsibility to society as a whole. Accountability implies flows of information into the public domain, including gender disaggregated data in – for example – company reports, and a willingness to engage in dialogue with those outside the organisation's boundary. This process can also extend the concept of 'expert' to stakeholders, identifying the benefits that accrue to the organisation from having the input of a broad range of stakeholders as part of quality improvement and other processes. Transformative gender mainstreaming often requires information to be made public and to receive input from actors external to the organisation, because it is a practice that intrinsically goes beyond existing neatly bounded responsibilities.

Within democratic theory, a focus alternative to that on substantive representation is the focus on deliberative democracy, which often draws on the work of Habermas and on his theories of communicative action (Habermas 1987, 1991): these are seen to offer the potential to achieve the resolution of initially conflicting priorities of diverse social groups and communities. Squires (2005) argues that deliberative democracy is essential in order to address gender mainstreaming in the context of diversity. She argues that the debates on gender mainstreaming demand a resolution of the tension between liberal individual egalitarianism and the politics of group recognition. It is only when diverse groups bring to the public agenda their respective views and experiences in order to engage in democratic deliberation that gender mainstreaming can move forward. One of the limitations of deliberative democracy, she notes, is that it depends on the institutional design of debate to ensure the inclusion of all groups, and the way this will happen tends to be under-specified in the theoretical literature – a point made more strongly by Fraser (1989). Nevertheless, Squires concludes that the debates on gender mainstreaming and on deliberative democracy have much to learn from each other.

In sum, while expertise and democracy have sometimes been seen as rival sources of legitimacy in governance, the case of gender mainstreaming suggests a strong interrelationship. This interrelationship may be conceptualised either as an alliance between individuals and groups or as a new, integrated form of community or network in its own right. These alliances, communities and networks often involve academics as well as more conventional political actors – such as elected politicians, civil servants and social movements. The analysis of gender mainstreaming thus involves a reconsideration of the nature of democracy so as to make it extend not only to the gender of the elected representatives, the institutionalisation of gendered interests in the gender machinery of the state and an active gendered civil society, but also to the nature and the incorporation of expertise, especially from academics.

Globalisation and Gender Mainstreaming

Gender mainstreaming often draws on transnational processes, involving transnational networks and agencies and transformations of the discourse of universal human rights, challenging the traditional focus on national processes. These developments are facilitated by the rise of global processes and institutions, such as the UN. Gender mainstreaming is a leading-edge example of the potential implications of globalisation for gender politics.

The principle of gender mainstreaming was initially developed by feminist development practitioners in the 1970s and launched at the UN conference on women in Beijing, in 1995 (Meyer and Prügl 1999). Its origins lie especially in the context of feminist work within development, where different ways of including gender equity into development processes and goals had long been explored (Kabeer 2003; Jahan 1995; Moser 1993). Gender mainstreaming has since been adopted by the European Union as a core part of its gender equality policy, which deepened and became more wide-ranging since the 1997 Treaty of Amsterdam (Pollack and Hafner-Burton 2000; Beveridge, Nott and Stephen 2000; Behning and Pascual 2001; Mazey 2000; Verloo 2005b), and this has given a further boost to global gender mainstreaming.

Gender mainstreaming is a global initiative, but it is not evenly developed globally. The implementation of gender mainstreaming is uneven even when it is led by a common transnational political entity such as the EU. Thus the understanding of gender mainstreaming raises complex questions as to the relationship between global, regional and national levels of governance. Unlike some more conventional forms of politics and policy, gender mainstreaming is not primarily situated within a national or country framework, but rather has been transnational from the start. This poses challenges to its analysis, since it requires a consideration of processes of policy development that involve international regimes, globalisation, transnational polities and practices of political and policy transfer from one location to another.

Gender mainstreaming practices vary between different countries in the context of divergent economic, political and social circumstances (Mósesdóttir and Erlingsdóttir 2005) – especially between North and South (Moser 2005; Pillinger 2005), all of which shape the process. Some polities tend to be 'makers' (developers of policy) while others are 'takers' (recipients) of gender mainstreaming policy (Behning and Pascual 2001; Mósesdóttir 2011). During this process the policies rarely remain the same: they are hybridised as they interact with different local conditions. The developing institutions of global governance and the political spaces that are associated with them, for example those of the UN and UNIFEM, also affect the process (Elson 1998; Meyer and Prügl 1999; Pietilä 1996; Rai 2003; True 2003), as does the developing discourse on universal human rights (Kelly 2005; Peters and Wolper 1995) and whether this is interpreted as a western, a globally hybridised, or a locally varied tradition (Ferree 2009; Woodiwiss 1998).

Gender mainstreaming is a practice that is at least as well developed (if not better) in the South as in the North (Moser 2005). It has often involved transnational actors, such as international aid agencies, in interaction both with northern funders and with southern planners. Further, there are important international political networks that support activities in ways that defy conventional notions of nation and state (Keck and Sikkink 1998; Moghadam 2005; Pillinger 2005).

The development of a discourse on universal human rights (Nussbaum 2000a), associated with the development of international organisations (Berkovitch 1999), fora and political spaces connected with UN developments, such as conferences for women, has been an important contribution to these processes (Meyer and Prügl 1999; Walby 2002). The UN declaration on violence against women and human rights in 1993 resulted from a global coalition of women from every continent, who created a new interpretation of human rights and lobbied for it (Kelly 2005). In this way it contrasts with the development of gender mainstreaming in employment and in related economic domains, which, in European countries at least, have been far more dependent upon developments within the EU than they were at the global level.

The transnational level has been a component of the development of gender mainstreaming in almost all places and domains. There is little policy development that has remained at a national level. The origins of gender mainstreaming were in development politics, involving transnational aid agencies. Feminists have made effective use of the emerging institutions of global governance, utilising UN and expanding the discourse of human rights so as to include women's rights to the elimination of male violence. The EU has become a transnational actor that is very important for the contemporary development of gender mainstreaming, with strengths in promoting the policy in the abstract, but with weaknesses in its implementation. The US is noteworthy for the absence of gender mainstreaming among its gender equality policies. Thus the transfer of the policy does not run simply from the most powerful countries to the weaker ones; it takes a more horizontal form, which hybridises according to local conditions. Gender mainstreaming often draws on transnational processes, involving transnational networks and agencies and the discourse of universal human rights. These developments are facilitated by the rise of global processes and institutions, such as the UN. Gender mainstreaming is a leading-edge example of the potential implications of globalisation for gender politics.

Conclusions

Potentially, gender mainstreaming is a powerful development in feminist theory and practice. While most frequently understood as a specialised tool of the policy world, it is also a feminist strategy that draws on, and can inform, feminist theory. Gender mainstreaming is essentially contested, since it is constituted in the tension between the 'mainstream' and 'gender equality'. There are many different forms of gender mainstreaming, not least because of the different visions and theories of gender equality, and because of the social and political processes that might constitute routes towards such a goal. These theoretical issues include the problem of whether gender equality is conceptualised through sameness, through the equal valuation of different gendered practices, or through transformation. Additionally, the outcome of gender mainstreaming depends on the diverse inequalities and further political projects with which it engages. In practice, gender mainstreaming works only if there are, simultaneously, both specific actions to promote gender equality and the inclusion of gender equality in mainstream policy practices.

Implicit within much of this analysis of gender mainstreaming is a theory of the state, of the political and of democracy. The state is a contested arena, with a mix of coherence and contradiction among a set of core institutions and complex linkages with other political and non-political domains. Gendered interests are socially constructed in complex ways rather than essentially related to simple conceptions of social–structural location, even though differences in resources associated with social position remain a key contribution to the environment within which political projects are constructed. The range of relevant forms of power include the representation of gendered interests not only through processes of formal democratic elections, but also through the constitution of specialised state gender machinery and through the constitution and articulation of gendered interests in civil society, both within NGOs and within the grassroots. Gender mainstreaming is constructed, articulated and transformed through discourse clustered within frames that are extended and linked through struggle and argumentation. Expertise is a form of power, often neglected in conventional analysis, which is increasingly deployed by those who represent gendered interests in and against the state, and is often articulated within epistemic communities that combine values, expertise and politics in order to become advocacy networks; and these are increasingly international. Gender mainstreaming is situated within the development of transnational global politics, of multilateral forms of governance such as the UN and the transnational polity of the European Union, as well as within the development of diverse global discourses of human rights that transcend country boundaries, each of which have disparate outcomes when in articulation with country differences. These gender mainstreaming debates position inequality and difference at the heart of the social and political theory of state and democracy, and not as a separate field of study.

6

Changes in the Context for Feminism

Introduction

Feminism varies according to its context. This context includes many different forms of the gender regime, of capitalism and of the socio-environmental relationship. The variation is linked to multiple forms of modernity, of which the two most important are neoliberalism and social democracy.

There is a complex relationship between projects and their contexts: projects do not simply derive from their context, but they are affected by them. A distinction is made between projects that are rooted in civil society, programmes that are governmental and more deeply institutionalised social formations. The present chapter focuses on social formations.

These social and environmental contexts not only shape the nature of feminism but can themselves be changed by feminism. Feminism has the potential to change the form of the gender regime, of capitalism, and of the socio-environmental relationship. The focus of this chapter is on the nature of the social formations that form the context of feminist projects. The final chapter of the book will address the implications of feminism for alternative futures.

Contexts for Projects

Although feminist projects are shaped by their contexts, this is not a simple determination by objectively given interests, derived from identity or from the economy. Rather, feminist projects are innovative practices that draw on and reinterpret previous civil societal and political repertoires and projects. They varyingly utilise perceived economic and rhetorical resources and face differently perceived political opportunity structures. These resources and opportunities were examined in detail in chapter 4, which dealt with new organisational forms of feminism. The purpose of the present chapter is to describe and explain the transformations that have occurred in the context that shapes the changing resources and opportunities on which feminism draws. The purpose is to encompass transformations in gender regimes, in capitalism and in the environment that constitute the context for feminism.

To begin with, this chapter identifies the context of the inequalities in which feminist projects develop and with which they engage. The concept of gender regime is used to help thinking about the interconnections between forms of gender inequality and the major forms of their variation. These variations are important in understanding why feminism takes diverse forms at different times and in different places around the world. The intersection of the gender regime with other inequalities and with the political projects linked to them is part of the wider context within which feminist projects develop. Changes in the regime of class inequality, of capital and of capitalism are important, as also are changes in the environment – such as climate change and global warming.

The concept of 'project' is used here in order to capture specific sets of ideas and practices that seek social and political change. A project is more than a set of ideas, but it is not as organised as a political party. There are many feminist projects, each subtly or strikingly different from others. Projects are flexible and innovative, responding in complex ways to changes in their context, as well as hoping to produce changes in that context. The meanings within projects are negotiated, indeed struggled over, by participants in the projects – as well as by outsiders, whether allies or opponents.

It is important not to conflate changes in gender regimes with changes in feminist projects, nor to conflate the intersection of sets of social relations with the intersection of political projects. These analytic separations are needed in order to avoid the problems of reductionism and essentialism. The relations between gender regimes and feminist projects are mediated in a multi-faceted way. Nevertheless, changes in regimes of inequality and in their intersection with other regimes of inequality are important in creating the context in which feminist projects are envisaged and developed, and also in producing potential allies – and enemies – for feminist projects.

Gender Regimes

Gender is constituted by the social relations between the sexes (Oakley 1974). Gender is not reducible to biology, or to a single facet of the social. It is not an absolute, and it undergoes significant change in form over time and place. There are many ways to analyse the causes of gender inequality and to explain variations in them (Hawkesworth 1997).

There is a challenge of avoiding 'essentialism', or the reduction of gender to a single base, whether biological (Firestone 1974) or social (Mackinnon 1989), in the course of attempting to theorise and explain gender inequality. Any essentialism in the analysis can potentially be used to support and entrench existing patterns of gender relations, and thus gender inequalities (Butler 1990; Brown 1995). The postmodern turn in gender theory developed as a strong reaction against the potential dangers of essentialism and meta-narratives. This turn has tended to prioritise thick descriptions over attempts at explanation, as well as a strategy of keeping categories of analysis dynamic, even nomadic (Braidotti 1994), so as to avoid their entrenchment. However, such a fluidity and refusal to stabilise categories makes it hard to engage in actual analysis (Felski 1997). A certain amount of abstraction is necessary for an explanatory analysis (Sayer 2000).

Gender is best analysed as a social structure (Risman 2004). Gender is here understood as constituted, simultaneously, at multiple levels, including both the micro-level of interactions and the macro-level of changes in social systems (Connell 2002; Walby 1990, 2009). The relations between levels are best captured by the complexity concept of 'emergence' (Archer 1995; Holland 2000; Walby 2007). In this way gender is not reduced to just one level or institution. Gender relations have ontological depth, which needs to be analysed in all the major institutional domains of economy, polity, violence and civil society.

The varied aspects of gender relations are sufficiently intercon-nected to merit being analysed as a social system, or as a gender regime. The explanation of different forms of gender regime requires the identification of the key elements associated with the major variations in the system (Connell 2002; O'Connor, Orloff and Shaver 1999). One attempt to identify key elements of variations in patterns in gender relations focused on the gendered welfare-state: it produced and refined a typology around the extent to which gender relations were marked by the presence of a male breadwinner in the family (Lewis 1992; Sainsbury 1996; Jenson 1997). While this was an important development, the gendered welfare-state literature is limited by its focus on a relatively narrow selection of elements; it has little to say, for example, about gender-based violence or about democracy. The approach used here adopts the method of identifying a limited set of key elements, but goes beyond it by broadening the range of elements involved so as to include the economy, the polity, violence and civil society.

A gender regime is 'a set of inter-connected gender relations and gendered institutions that constitutes a system' (Walby 2009: 301). This kind of system can take a variety of forms, with key distinctions between domestic and public gender regimes, and, within the public form of the gender regime, between its neoliberal and its social democratic forms. The gender regime is a special instance of a regime of inequality and involves the four major institutional domains of economy, polity, violence and civil society. The traditional definitions of these four institutional domains need to be revised and broadened in order for gender to be taken more adequately into account.

The phrase 'gender regime' means the same as the term 'patriarchy'; they refer to the same underlying concept. The phrase 'gender regime' is used here because of a tendency for the term 'patriarchy' to be misinterpreted. All too often, 'patriarchy' is incorrectly presumed to entail an ahistoric, essentialist, unchanging, reductionist approach to the analysis of gender relations (Pollert 1996). In order to avoid this misunderstanding, I use here the phrase 'gender regime'.

The economy encompasses both the domestic and unpaid economy and that part of the economy that is organised through markets (Oakley 1974; Bakker 1998; Himmelweit 2002). The polity includes not only conventional states and the EU, but also those organised religions that have the capacity to regulate important aspects of social life, such as intimacy. Violence is additionally included as an institutional domain, in order to grasp the significance of inter-personal violence for gender relations. Civil society includes not only culture, knowledge institutions and the media, but also sexuality. The gender regime involves the interrelationship between all four of these institutional domains and is not reducible to any one of them.

The gender regime may be analysed at different levels of abstraction. These include the different forms of the gender regime as a whole; the relationship between the four institutional domains of the gender regime; gendered practices, which exist at a lower level of abstraction, for example occupational segregation by sex in employment; and also individual and group experiences of gendered events (see Walby 2009 for a more detailed account). The nature of the gender regime varies across time and place due to the process of transformation from domestic to public form, according to whether the public form is neoliberal or social democratic, and according to the way in which it intersects with other regimes of inequality.

The patterns of gender inequality have been changing significantly in many countries. There are considerable variations in these changes – between the global North and the global South, between neoliberal and social democratic countries. Despite these changes, there remain significant gender inequalities in economy, polity, violence and civil society in most countries of the world. Some of them have seen reductions in some of these inequalities in recent years; but unevenly so. There remain significant inequalities in relation to employment, for instance in pay and in representation on decision-making bodies; in relation to the state, for instance in the matter of representation in parliament and in government ministeries; in relation to violence, for instance in the extent of rape and partner violence committed by men; and in relation to civil society, for instance in the matters of pornography and prostitution (Walby 2009).

One of the most important differences between gender regimes is the difference between its domestic and its public forms. In the domestic gender regime the processes of power are predominantly exclusionary: they exclude women from locations of power and influence. In the public gender regime, they are more often segregationary, in that, while women are present in the public sphere, they are segregated through placement in positions of lesser influence and power. There is a major ongoing process of transformation of the form of the gender regime from domestic to public – which, although far from complete, is having significant implications for the shape of feminist projects. In most of the global North, the transition from a domestic to a public gender regime is well advanced – but not so in the global South.

In the domestic form of the gender regime there are intense gender divisions in each of the four institutional domains. In the economy, there is a gendered division of labour, women being much more often engaged in unpaid domestic care work, while men are much more often engaged in employment outside the home and are much more often marketised as wage labour. In the polity, men are much more likely than women to hold positions and to have effective power in political decision-making, even if this privilege is confined to elites. In relation to violence, men are much more likely than women to be engaged in its practice and deployment, as well as to hold power over its regulation. In civil society, men are more likely than women to participate in, and to have influence over, decision-making. In the public gender regime the gender divisions in presence and participation are much less intense than in the domestic gender regime, so that women participate in waged employment, in education, in the polity, and in civil societal organisations. However, the degree of gender inequality may not necessarily be less intense, since there often still are inequalities, for example gender pay gaps in employment; further, even when women participate in an activity, this does not necessarily mean that they are involved in the associated decision-making.

Despite the ongoing transformations, women are not yet in employment in equal numbers with men; men are not yet contributing to care work equally with women; childcare is still disproportionately performed by women in the domestic sphere, in spite of some development of public childcare; the state does not yet have a monopoly over legitimate violence, while there remains violence against women that is not fully criminalised. Nevertheless, there is a very significant process of transformation of gender relations, and this has implications for the environments in which feminist projects are shaped.

There is an ongoing transformation of the gender regime from domestic to public form within many countries, but this process is not yet complete even in the global North, and it is far from advanced in the global South. The differences between global regions in the extent of this transformation have implications for its trajectory and for the shape of feminist politics. In those countries where the gender regime is more domestic, maternalist feminist strategies have different implications from the ones they have in countries where the regime takes a more public form. Another difference between the global North and the global South lies in the timing of transformations across institutional domains. For example, transformations in the global South more often involve changes in education and suffrage before rather than after changes in employment – unlike the trajectory of development typically found in the global North; and this has implications for the trajectory of the development of feminism and for its priorities.

The transformation of the gender regime is sometimes understood as a process of linear modernisation driven by economic development (Bergmann 1986; Beck 1992; Giddens 1992). However, it is more complicated than this description suggests, having more than one trajectory of development (Inglehart 1997; Inglehart and Norris

2003). There are important differences between emerging forms of
public gender regime. They generate at least two major varieties in the
global North – neoliberal and social democratic – as well as others in
the South, such as the state-dominated form in China (Walby 2009).

The neoliberal and social democratic forms of the gender regime
are distinguished in each of the four institutional domains of
economy, polity, violence and civil society. The most important
differences are those pertaining to the depth of democracy and to the
degree of inequality. The detailed differences will be discussed later
in the chapter.

Capitalism

Feminism shapes and is shaped by capital/ism. Capitalism is a regime
of class inequality in which capital is the dominant locus of power.
The nature of the relationship between capital as a specific accumulation of power and capitalism as the wider social formation, which
capital structures and within which it is embedded, is central to the
question of the nature and effect of feminism on capital/ism. The
nature and extent of the potential impact of feminism on capital/
ism depends on the nature of capital/ism, as well as on the nature of
the interaction between them. The form of capitalism is changing,
with implications for the form of the gender regime and of feminism.
Feminism, itself changing as both capital/ism and the gender regime
change, has implications for capital/ism.

In order to assess the potential significance of feminism for
changing capitalism, it is necessary to address two issues. The first
is whether there are significant variations in the form of capitalism around the world, or whether one form is globally hegemonic.
The second is whether the democratic forces, of which feminism is
one, are significantly a part of what causes these differences. These
two questions are interrelated, since one of the potential sources of
variation in forms of capitalism is democracy. They underlie another
question, namely whether there are significant varieties of capitalism shaped by variations in the depth and practice of democracy –
including variations between neoliberal and social democratic forms.

If capitalism is understood as a single world system (Wallerstein
1974, 2004; Arrighi 1994; Chase-Dunn 1998; Jessop 2002; Robinson
2004), then there is little possibility that feminism can change it.
'World systems theory' analyses capitalism as a single system in
which the parts form a whole, and in which capital is the major

structuring force. It subsumes the role of states, militaries and ideologies within the larger system. Change is theorised in two ways: according to one, countries can go up or down the core–periphery hierarchy (Wallerstein 1974, 2004); according to the other, one global hegemon gives way to another, so that the global capitalist system is led in slightly different ways (Arrighi 1994). Neither of these approaches to change has any role for feminism. This is because gender relations are subsumed to class relations without any autonomous efficacy. The only way in which the world systems approach can encompass a role for democratic change would be if the global system as a whole were to be democratically overthrown, as Hardt and Negri (2000, 2006) suggest, though there are few signs of this.

However, in the world systems approach, the integration of the world capitalist system is overstated at the expense of variations between countries and between multiple regimes of inequality, including gender. There are variations in the form of capitalism even as capital expands its spatial reach (Castells 1996, 1997, 1998; Sassen 2001, 2006), and even as its depth in structuring other social relations increases (Harvey 2005). While there are important global connections concerning some phenomena, for example finance, few are comprehensively globalised. Some things are more global than others, and in this order: finance capital; productive capital; commodities (e.g. traded goods such as cars); then polities, which are subjected to global and non-global pressures; violence, where the projection of military force is transnational, but rarely fully global; civil societal and political projects; labour, as workers increasingly migrate but are far from being fully global. There is tension between the different degrees of partial globalisation in these different phenomena. This tension can be seen, for example, as the aftershocks of the 2008 financial crisis reverberate through diverse 'real' economies, causing varying depths of recession, unevenly provoking sovereign debt crises, and re-balancing the political forces involved in government budget cuts and in nationalist responses. The circulation of finance is more global than the political forces that engage with it.

Today there are competing hegemons rather than a single one (Zakaria 2008). While the US is the most powerful hegemon, it is at the risk of an over-reach of its powers: its over-extended military (Mann 2003) and financial exuberance (Greenspan 2008) are indicative of economic decline and of the end of the US period of global hegemony (Arrighi 1994). There are potential rival hegemons, including the EU and, in the near future, China, with (re-) emerging strength in the other 'BRICs' (Brazil, Russia, India). The varieties of gender regime and capitalism carried by these alternative global hegemons are of great significance, and not only for the hegemon, but for the rest of the world. The EU has a distinctive model of intersecting capitalism and gender regime, which promotes a public gender regime, in a set of arrangements that encourages full employment and highly skilled work, even though this model is not fully implemented. However, the EU's lack of internal cohesion may mean that it will not achieve the position of global hegemon.

The form of capitalism is not impervious to political forces, including those mobilised in democratic practices. The traditional reading of Marx's analysis of capitalism has viewed the economic as determining the other aspects of the social formation. But the origin of this interpretation pre-dated the development of parliamentary democracy; hence it necessarily underestimates the significance of democratic forces. There is a more complex relationship between capital and the state in contemporary capitalist social formations (Tilly 1990; Arrighi 1994; Chase-Dunn 1998; Sassen 2001, 2006; Robinson 2004; Wallerstein 2004). Democratic forces in civil society and in the polity play an important role in shaping the contemporary state and the capitalist social formation (Moore 1966; Gramsci 1971; Hardt and Negri 2000, 2006; Keane 2003; Berman 2006; Wright 2010). Since democratic forces are important for the form that capitalism takes, feminism is potentially significant for it too.

Changes in Class and Gender Inequalities

During the last thirty years or so of neoliberalism in North America and Europe (and, to varying extents, in other countries), there has been an increase in class-based economic inequalities in income and wealth – inequalities consequent upon the development of an under-regulated financialisation; a process of de-democratisation in the full, or of partial privatisation of major services (such as health, education, transport, water); and thus a movement from democratic state control of these services to governance by the market, an increase in the deployment of violence by the state in war, and a more commercialised civil society.

However, there are significant differences in these changes according to gender and class. During the last thirty years, in North America and Europe, there has been an increase in class-based economic inequalities, in the overall wage spread, and in the Gini index measuring income inequalities between households. However, at the same time there has been a narrowing of gender gaps and inequalities in employment, as women's employment has risen and gender pay gaps have decreased. Despite a process whereby important institutions were taken out of democratic governance, there has been an increase in women's presence in parliament and holding ministerial jobs.

Changes in regimes of inequality do not necessarily move in the same direction, even if they coexist in the same country at the same time and intersect. These contrary movements in regimes of inequality are possible because the regimes in question have autonomy from each other, even though they adapt to each other as they intersect. For example, the gender regime is not nested within the class regime; rather, these regimes coexist, each taking the other as part of its context. Gender inequalities do not derive from capitalism, although they are shaped by it as well as shaping it.

Neoliberal and Social Democratic Forms of Class and Gender Regimes

Neoliberalism and social democracy are different types of social formations, as well as being projects and governmental programmes. They differ in the institutional domains of economy, polity, violence and civil society. There has been a long literature that identifies the distinguishing features of social democracy.

Polanyi (1957) has perhaps the broadest approach to social democracy, although he does not use this phrase, pointing to the intrinsic limits to the commoditisation of labour, land and money. If labour is treated as if it were only a commodity, then there is danger of death by starvation as economies fluctuate. If land, by which is meant nature and the environment, is treated as if it were only a commodity, then it will be exhausted and it will not be sustainable in the long run. If money, which means finance, is treated as a mere commodity, then its fluctuations could destroy the industrial economy it is supposed to support. Capitalism thus has the potential to destroy the conditions of its own existence if commodification is carried out to excess. Polanyi argues that there is no such thing as a self-regulating market. The regulation of the markets for labour, land and money, which are needed not only for human well-being but also for the survival of capitalism, requires state intervention.

The regulation of finance is a key part of social democracy. Polanyi (1957) referred to it as the regulation of money – a free market which, unregulated, would destroy the rest of the economy. The destructive consequences of unregulated finance, demonstrated in the great crash and depression in the 1920s and 1930s, informed the analysis of Galbraith (1975) and Keynes (1936); while the problems of global finance in the 1990s informed the work of Stiglitz (2002, 2006), and the crash of 2008, the work of Krugman (2008).

Most of the contemporary debates on the nature of social democracy focus on the welfare state. This topic has a long history, drawing on the work of Marshall (1950), who developed and extended the concept of 'citizenship' so as to make it include not only political, but also civil and socio-economic aspects. In particular, social citizenship requires material resources sufficient to enable full participation in society, and it is the remit of the state to ensure that these resources are provided if they are not otherwise forthcoming. The work of Esping-Andersen (1990, 1999, 2002) embeds the discussion of welfare states in a wider context of welfare state regimes, which extends to the organisation of employment relations. Esping-Andersen (1990) makes a distinction between different types of welfare state regimes, distinguishing not only the liberal from the social democratic, but also the conservative corporatist, and indeed further forms and hybrids (Esping-Andersen 1997). The way in which the state is used in the provision of welfare may potentially lead either to the redistribution (social democratic regime) or to the maintenance of existing hierarchies (conservative corporatist regime). However, Hicks and Kenworthy (2003) find that there is actually a single continuum rather than three separate clusters, which Esping-Andersen (2002) concedes. The conclusion drawn here is that there is a single continuum, from (neo)liberalism to social democracy. The term 'neoliberalism' is used in preference to 'liberalism', which, in the US at least, is confusing on account of its many overlapping and divergent meanings.

One of the key contemporary debates about social democracy and the welfare state is over the location of the boundary between social democracy and neoliberalism. Giddens (1994, 1998) offers the vision of a renewed social democracy, a 'Third Way', which includes a larger presence of markets. But, while some see the application of 'markets' and 'choice' to the development of public services as an important and positive contribution to the contemporary social democratic project (Le Grand 2007), others see it as a step outside of this project, into neoliberalism (Arestis and Sawyer 2005).

The regulation of employment relations is also a key component of social democracy (Esping-Andersen 1990; Streeck 1992), although it has sometimes been regarded, more generically, as a 'coordination' of the market economy (Hall and Soskice 2001).

Social democracy stretches the boundaries of the economy and of the state. In his analysis of the donation of blood, Titmuss (1972) showed that commercialisation, as manifested under the form of payment for blood, was not as efficient as free donation in generating supplies of blood. In this social democratic stance, mutualism, which is based in the civil society practice of gifts, can be a more effective basis of social policy than commercialisation. There are public goods, not only private ones.

Violence can also be considered from a perspective that differentiates social democratic from neoliberal practice, though much of the current analysis concerns changes over time rather than coexisting systems. Garland (2001) analyses a shift from a penal welfare to a punitive criminal justice system in the US and UK since the 1980s, a change that can be re-described as movement from social democracy to neoliberalism. Wacquant (2009) analyses the development of a punitive criminal justice system in the US, which involves the incarceration of ever increasing numbers of the poor in prisons. These analyses could be further developed, since there are continuing differences between countries in the regulation and deployment of violence, including in the criminal justice system – differences that can be conceptualised as differences between social democracy and neoliberalism.

Most of the discussion of social democracy concerns class relations, with little reference to other sets of social relations of inequality. There are some exceptions to this: the inclusion of gender as a topic, albeit not as one seen to be part of the theory of change; the inclusion of women in detailed historical accounts of the development of social democracy, but accounts not integrated into an overarching narrative of this development. What difference would it make if gender and other inequalities were adequately included?

One partial exception to the omission of non-class inequalities can be found in the work of Esping-Andersen (1990, 1999), who tries hard to include women in his analysis; but gender inequality is nevertheless still treated primarily as the outcome rather than the cause of differences between his various welfare state regimes, so it is of little theoretical interest in his typology. This is a result of his locating gender within the family, whereas the causal drivers in his analysis are located in employment and in the state.

Most of the attempts to build a gendered typology of welfare state regimes on the basis of a critique of Esping-Andersen's work leave behind his concepts of liberalism and social democracy, focusing instead on the gender relations – for example (and in particular) on the male breadwinner versus the dual earner model (Lewis 1992). These attempts do not go far beyond Esping-Andersen's narrow range of relevant institutions – those of employment and of the welfare state – not adding much beyond that of the family.

Other writers on social democracy have texts on gender that are relatively separate from their main work on social democracy, or where the gender changes are seen as deriving from those in capitalism or the market economy. For example Giddens' (1992) work on the transformation of intimacy has this characteristic, even though the text is important for its linking of gender equality, capitalist change and intimacy within a social democratic framing.

The neoliberal and social democratic forms of social formation diverge in each regime of inequality and in each of the four major institutional domains of economy, polity, violence and civil society. The neoliberal variety of modernity is marked by high levels of inequality and shallow levels of democracy in its regimes of inequality, while the social democratic variety has lower levels of inequality and deeper democracy.

The distinction between neoliberal (sometimes 'liberal') and social democratic social formations has been more developed in the analysis of class relations than in the analysis of gender relations (Esping-Andersen 1990; Hall and Soskice 2001; Hicks and Kenworthy 2003). In relation to class, the focus is on political economy, in particular on the extent to which the state coordinates and regulates economic markets. However, it is important not to reduce patterns in gender relations to patterns in class relations, but to recognise and analyse their specific dynamics. Also, the nature of the variations in the form of modernity goes beyond political economy to other domains – not only to the economy and the polity, but also to violence and civil society.

Drawing on this literature, I propose here the following distinction between neoliberalism and social democracy. It encompasses the economy, polity, violence and civil society. It identifies the specifically gendered aspects of the distinction between neoliberalism and social democracy in each of these institutional domains.

In the economic domain, the neoliberal variety is marked by lesser regulation of finance and employment than the social democratic variety, and by lesser provision of state welfare. The regulation of finance is to ensure that finance is subservient to wider economic and social ends rather than allowed autonomy. The regulation of employment concerns especially preventing discrimination against women and minorities and providing a balance between employers' and workers' interests in continuity of employment. The state provision of welfare operates in a way that is subject to democratic control and to the maintenance of minimally decent standards of living. The gendered specificity includes larger gender gaps in pay in the neoliberal rather than in the social democratic variety and lesser state provision of services that socialise care-work, but not necessarily any differences in the extent of female employment, which is at a high level in both.

In the polity, democracy is less deep in the neoliberal than in the social democratic variety, being usually restricted to suffrage rather than including presence or range (Walby 2009). Ten items are used to identify the depth of democracy: (1) no hereditary or unelected positions, such as those of monarch and of members in either chamber of the parliament; (2) no colonies; (3) no powers of governance held by additional non-democratic polity, such as organised religion; (4) universal suffrage, *de facto* as well as *de jure*; (5) elections, especially free, fair and competitive, in a context of free speech, free association, and developed civil society associations; (6) low cost of electioneering, either by law or by custom; (7) an electoral system with proportional representation; (8) an electoral system with quotas for under-represented groups such as women; (9) the proportionate presence of women and minorities in parliament; and (10) a range of institutions (e.g. welfare services) that are governed by the democratic polity (Walby 2009). The gendered specificity of the depth of democracy focuses on 'presence democracy' in the extent to which women are present in parliament and in the mechanisms within the electoral system that facilitate rather than restrict this principle – such as quotas, proportional representation and low cost elections. It also focuses on the range of institutions that are governed democratically rather than by the markets and by capital – for example health, education, transport and care work – since these are so important for the form and inequality of gender relations.

In the domain of violence, the neoliberal variety of modernity has higher levels than the social democratic variety in the deployment of violence by individuals and by the state, and lesser regulation of inter-personal violence targeted against the disadvantaged. Neoliberal states are more likely to be militarised, to deploy harsh practices in their criminal justice systems, and to have higher rates of inter-personal violence. The neoliberal form of the public gender regime has a less developed regulation of men's violence against women than social democracy has. Democracy and violence are inversely related. An increase in democracy leads to less inter-state war and to the regulation of violence from powerful to less powerful groups, which discourages these forms of violence. An increase in violence, especially inter-state and inter-group violence, is linked to a reduction in civil liberties and thereby in democracy. Securitisation and democratisation are processes in opposition to each other.

In civil society, the neoliberal variety of modernity is marked by greater inequality and commercialisation, as compared with greater mutualism in the social democratic variety. The neoliberal variety of the public gender regime has higher rates of unequal and commercialised sexual practices, such as prostitution and pornography, than has the social democratic variety.

This theoretical distinction between neoliberalism and social democracy can be applied in practice to particular countries or social formations. The distinction is best understood as a continuum with countries distributed along it and with only a few countries at the extreme poles. The best example of a neoliberal country is the US, and the best example of social democracy is Sweden. The EU is more social democratic than the US (though not as much as Sweden). (See Walby 2009 for an empirical analysis of the location of Organisation for Economic Cooperation and Development [OECD] countries along this continuum.)

The distinction between neoliberal and social democratic forms of public gender regime has important implications for the analysis of disagreements between feminist projects. Sometimes feminists imagine that the only form of the public gender regime is that of neoliberalism. In this view, the alternative to domesticity would expose women to the harshness of the market – not only in the economy, where it may mean low paid, poor quality jobs, but also in the construction of intimacy, where it means commercialised pornography and prostitution rather than mutuality. However, when the vision of the social democratic form of the public gender regime is brought into focus, a new set of alternative opportunities and possibilities to that of the domestic gender regime can be seen to emerge. For example, if the only alternative to domestic care work is seen to be low paid, poor quality waged work, then it is unsurprising that the domestic may be preferred to public forms of the gender regime; when decent work with good pay and conditions is an option, then this may more often be perceived as preferable to domestic care work. If the only alternatives to life-long marital sexual fidelity are abandonment after youth and prostitution, then it is not surprising that women's projects promote life-long marriage; when independence and mutual respect within serial sexual relationships is a realistic alternative, this may be perceived as an appropriate alternative to life-long marriage.

Globalisation

Globalisation has changed the context in which feminist projects co-operate by facilitating new spaces, institutions and rhetoric, which constitute a new location for the framing of feminist politics – one that assists the change in discursive presentation and new opportunities for argumentation. Globalisation impacts on the nature of feminism especially by creating changes in political opportunities. By globalisation I mean a process of increased density and frequency of international or global social interactions relative to local or national ones. This process has economic, political and cultural dimensions. This formulation closely follows the definition of Chase-Dunn, Kawano and Brewer (2000). I resist a definition in terms of supraterritoriality (Scholte 2000), as it underestimates the extent to which global processes still have a territorial component (Sassen 2001, 2006). The definition is deliberately minimalist, in order to avoid conflating the causation of globalisation with its definition and to allow for the possibility of multiple waves with different causes.

Much of the analysis of globalisation has concerned itself with social processes primarily connected with changes in capitalism and in the associated class, political, economic and cultural relations (Held, McGrew, Goldblatt and Perraton 1999; Ohmae 1995). However, this choice is unduly restrictive. When the focus includes differences due to gender, ethnicity and religion, a wider set of politics comes into focus. The extent of globalisation can be overestimated and remains highly uneven, with countries differentially integrated into global networks (Hirst and Thompson 1996). Of course, globalisation has not homogenised the world, and many national differences remain (Whitley 1999). Globalisation does not simply entail an economic process which diminishes the political capacities of nation-states (Cerny 1996; Ohmae 1995), but rather it is more complexly implicated in the restructuring of workers' repertories of political action (Piven and Cloward 2000) and of regional polities (Hettne, Inotai and Sunkel 1999) such as the European

Union (Walby 1999a), and in the development of forms of global governance (Held 1995) and of global civil society (Berkovitch 1999). The changes in time–space relations involved in globalisation produce contradictory effects. Globalisation has sometimes been considered to be a process hostile to feminism (Peterson 1996), in which emerging forms of global economic governance are in opposition to women's interests, as is suggested in the case of neoliberal strategies for micro-credit to women (Rankin 2001) and in structural adjustment policies of the IMF (Sparr 1994); consequently, feminist responses are primarily ones of opposition (Haxton and Olsson 1999; Rowbotham and Linkogle 2000). However, increases in international linkages have also been used for political projects designed around women's perceived interests (Moghadam 2000; Moser 1993; Ramirez, Soysal and Shanahan 1997). Globalisation restructures gendered political opportunities and resources in complex ways. Of course, there are contradictory impacts of global processes, since in some places the rhetoric of globalisation has been used to legitimate the erosion of some dimensions of welfare provision in nation-states that perceive themselves as being under threat from global economic competition. However, globalisation is not simply an economic process involving the development of global financial and capital markets. Rather it is a political process as well, which has involved the restructuring of the political environment and the re-positioning the nation-state in a web of transnational networks and institutions. In this new context feminists have been adept at utilising these networks in order to promote their demands.

Financial Crisis

The 2008 financial crisis and its aftermath created a new context for feminism. The neoliberal deregulation of finance enabled finance to engage in excessive expansion at the expense of the 'real' economy. The ensuing waves of the crisis have offered different opportunities and threats for neoliberal and social democratic projects. The 2008 crisis is the latest and largest in a series of financial crises with focal points in different parts of the world.

The first wave of the 2008 crisis was the near meltdown of the financial system, which was triggered by a collapse in value of predominantly US sub-prime mortgages, packaged and sold around the world in specialised financial instruments. The threat of financial meltdown led to the bail-out of the banks by governments, which transferred massive quantities of tax-payer funds to financial institutions in order to prevent the collapse of the banking system. The second wave of the crisis consisted in the deep economic recession triggered by the financial disaster. This was met in many countries of the global North with a Keynesian social democratic response intended to stimulate the economy and prevent the recession from turning into depression. The third wave of the crisis is the threat of sovereign debt default, as governments struggle with the cost of the bail-outs and stimulus packages, in the context of reduced tax revenues due to recession. This threat is being met by a neoliberal response to reduce the deficit in government budgets at unprecedented speed, risking a further round of recession. Since the proximate cause of the crisis was the failure to regulate the financial system appropriately, there have been calls for increased regulation (a social democratic move), but developments by 2010 have been relatively meek (Stiglitz 2006; Krugman 2008; Soros 2008).

The crisis is gendered in several ways. First, the governance of finance by a homogenous, almost all-male clique encouraged herd-like behaviour rather than critical thinking (van Staveren 2002). Second, the loss of jobs is gendered, though differently in different periods of the crisis. At the start, more male jobs were lost, as male-majority industries such as construction were initially the most affected ones; in the later phase, women's jobs are most affected by cut-backs in public expenditure on state services. Third, the reduction of the deficits by cutting public services and benefits affects women more than men, since they are more dependent on these services and they are poorer.

The neoliberal and social democratic responses to the financial crisis are also gendered. The neoliberal response cuts the income of the poor and of women at a time when cuts in public services affect women disproportionately. The social democratic response has gender implications: increased regulation of finance can include more women (though this has been confined to Nordic countries); the stimulus packages of the second phase typically supported men's jobs (as in the scheme that supported the predominantly male workers in the car industry by paying for old cars to be scrapped so as to encourage new ones to be bought); and support for continuation rather than cutting state expenditure on public services, which is so important for women.

The diverse interpretations of the financial crisis have different implications for the future of feminism. The crisis may be a bubble, a routine occurrence in the history of capitalism (Perez 2009), giving rise to a response that this is merely 'business as usual' and does lead to major changes. It may be the exhaustion of the current regime of accumulation, which, routinely in the macro-history of capitalism, triggers a change in the global hegemon, a process often involving war (Arrighi 1994). It may be a tipping point or a critical turning point, either an opportunity for the right to gain ground, as in other examples of 'disaster capitalism' (Klein 2007), or an opportunity for the resurgence of the social democratic project.

Environmental Crisis

Economic growth depends upon the natural environment to provide raw materials and to absorb waste. Economic development is reaching the limits of nature. Peaks are approaching in many of the good environmental resources previously taken for granted: peak oil, peak gas, and peak benevolence in world temperatures. If there is no mitigation, these are likely to lead to peak standard of living and GDP and to peak longevity, first in the global North, then on the rest of the planet. This is a difficult context for feminist advances.

The planet is reaching its limits in absorbing the carbon dioxide produced – especially, but not exclusively – in burning oil and coal without raising the temperature to levels that are harmful to human survival. The change in the climate that results from the warming, or better the heating, of the planet threatens extreme weather events, from floods to drought, with a consequent destruction of the capacity for agricultural production and a rise in the sea level that would drown significant human settlements. The consequences include reduction in food production and in food availability and deaths by flooding caused by extreme weather events and by rise in the sea level. Indeed, some of these effects can already be seen. They are likely to intensify even further the struggle over scarce resources (Monbiot 2006; Stern 2007; Giddens 2009; Intergovernmental Panel on Climate Change 2011; Urry 2011). These consequences would be experienced unevenly around the world, between men and women, rich and poor (Roberts and Parks 2007; Holmes, Jones and Marsden 2009).

The extent of production of carbon dioxide (CO_2), the greenhouse gas that lies at the root of global overheating, is very varied. Rich, developed countries produce more than poor, less economically developed countries. As the world becomes increasingly developed, the output of CO_2 is steadily rising. Some countries produce more CO_2 for the same amount of economic output than others, for example Sweden produces less CO_2 per \$GDP than the US (0.22 kg Sweden, 0.32 kg the EU, 0.56 kg the US; World Bank 2007; Walby 2009). Modern economies that are organised on social democratic lines produce less CO_2 per unit of production than those organised on neoliberal lines. It is possible to reduce the production of CO_2 through the development of sources of energy other than the burning of hydrocarbons such as oil and coal, for instance by harnessing the energy of the sun (through solar panels and reflectors), of wind (through wind turbines), of waves and falling water (through hydro-electric schemes). This requires expensive investment in new technologies, the production of which depends on the structuring of the markets for these technologies and for their outputs by political as well as economic forces. These forces are not only national, but also global. Some of the most important initiatives have come from UN bodies and conferences, though these have been subject to controversy and conflict and have not always resulted in substantial outcomes. The UN conference on climate change in Kyoto set some limits on emissions, but that in Copenhagen (2010) was subject to controversy over the role of the US and China and did not produce such substantial outcomes, despite the efforts of the EU.

Oil followed coal as the fuel of choice of the industrialised economies. It is essential for the car- and truck-based mobility of the North. It is also widely used to generate the electricity that runs industry and lights and heats offices and homes. Thus most developed economies are dependent on oil.

Oil is a finite resource, and it is running out. After the peak of production, its availability reaches a plateau and then declines. Peak oil in the US was in the 1970s. Global peak oil is probably occurring round about now (2011). There are attempts to access ever more difficult and polluting oil reserves, such as the tar sands of Canada and the deep sea drilling off the US coastline in the Gulf of Mexico (site of the 2010 spill), which can have destructive environmental consequences. Gas production is expected to peak a little later, as the reserves of this finite hydrocarbon are also exhausted.

Yet there is increasing demand for oil, as economic growth continues in the North and the global South industrialises. As the decline in production meets this increase in demand, there is a potential for fierce conflict over the remaining supplies. This has perhaps already begun, if the US invasion of Iraq is interpreted as a quest for control over its oil supplies, as is asserted by Greenspan (2008: 463): 'the

Iraq war is largely about oil'. Western support for, and arming of, the feudal regime in Saudi Arabia, despite its absence of democracy and its violations of human rights, which are criticised in other countries, is perhaps an example of the diplomatic compromises made in order to secure oil supplies. Al-Qaida's leader, Osama bin Laden, initially emerged in opposition to the Saudi regime's closeness to the US. Organised violence over control of oil is likely to grow rather than diminish, as the shortage of oil develops.

The price of oil will rise after the peak in its production if economic growth continues in its current form. As consumers pay more for oil (petrol, heating, light), they will have less money to buy other things, and their standard of living will fall in consequence. Further, this price rise is unlikely to be steady and linear, but rather fluctuating, with sudden spikes. This is partly the consequence of financialisation and the development of speculative markets in the future price of oil. Spikes in the oil price have already occurred. The rise in the price of oil has been linked to fluctuations in the price of housing in the US, which suggests that interactions between speculative markets in commodities and assets such as oil and property can trigger wider financial crises if there is vulnerability in the financial system. Thus the rises in the price of oil that will follow peak oil may trigger further economic and financial problems, in addition to a reduction in living standards.

The standard of living is likely to be approaching its peak, although unevenly around the world. This is due partly to the rise in the price of oil, and hence of food, as oil production peaks, and partly to the cost of repairing damage from extreme weather events.

To repeat, as the rising cost of increasingly scarce oil takes an ever higher proportion of an individual's income, there will be less money to spend on other things, so there will be a decline in the standard of living. And, as the temperature rises, food production around the world becomes more difficult and unpredictable in the face of droughts, floods and other extreme weather events; this is likely to lead to a rise in the price of food, which, again, will leave less money for other things.

As the climate changes, extreme weather events become more common, causing death and injury to humans and damage to property and to economic infrastructure. Building protection in advance of storms (e.g. raising sea wall defences), ameliorating harms (e.g. health care for the injured), and reconstruction after damage (e.g. rebuilding homes) will divert resources from use on the current standard of living.

Investment in the energy technologies necessary to prevent the rise in temperature would in the short run require a diversion of the resources that would otherwise be spent on the current standard of living (Stern 2007). While such investments might ameliorate the rise in temperature, few now expect them to be made with the speed and on the scale needed to prevent some rise in temperature and its untoward consequences.

Longevity is improved not only by good medical care, but also by a good standard of living, the absence of war, and a good diet. These factors are likely to have peaked, though unevenly around the world. The limits to economic growth imposed by peak oil and by the environmental crisis are also limits to the standard of living and to longevity. Increases in the standard of living are important in contributing to longevity. A peak standard of living is likely to occur in the near future, as a consequence of peak oil and of global warming.

In the global North there is an epidemic of obesity, which is related to the growth of a poorly regulated 'food' industry. In this industry food is often altered, not so much to improve its nutrition and health-giving qualities, but rather for the sake of saleability. This process has sometimes involved increasing the tastiness and addictiveness of foods through the addition of sugar, salt and fat. The countries with the highest industrialisation of food and lowest regulation of its quality are also the ones with the highest proportion of obesity in the population: 39 per cent in the US; 23 per cent in the UK; 11 per cent in Sweden (World Health Organization 2007).

Current longevity varies considerably around the world. While overall there is correlation between longevity and income per person, those living in the US live shorter lives than those who live in Sweden, in the UK and in the EU. Neoliberal economies are less effective than social democratic ones in converting resources into longevity.

The planet is reaching the peak that the environment can offer humanity, with a decline likely thereafter. There is peak benevolent temperature and peak oil, with the prospect of peak standard of living and peak longevity following on. The context for the future of feminism is one of increasing problems linked with the depletion of the environment. The remedies needed to re-balance society and the environment require the regulation of the form of economic growth, especially of energy production and of energy use. This is unlikely to happen in an era of neoliberal deregulation; and it is more likely to happen if there is greater democratic control over the forms of economic development. Feminism has a contribution to make to environmental and social democratic projects as part of its shared concern for the democratic regulation of the economy. The concern of the feminist project with deepening democracy overlaps with the environmental project, which also requires a deepening of democracy in order to secure change.

Conclusions

The future of feminism depends not only on the internal resources of the project, but also on the resources of its wider environment. These offer both threats and opportunities for the development and influence of feminism.

As the nature of gender inequalities changes, so too do feminist projects, and this change involves complex processes of innovation and adaptation. There is no simple, monolithic, timeless category of 'woman', whose 'interests' would be obvious; rather there are changes in who women are, in how they are positioned, and also in how they perceive their interests and imagine them being taken forward. Changes in gender regimes alter the nature of what constitutes women and gender relations, with implications for the development of, and changes in, feminist projects. The different forms and varieties of the gender regime provide quite different environments for the development of feminist projects. They produce the context for the development of distinctive goals and priorities, as well as the organisational capacity and form that the project takes. They offer varied prospects, both for political opportunities and for potential political threats. The form and variety of the gender regime varies over time and place; the current period is different from previous ones, while the global South and global North contain many further variations.

Feminist projects are shaped by and have implications for capitalist development, in its institutions of economy (with the availability of women as wage labourers), in the polity (with demands for deeper democracy), in violence (with demands for less of it), and in civil society (with demands for the prioritisation of mutualism over commercialism in sexuality).

The current context for feminism is increasingly hostile, containing as it does a resurgent neoliberalism, de-democratisation, a financial crisis and its after-shocks, and an environmental crisis with peak oil and global warming. These constitute challenges to the further development of feminism. The goal of reducing gender inequality will not be achieved unless these other challenges are successfully addressed. Not only must feminism engage with these difficult developments if it is to realise its goals; but, unless feminism does engage with them, they will not be overcome. Feminist projects are not separate from these wider social changes.

7

Feminist Intersections

Introduction

Feminism changes other political projects, as well as being changed by them. There are mutual adjustments between projects as they intersect. These intersecting political projects take a wide range of forms. Some are linked to other kinds of social inequality, such as ethnicity/race, disability, age, and sexual orientation (Verloo 2006; Kantola and Nousiainen 2009; Equality and Human Rights Commission [EHRC] 2010; Walby, Armstrong and Strid 2010a). Others concern national, religious and ethnic projects (Anthias and Yuval-Davis 1992; Yuval-Davis 1997).

Feminist projects also intersect with mainstream governmental programmes, as was shown in the chapter on gender mainstreaming.

Two key political projects that overlap with feminism are those of human rights and of social democracy. Human rights and social democracy have different traditions and priorities, one being associated with progressive, though individualist liberalism, the latter with collectivism and socialism. This alterity between individualism and community is a long-standing theme in political philosophy, and it is characterised by frequent failures to make a satisfactory compromise or synthesis between them (Rawls 1978; Habermas 1987, 1991; Kymlicka 1995; Bauman 1996; Benhabib 1992; Sen 2009). Feminism may either be construed as facing a choice between the two approaches to justice, or it may be seen as a route to their effective hybridisation or synthesis into something new.

This chapter addresses the topic of the intersection of feminist projects with other progressive projects. It examines the relationship of feminism with anti-racism and nationalism, with environmentalism, with human rights and with social democracy. It considers how human rights and social democracy can be reconciled; and it offers a view as to a possible synthesis of feminism, human rights, social democracy, economic growth and sustainability.

Intersecting Projects: Feminism, Anti-Racism and Nationalism

The analysis of intersectionality has often focused on the intersection of sets of social relations, for example between gender and ethnicity. Here the focus is a little different; it is on the intersection of political and civil societal projects. Crenshaw (1991) makes a similar distinction between structural and political intersectionality. The relationship between such multiple projects, which are addressed in debates on intersectionality, is complex and contested (Crenshaw 1991; Hankivsky 2005; McCall 2005; Phoenix and Pattynama 2006; Verloo 2006; Hancock 2007).

Crenshaw (1991) is highly critical of the way in which black women can be rendered invisible at the intersection of 'race' and gender projects and offers a critique of the identity politics that obscures groups at such points of intersection. Several different ways of analysing the 'intersection' of multiple inequalities have since developed (McCall 2005; Hancock 2007), though this is not a new area, since there is a long-established debate on the relationship between class and other kinds of inequalities (Hartmann 1976; Davis 1981; Westwood 1984; Walby 1986; Phizacklea 1990; Acker 2000). The new debates on intersectionality have prioritised the relationship between gender and ethnicity, as well as those intersections that involve mutual changes in the systems of inequality involved (Crenshaw 1991; Hancock 2007), though not all of them insist on such features (McCall 2005).

It is important for the analysis of intersectionality to avoid the temptation of conflating structural inequality and political projects, or else the political projects would be reduced, in an essentialist manner, to the associated set of social relations. While Crenshaw (1991) succeeds in avoiding such reductionism, many others fall into this trap and reproduce the essentialism that they try so hard to avoid, albeit now at the micro-level of small groups at points of intersection, as McCall (2005) notes. It is important to distinguish between, rather than conflate, the structural inequalities and the projects associated with them. While the previous chapter concentrated on sets of social relations, this one concentrates on projects.

In bringing into focus the significance of relations of inequality previously neglected, there has been a temptation to treat them as if they were equally significant, as if the pursuit of equality required the assumption that each form of inequality has the same level of impact on the social formation. For example, Hancock (2007) writes critically of what she calls the 'oppression Olympics', which treat some inequalities as being more significant than others. However, this is a normative approach rather than one based on evidence. The evidence does not always support the claim that each set of social relations is equally important in structuring the social formation. It is more appropriate to treat the relations of power between structural inequalities and between political projects as contingent and open to empirical investigation. The relations between the projects may be equal and symmetrical, but they are more likely to be unequal and asymmetrical; this is an empirical matter. The projects are likely to be mutually adaptive, but whether they retain separation or merge is an empirical question about contingencies (Walby, Armstrong and Strid 2010b).

The relationship between gender and nations is a two-way process, in which gender and nation shape each other (Yuval-Davis 1997; Walby 1992, 2006). These relationships are mediated by associations with other phenomena, including democracy and militarism; for example feminist projects typically, though far from always, are unsupportive of militarist nationalism (Woolf 1938; Roseneil 1995).

The creation of a nation often involves a process of looking back, towards a myth of common origin (Smith 1986); it is a process that involves an imagined community (Anderson 1983) and draws on collective memories of perceived common experiences (Gellner 1983) and invented traditions (Hobsbawm and Ranger 1983). The selective interpretation of the past is a potent method of legitimating present political projects (Delanty and Kumar 2006). A choice has to be made as to which model of gender relations is to be included in this cultural assemblage in order to support national identification and renewal. A particular model of womanhood may be used as a symbol of nation (Yuval-Davis and Anthias 1989), but it is important not to treat women only as passive symbols, not to ignore their own, actively articulated preferences (Jayawardena 1986; Kandiyoti 1991), and not to essentialise the imagery and practice either of gender or of nation (Cockburn 2000). There may be struggles within the nationalist project over the model of gender relations that is preferred

(Ward 1989). In particular, there is a not infrequent tension between a backward-looking, domesticated version of womanhood and a version that attempts to mobilise women as full citizens in the public sphere (Walby 2006). For national projects, feminism may be a welcome partner and it may organise part of the agenda setting of the overall project; or it may be a critical insider, trying to shape the other project the better to fulfil its own. For example, nationalist projects may promote women as full citizens engaged in the public sphere, or they may attempt to promote a romantic or fundamentalist myth of domesticity. Feminist projects may support or oppose the representation and location of women in these national projects (Walby 2000, 2006).

Since nations and national projects are gendered, the relations between nations and national projects are also gendered. Thus competition and contestation between nations and other polities is often a gendered competition and contestation, in that changes in the dominance of one nation or polity over another can have implications for the gender regime in those nations and polities. Changes in the relations between imperial powers and colonised nations (Enloe 1989, 2007) and between the European Union and its member states (Hoskyns 1996; Walby 2004a) are gendered changes. Global processes offer the potential for new forms of relation between local, national and global politics (Keck and Sikkink 1998).

The moments when national and ethnic projects are re-shaped or the relations between them are re-balanced, such as those of the formation of the EU and decolonisation, constitute important points when feminist projects potentially build new relations with intersecting national and ethnic projects.

Feminism and Environmentalism

The green agenda has been growing substantially in scope and significance in recent years. It now encompasses climate change, the overheating of the planet, peak oil and the reduced availability of this mobile fossil fuel, together with its implications for transport and mobility, floods, pollution, toxic waste and its dumping, biodiversity, water shortage and food shortage (Monbiot 2006; Stern 2007; Urry 2011). There has long been some affinity between the green agenda and feminism (Mies and Shiva 1993; Plumwood 1993; Cudworth 2005), for at least three reasons: women's vulnerability to environmental crisis; their positioning, which fed perceptions about the importance of green issues; and shared organisational forms. However, not all green writers and activists include a gender dimension in their work (Jackson 2009).

Women are a disproportionate component of the disadvantaged and they are most likely to suffer the downside of environmental changes, being most vulnerable to environmental disasters and least able to buy their way out of them. When there are food shortages, women are more likely than men to go hungry. When there is flooding, women are less likely than men to escape. The gender inequality dimension of environmental issues is related to the more general issue that the poor and disadvantaged suffer most from environmental degradation and crisis (Shiva 2005; Roberts and Parks 2007).

Groups of women may be particularly sensitive to environmental issues not only because of their position as the losers in environmental crises, but also because of their location in the forms of agriculture and production most affected and because of their commitments to children, which raises the significance of inter-generational justice (Mies and Shiva 1993).

Feminist and green projects not infrequently share similar perspectives on organisational form, with commitments to democracy, openness and the flattening of hierarchies within political organisations. Both feminism and environmentalism are more recent arrivals into formal politics (although the projects themselves have long histories) and the relative newness of this engagement between civil societal projects and the state offers a shared location and perspective on how the engagement should proceed.

The alliance between feminist and green projects takes a multiplicity of forms. Often alliances have been local and informal, but the projects have also engaged at the national, European and international level. There have been several significant attempts to move, beyond alliance, to a synthesis of green and feminist projects. In particular, there is an attempt on the part of green groups to develop the organisational form of a political party by drawing on alliances with feminists and others.

There has been a significant (if early and small) development of green political parties in Europe, at the levels of the EU and of specific countries; these include the UK, but more particularly Germany. Green parties are led by environmentalists, but they draw on alliances with feminist and social democratic groups. Women have been key members in the leadership of these new parties (e.g. Caroline Lucas in the UK and Petra Kelly in Germany), to a greater extent than in many of the older political parties. Green political parties have sought to make progressive interventions on a broad range of issues concerning sustainability, not only environmentalism, but also what are perceived as the deeper causes of the problem that lie in unregulated capitalism. While all green parties promote not only environmental policies but also democracy and gender equality, there are variations in these alliances. For example, in the European (Union) Parliament (EP), there are members (MEPs) of both the European Green Party (2011) and the European United Left-Nordic Green Left (GUE/NGL) (2011). The first places greater priority on green issues but does so in a left social democratic framing, as in the manifesto of the United Green Parties of Europe (2009) for a Green New Deal, which states: 'As economic, social and environmental crises converge, it is time to shift our course from destructive short-term profiteering towards sustainable, long-term prosperity.' The second has policies that are more radical on issues of gender equality and, further left, on issues of social democracy and peace, but which include green policies among several others.

However, not all green interventions have a feminist dimension. For example, Jackson's (2009) otherwise excellent discussion of how prosperity could be obtained in a manner consistent with sustainability by stopping economic growth is silent on gender issues, though there are references to the relevance of inequality.

The potential advantages for feminist projects that have developed alliances with greens include having only rarely to compromise on their own content, shared perspectives on organisational form, and the greater active presence of women. However, there are potential disadvantages too: when a project is led from green issues, feminist issues are often included, but they are rarely made fully visible and sometimes they are omitted. The most important shared platform appears to be that of deepening democracy so as to facilitate the development of an appropriate regulation of capital.

Feminism and Human Rights

'Rights' has a long history as a basis of claims-making by feminism. Since Mary Wollstonecraft (1992) and her repost to Thomas Paine's (1984) *Rights of Man* about the rights of women alongside those of men, the discourse of rights has had a far-reaching resonance. The UN Declaration of Human Rights in 1948 is currently the most authoritative statement on rights. However, this text has been subject to reinterpretation, for example so as to give greater weight to economic issues in the UN Covenants; another example is the statement that women's rights are human rights and include the right to be free from male violence (United Nations General Assembly 1993). Rights have been codified in a variety of legal regimes, including constitutions (such as that of the US), conventions (such as the European Convention on Human Rights) and laws (such as the equality Directives of the European Union that are transposed into domestic legislation in the member states). The claim to rights was a key legitimating principle, though not the sole one, during struggles for suffrage for women (Banks 1981; Jayawardena 1986; Ramirez, Soysal and Shanahan 1997). It is present in claims to equal worth, equal pay and equal treatment at work in the European Union (Pillinger 1992; European Commission 2007), in Japan (Yoko, Mitsuko and Kimiko 1994) and elsewhere around the world (Nelson and Chowdhury 1994). The discourse of 'rights' can be stretched or shrunk so as to encompass a wider or a narrower range: civil rights, equal rights and human rights (Ferree 2009). One of the strengths of 'rights' as a basis for justice claims lies in its appeal to the notion of the 'universal', which is especially pertinent in a globalising era. Its potential weaknesses lie in its focus on individuals rather than on social groups and systems and in its difficulty with issues of diversity and difference.

The discourse of women's rights as human rights has a powerful resonance in the new global context. While traditionally this political discourse has been associated with a liberal feminism which was too meek to make a difference, today this is not always the case. Rather, it is a discourse that has been strategically utilised by collectively organised women, in the context of developing powerful transnational political institutions. Globalisation is being used creatively, as a new framing for feminist politics. It is not possible to limit the horizon of feminist politics to that of local or national situations (Benhabib 1999). Although there is concern to ensure that feminist analysis is situated (Haraway 1988), that situation is now not local, but global (Walby 2002). This is only partly the result of the enhanced capacities for communication across national boundaries. As importantly, it is a result of emergent global institutions and fora, which provide spaces for the development of feminist ideas and practice.

The appeal to the notion of universal human rights has been a continuous strand in political life for centuries (Paine 1984; Held 1995), although it was subject to criticism from socialists and feminists seeking more radical transformations (Young 2000). This appeal to universal human rights is newly re-invigorated by the development of global institutions and perspectives. The appeal to universal human rights depends not only upon a philosophy and a commonly accepted rhetoric, but also upon a set of institutional practices, which may give it practical expression. This set of institutional practices is increasing with globalisation. There are at least four elements here. First, enhanced global communications shrink the distance in time and space between events, so that live news footage of a conflict can be beamed to millions around the world. This increases the awareness of quite general publics about incidents beyond their own country. Second, enhanced global communications make for easier interconnections between political activists – especially the internet, cheaper air travel, faster trains, and the development of cheaper and more reliable phone, fax and email connections. These connections facilitate the exchange of ideas and practices between people located in different countries and regions of the world. Third, the development of global institutions, events and conferences has increased the number of spaces where international interactions, dialogues and networking between activists can take place. These spaces include international conferences and agencies like the World Bank and the International Monetary Fund, whose salience has increased. Fourth, the salience of the UN custodian of the Universal Declaration of Human Rights has increased through its global conferences (e.g. the UN Beijing Platform for Action, 1995), and the diverse activities of UN agencies.

This claim to universalism is often 'knowing', by which is meant that the protagonists know that the 'universal' is but a contingent social construct (Bunch 1995). The appeal to the global level is often presented as if it were an appeal to a timeless universal. This is an increasingly common feature of feminist (Peters and Wolper 1995), environmental (Roberts and Parks 2007), development (United Nations Development Programme [UNDP] 2009), and labour movement politics (Valticos 1969), as well as extending into the treatment of international war crimes and other issues. This appeal to a global level occurs especially during attempts to mobilise practices in support of the principle of 'universal' human rights. A successful elision of the global and the universal is an important move in contemporary politics. The ability to claim access to a universal standard of justice has been used in an increasing number of political projects as a powerful form of legitimation. The conflation of the concept of the 'universal' with that of the 'global' lies at the heart of this development. It is implied that, if all the world agrees to something through open debate in fora of persons selected in a representative manner from each country, then the Habermas-type conditions of procedure have been met, which in turn means that truth is approached as closely as is humanly possible. Simultaneously there is an appeal to the liberal principle of universal individual human rights, as if this were above time-bound and space-bound calculations of interest. In these developing global fora political activists devise and change those principles of justice understood as human rights. They successfully treat the global as if it were the same as the universal, the better to claim authority for their actions.

A significant amount of feminist activity is devoted to redefining and reconstructing what constitutes 'universal' human rights (Peters and Wolper 1995). This process occurs in UN conferences, which attract a massive attendance of feminist activists from all around the world, including both North and South, who supplement and influence the official delegations. For example in 1993, in a UN conference in Vienna, violence against women was construed for the first time as a violation of women's human rights, and thus of human rights (Bunch 1995). This UN conference concluded with a statement to the effect that violence against women is a violation of human rights, and thus that national governments must strengthen the response of their criminal justice systems in support of women. The statement presented this as an already existing universal human right, even as its proponents knew that it was developed recently and through struggle. The statement involves a major reconceptualisation of the issue of male violence against women. It involves a shift away from constructing men as the beneficiaries of this form of power, towards seeing such violence as a minority form of socially unacceptable conduct. Since this conduct is now held to violate women's human rights, which are newly considered human rights, the issue becomes one on which progressive men can stand as allies with women in a human rights struggle, rather than uncomfortably on the margins. This reconfiguration makes it harder to reject actions opposing violence against women on the grounds that the analysis is extreme; rather, all humanity is considered to have an interest in the elimination of such violent conduct (Bunch 1995; Davies 1993; Heise 1996; Peters and Wolper 1995).

This framing of feminism in terms of universal human rights constitutes a challenge to some forms of feminist treatments of difference. The analysis of diversity is a major development in contemporary social science (Calhoun 1995; Taylor 1994). One of the major issues for contemporary feminist theory has been how to theorise differences between women without reifying them (Braidotti 1994; Squires 1999; Young 1990), and simultaneously address commonalities. While a considerable amount of western feminist theory has focused on the 'doxa of difference' (Felski 1997), for example in the debate about the ethics of care (Fraser 1997; Gilligan 1982; Sybylla 2001; Tronto 1993) and about ethnic, national, religious and racialised divisions between women (Mohanty 1991), a new wave of international feminist practice has embraced the discourse of human rights (UNIFEM 2000). This opens fundamental questions as to the nature of the basis on which claims for justice are made and the implications of the use of the concept of the 'universal' (Nussbaum 2000a, 2000b; Menon 2002; Sen 1999, 2009). The notion of human rights has sometimes been thought to be limited by its Eurocentric origin and by its consequent closeness to western rather than universal ideals of the autonomous individual. However, the range of human rights legitimated by the UN includes not only the individual civil and political rights of the western heritage, but also the list of economic and social rights developed in the Soviet Union and Asia, which was integrated into the UN list of human rights in 1966 – so that these UN legitimated human rights now take a hybridised rather than purely western form (Woodiwiss 1998). Because of its recent and various additions and reinterpretations, the reformulation of the list of universal human rights endorsed by the UN is, obviously, a social construction, even as its invocation of the 'universal' as a source of legitimacy attempts to stabilise it as an absolute. Formulating the conception of feminism in terms of rights is, of course, not itself new (Banks 1981; Ramirez, Soysal and Shanahan 1997), but the nature of its current deployment, globally, appears to have some new features (Berkovitch 1999). Is, then, the 'traditional' feminist focus on difference being undercut, transformed, or restructured in a new global context? Is there an emergent unifying framework for feminism in which an increasingly global discourse invokes the notion that women's rights are human rights – and, if so, how important is this framework? How important is the practice of complexity and alliances (Jakobsen 1998), coalitions (Ferree and Hess 1995) and networks (Castells 1997) as practical forms of engagement with difference?

One of the problems raised about the tradition of rights is that it is considered too individualistic and too close to neoliberalism to be able to address issues of collective and structural disadvantage (Young 2000). Critics suggest that the rights discourse leads to strategies which are individualistic and divided, and which therefore cannot deal with institutional and collective obstacles. However, this philosophical concern is in practice misplaced, since the articulation of the claim through the rhetoric of equal rights does not necessarily determine the form of the politics through which these rights are pursued. In the case of improving women's conditions in paid employment or in relation to violence from men, the pursuit of the goal through the rhetoric of rights to equal treatment does not preclude its political articulation in a collective form. This can be seen in examples drawn from the politics of equal rights in employment and in cases of violence against women. While it is hard for an individual to pursue a legal case through a series of expensive and time-consuming tribunals and courts in a search for redress in the UK, many of those who resort to equal opportunities legislation do so collectively rather than individually, as a consequence of receiving support from collective bodies (Gregory 1987). There are many instances of successful prosecution of discriminating employers, which have involved either trade unions or the Equal Opportunities Commission bearing the legal costs and providing support during the long tribulations of legal processes and contested workplace relations. That is, implementation of these laws depends, at least partially, upon collective actors who would take forward individual grievances. Indeed trade unions today will often take forward legal claims on behalf of groups of workers who share similarly discriminating employers. So, despite the absence of a clear formal legal route for the collective pursuit of claims in the UK (as compared with class actions in the US), in practice, nevertheless, collective cases often occur, as a result of the device of taking to court a representative claim, or a small group of representative claims (Willborn 1989; Gregory 1987, 1999). There is hard evidence of the impact of equal opportunity legislation on the pay gap between women and men. Econometric analysis, based on the decomposition of the wages gap into education, work experience and discrimination, has shown that the 1970s equal pay and sex discrimination acts in the UK produced a significant narrowing of the gender wages gap (Harkness 1996; Joshi and Paci 1998; Zabalza and Tzannatos 1985).

Framing feminist demands through the discourse of human rights has advantages and disadvantages. It has the advantage of a broad appeal around the world through codification into binding legal codes. It has the disadvantage of appearing to support an individualisation of justice claims, when the root of these disadvantages lies in collective processes within social systems. However, the articulation of political demands through the vocabulary of rights does not necessarily have to lead to a strategy of pursuing claims individually. Potentially, the notion of human rights as applied to women could be seen as an addition to the varied political repertoire of feminism.

Feminism and Social Democracy

Modernity (in capitalism or in public gender regimes), it is argued here, comes in significantly different varieties. This position is taken in contrast to modernisation theory and world-systems theory, which presume a single major form. Social democracy variously takes the form of a project – a governmental programme or a social formation. In this chapter the focus is on social democracy as a project; in the previous chapter the focus was on social democracy as a social formation. The main 'other' of social democracy in the contemporary modern world is 'neoliberalism'. This section starts with a review of the main literature on the nature of social democracy, by identifying the principal issues and themes and by noting the various omissions of gender issues.

Social democracy is a project for a form of capitalism, of gender regime and of social/environmental relations, that is moderated by democracy. A range of theorists have drawn attention to different aspects of the social democratic project, jointly setting the foundations of the analysis discussed in detail in chapter 6. These authors are early twentieth-century Swedish theorists on democratic aspects of social democracy (Burman 2006); mid-twentieth-century writers on the limits to the commoditisation of labour, land and money (Polanyi 1957), on regulating finance (Galbraith 1975), on state intervention in the economy (Keynes 1936), on the extension of citizenship beyond the political, to civil liberties and socio-economic standing (Marshall 1950), and on the value of mutualism in civil life (Titmuss 1972); late twentieth-century writers on the welfare state, for instance Esping-Andersen (1990, 1999, 2002) and arguably Giddens (1994, 1998); and early twenty-first-century writers on global finance (Stiglitz 2002, 2006; Krugman 2008) and on the society/environment relationship (Monbiot 2006; Roberts and Parks 2007).

Historically, the social democratic project has drawn on a range of constituencies. The conventional history is that the project has been particularly supported by male manual workers in manufacturing who have organised themselves through the trade union and labour movement, but the industrial base for this constituency has been contracting. However, it is important not to marginalise the contribution of feminism to the development of social democracy even in its early decades, when there was much argumentation and negotiation about the centrality or marginality of feminism to the project. There are many detailed accounts of the role that women played in the development of social democracy. These accounts discuss the ways in which gender equality issues – such as childcare and equality regulations in employment – are inserted into the social democratic agenda. And they deal not only with the countries where social democracy became an entrenched part of the social formation, such as Sweden (Qvist 1980; Haavio-Manila 1985; Ohlander 1992; Karlsson 1998), but also those where it did not, such as the UK (Middleton 1977).

In recent decades there had been an intensification of support for the social democratic project from women who had been increasingly employed and organised within trade unions, although traditional support for this project has diminished during this time. This shift in the gender composition of the key constituencies supporting the social democratic project is also linked to the higher prioritisation of its gendered goals. The stronger mobilisation of women in trade unions and NGOs contributes to this project. Today, the contemporary social democratic project involves not merely an alliance or coalition between feminist and labourist forces, but a melding, hybridisation or synthesis into a new project, which encompasses both these processes.

There are several contemporary attempts to create a synthesis out of the various components of progressive politics – components such as feminism, human rights, social democracy and environmentalism – in a way that, additionally, is conducive to the goal of economic growth. These occur despite the increasing difficulties in the wider context for progressive politics. The following are examples at UK, EU and global levels. In the UK, Compass seeks to take forward feminist goals as part of a wider progressive alliance. Compass is centred in the Labour Party, although explicitly in its left wing, and engages with ex-members of the Labour Party as well as with Greens and others. Feminist goals are included in the project. In the EU, an example is the European United Left/Nordic Green Left European Parliamentary Group (GUE/NGL) established in 1995, which is an alliance of green and left social democratic parties with a strong feminist presence, and treats eliminating violence against women both as a human rights issue and as a socialist (GUE/NGL 2011). Globally, a major project is that of the World Social Forum (2011), an annual gathering of progressive activists around the world, with an agenda of global justice that includes gender equality (George 2004).

Feminist projects have often adopted, pragmatically, whatever framework was most easily to hand, adapting and innovating as the opportunity arose. However, this does not mean that tension between different justice frameworks does not exist.

Can Human Rights and Social Democracy be Reconciled?

Human rights and social democracy are the two most important progressive justice projects in the contemporary world. Feminism has developed projects that engage with both of them. Each has potential strengths and weaknesses for future development. Are they reconcilable or not, and, if they are, how? Assessment of this issue will be approached first at the level of political philosophy and secondly at the level of political practice.

The dilemmas articulated here by philosophers and social theorists centre on the nature of the grounding of the rules by which the justice of political and ethical claims may be judged. The underlying dichotomy between community and individualism/universalism is a key theme in social philosophy (Bauman 1996; Lash 1996). On the one hand, liberalism and universalism appear to offer a plea for a free-floating form of reason, which would be universal, drawing on the Kantian heritage. They make a claim to the existence of some universally valid truth, and such claims usually assume that the seeker/knower is a coherent individual. On the other hand, communitarianism appears to offer grounding in the specific standards of a given community (Sandel 1998; Taylor 1994). It works with the notion that truth is always partial and situated, that we are limited by the communities in which we are located.

Of course, in practice, most contemporary writers reject these polar extremes as untenable. Some simultaneously reject both poles, and with them the search for certain foundations for contemporary ethics and for political projects (Bauman 1991, 1996). Bauman's rejection of both these options follows from his earlier rejection of the morality of modernity, on account of its association with the holocaust (Bauman 1989). Others seek a compromise, either by refining the procedures for assessing justice claims (Habermas 1987, 1991; Benhabib 1992) or by integrating the concerns of the individual and those of the community (Kymlicka 1991, 1995).

There have been many attempts to find a resolution to this debate. Habermas (1987, 1991) proceeds by attempting to establish universally valid procedures through which truth may be established; he uses the dynamics of an assumed desire to communicate as a driver of this process, and locates the process itself in an idealised situation of equality of contribution. However, in spite of his intentions, Habermas does not reach the universality of the conditions for truth, since the processes of democratic contribution are socially specific and hence uneven, not equal. Benhabib's (1992) attempt to overcome the same dualism by requesting a focus on the other has similar strengths and weaknesses, although she tries to move beyond Habermas (Hutchings 1997). Benhabib seeks to avoid commitment to the communitarian stance by appealing to an ostensibly universally valid criterion of judgement: that of recognising the standpoint of the other. But the process of recognising the standpoint of the other is not natural and automatic; it depends upon socially variable conditions. Thus Benhabib merely displaces the problem of universalism onto these new procedures for judgement, which are not sufficiently universal to be adequate to the task demanded of them. The act of 'recognition' requires a social process of assessment as to what constitutes the same as, or different from, oneself. The abstractions of social philosophy constitute a serious limitation here, since they neglect the complex social dimensions of the processes involved.

Sen (1999, 2009) attempts a different accommodation between individualism and collectivism, namely through the introduction of the concept of 'capabilities'. Sen (1999) uses a positive conception of freedom, defined as what people can actually do and be – an approach which is often associated with social democracy rather than liberalism. He wishes to go beyond money as an end in itself, valuing instead human life and its capabilities. Sen defines capabilities as capacities to achieve functionings; capabilities are opportunities and freedoms. However, by defining capabilities in terms of choice and opportunity, he returns to liberal individualism. Thus he fails to bridge adequately the chasm between liberal and collective approaches to justice (Walby 2010).

Kymlicka (1991, 1995) tries to find a way forward by softening the polarities of the debate, by grounding them in a comparative analysis of practical attempts to resolve them. Kymlicka (1991) analyses the special rights given to aboriginal minorities in order to protect their cultural heritage, and the way in which these rights might appear to cut across individual rights to Canadian citizenship. His aim is to reconcile principles of justice so as make them able to sustain cultural communities (such as those of aboriginals, with their lifestyles), and at the same time to leave intact liberal principles, which protect other social groups from discrimination. He seeks to achieve this through a reconsideration of the theory of the self within liberal

theory, effectively putting across a more social and more socio-
logically grounded conception of the self than is customary within
abstract philosophy. Kymlicka argues that, in practice, liberalism
has respected the collective rights of minority communities and has
understood this attitude as part of a liberal respect for one's freedom
to choose one's own way of life, which involves the recognition of
communities as a whole within a larger polity; and he claims that all
this can be articulated theoretically within his modified account of
liberal philosophy.

Kymlicka's work is at its strongest when he is engaging with communities defined in terms of ethnicity or nation, where there is a fully
rounded and cohesive culture. It is at its weakest in relation to cross-
cutting forms of difference such as gender, when these forms do not
coincide with holistic communities. This is because of Kymlicka's
use of the notion of 'community' as his dominant conceptualisation
of the social. His analysis is strong when the forms of difference are
articulated through cohesive communities. But he is unable to offer
solutions to the reality and complexity of modern social life where
there are divisions and social fractures which cross-cut ethnic and
national groups, such as gender. The full range of differences that he
notes empirically fails to get integrated into the theory as a result of
what was signalled above: the choice of the concept of 'community'
as a metaphor for the social. The use of 'community' pulls Kymlicka
back into the simplicities which he has tried so hard to escape. In the
end, his analysis can deal with one set of differences, but not with the
diverse range of cross-cutting and multiple differences that actually
exist in the world, nor with the dynamics of the changes resulting
from their mutual adaptations. Cohesive 'communities' devoid of the
internal divisions of gender, class and ethnic and religious minority
groups do not exist in the modern world. The concept of 'community' does not capture the nature of the social, as it is actually riddled
with a plurality of intersecting differences.

The alterity between liberalism and communitarianism provides a
creative tension in political thought, once it is recognised that both
polar positions are untenable. The route out of this philosophical
dilemma is via sociological analysis. The concept of 'community'
is a poor and overly narrow operationalisation of the concept of the
'social', and one which is unable to articulate sufficiently the complexities of cross-cutting differences. Rather we should invoke a wider
range of sociological concepts of social divisions, accepting that they
intersect in complex ways. It is important to utilise concepts of multiple and complex inequalities, alliances, coalitions, networks and joint

projects in order to straddle the gulf that otherwise exists between the individual and communitarian routes to conceptions of justice. Some modern political actors have already found a way through the dilemmas of difference, and have also formed the desire for a less particularistic conception of justice. This has happened through the use of networks and coalitions and through the overt abandonment of the assumption that political projects are to be based on culturally cohesive communities. In particular, we need to abandon any notion that ethos and polis do or should map onto each other. The purity demanded by such a project is unachievable in the modern world.

The way forward in the debate on rights and social democracy is to treat individual human rights as a part of the social democratic vision, as already within it and not separate from it. Social democracy is necessary in order to achieve human rights. Social democracy is as much about the route to achieve goals as it is itself a set of goals. By contrast, human rights have little account of the means that can achieve them, other than rhetoric and occasionally the law. 'Human rights' do not form a theory of how society functions, they are merely a list of goals.

Synthesising Social Democracy, Feminism, Human Rights, Economic Growth and Environmental Sustainability

The social democratic project is more ambitious in its goals than is that of human rights. The inclusion of feminist goals at the heart of the social democratic project has been a significant development. In terms of range of the issues covered, the strengths of the feminist social democratic project lie in the potential breadth of its coverage and in the understanding of the interconnections between them, while its historic weaknesses – an excessive focus on the economy and a relative neglect of violence and civil society – can be remedied.

Building on and going beyond these accounts, a new model of a social democratic social formation is constructed here. This is an ideal type, situated at one pole of the same continuum that stretches at the other end to neoliberalism. The new model differs from the accounts reviewed above by increasing the range of institutional domains and of inequalities that are encompassed. There are four major institutional domains: economy (regulation of financial and industrial capital; domestic economy; and state welfare); polity (especially the depth of democracy); violence (its regulation and deployment), and civil society (commercialism versus mutualism).

The regimes of inequality include not only class, but also gender and ethnicity.

Social democracy means more than state expenditure on services, despite the contemporary focus on this issue. Social democracy is gendered; or, rather, it is gendered in its fully developed forms. Gendering social democracy inflects the traditional arenas – state spending – and also introduces new ones: employment equality regulations, finance regulations, the deepening of democracy, the reduction of violence (inter-personal and in war), resistance to the commercialisation of sexuality in pornography and prostitution. Economic growth has always been a key part of the social democratic agenda; but this is unachievable unless gender inequality is dealt with, since women, together with recent migrants, form the group that is most often concentrated in a low wage, low skill part of the workforce; while a social democratic economy requires the reduction, even elimination of this sector and its replacement by high wage, high skill work. Social democracy reaches its full form only when it subsumes the best parts of the human rights agenda, for example the condemnation of state violence against individuals, and extends its own agenda to other fields, such as autonomy for women over their own bodies in issues of violence and in sexual and reproductive matters (including contraception and abortion).

The feminist project can be approached through social democracy. The social democratic project is marked by a commitment to deepening democracy and diminishing inequality. The state is seen as an important instrument in achieving these goals. In the economy, social democracy means regulating employment and finance so as to reduce inequalities and increase fairness and productivity; its gendered specificity includes regulating employment for equality and providing public care, for example for children and the frail elderly. In the polity, social democracy means deepening democracy beyond the surface of suffrage, so as to ensure widespread participation in political decision-making and the extension of the democratic principle to a wide range of social institutions; its gendered specificity includes electoral devices that ensure the equal participation of women in parliament and ministerial positions. In relation to violence, social democracy means limiting the deployment of violence by states, groups in wars, and militias, and regulating inter-personal violence through its criminalisation and other policy devices; its gendered specificity includes policies designed to reduce violence against women. In relation to civil society, social democracy means embracing the principles of mutuality and equality.

The economic growth project is sometimes regarded as intrinsically neoliberal (Eisenstein 2009; Fraser 2009). But this project has taken a social democratic form in the past (e.g. Swedish social democracy), and this can happen in the future too. Yet it will only take a social democratic form in the future if feminism is integrated into the social democratic project.

Increasing the rate of economic growth is the most important mainstream project and governmental programme. It is adopted by almost all national governments (e.g. UK's HM Treasury 2010), by the EU (European Commission 2010d), and by global financial institutions such as the International Monetary Fund (Strauss-Kahn 2011). Sometimes there are caveats, for example a concern for the distribution of the benefits of economic growth, but these are more often nuances on how to achieve economic development than an alternative to it; for example the goal of gender equality in education in the *UN Millennium Development Goals* (United Nations 2011) is considered to increase economic growth as well as to promote gender equality (Klasen 2002). Occasionally there are significant competing goals, such as national or imperial domination, which may compromise economic growth (Mann 2003), but these goals are often entwined rather than fundamentally opposing, for example in wars for oil (Greenspan 2008). A major possible exception is that of the green agenda concerning climate change (Jackson 2009).

There are major disagreements as to how economic growth is to be best achieved and sustained, especially between neoliberal and social democratic approaches. Economic growth projects take different positions on class inequality and on the extent of state regulation (Esping-Andersen 1999; Hall and Soskice 2001; Kenworthy 2004). In addition, and at least as importantly, they differ in how they engage with gender relations, especially around issues related to the use of women's labour. They may promote the domestication of women as care workers or their full employment in the market economy. The promotion of female employment may encourage high levels of education and skill or, alternatively, their use as a marginal low wage, low skill source of labour (O'Connor, Orloff and Shaver 1999; Rubery, Smith and Fagan 1999; Walby, Gottfried, Gottschall and Osawa 2007; Gottschall and Kroos 2007; Shire 2007). Economies need to be well regulated in order to be sustainable, otherwise short-term interests trump long-term ones. This is more likely to happen under a social democratic form of governance, where democratic regulation is an integral part of the model of the economy.

Engaging with a strong feminist project means there is a greater likelihood that the economic growth programme will include the increase in female employment and the narrowing of the gender productivity gaps as part of the programme. In the absence of such a project, an increase in female labour is less likely to be considered an important contribution to economic growth, and the narrowing of the gender pay gap may even to be treated as if it were a competing goal, on the grounds that it increases labour costs. The European Union, which engages with a strong feminist project in the European Women's Lobby, in trade union representatives, and in its own internal gender equality unit, recommends policies to narrow the gender gaps in employment and pay through reducing discrimination and reconciling employment and care work (European Commission 2010b). However, while the European Union's legislative programme against discrimination is very strong, the mobilisation of economic resources, for example for childcare, behind the programme in member states is much weaker (Randall 2000). The economic growth programme of the Nordic countries (Sweden, Denmark, Norway, Finland) engages not only with a strong feminist project, which is articulated in NGOs, trade unions, political parties and governmental programmes, but also with a wider social democratic project and programme. In consequence, the Nordic model of economic growth includes full female employment, supported not only by legislative and collective bargaining efforts to reduce discrimination, but also by state welfare, which funds nurseries and leave in order to facilitate the combination of employment and care work. Countries without such strong feminist projects and countries where the feminist project does not receive support from an alliance with a strong class project are much less likely to produce programmes for economic growth that promote female employment and productivity.

The social democratic project for the polity is to deepen democracy. Most modern countries have achieved a basic level of suffrage democracy, in which there are regular elections for political positions that are free, fair and competitive. However, this is a rather shallow democracy. Even then there are often exceptions to legislative positions being filled only through elections, such as in the UK, where there are 92 unelected peers in the upper legislative chamber known as the House of Lords. There are feminist campaigns to deepen democracy, to move towards the equal presence of women in political decision-making by reforming the technical procedures of the electoral process. Such procedures include proportional representation, capping the cost of elections, and quotas for under-represented groups such as women. The provision of major services under demo-cratic control is a further example of the deepening of democracy through an increase in the range of institutions subject to democratic governance.

Social democracy depends upon the identification of the unit within which democracy and redistribution are to be delivered (Held 1995, 2004; Held, McGrew, Goldblatt and Perraton 1999). Traditionally such units have been specific countries, represented under the mythological notion of a 'nation-state' (Walby 2003), in which a collective entity within which democracy is to be achieved is defined as the 'nation' (Marshall 1950). In a globalising world, in which the boundaries between countries are ever more porous to flows of capital, finance and people (Castells 1996, 1997, 1998), the identification of the unit within which democracy, mutuality and exchange takes place becomes more difficult to establish. While there is an aspiration for social democracy to be practised at a global level (Held 2004), defining the unit of mutuality is a challenge, especially if its goals are to be more than the minimal level of human rights. One response has been the development of stronger regional entities (Hettne, Inotai and Sunkel 1999), of which the most established is the European Union.

The social democratic project varies as to whether the reduction in violence is integrated into its core or left on the margins. The illegiti-macy of extreme violence committed by states against individuals, for instance torture and the death penalty, is more often profiled as part of the human rights project (Amnesty International 2011). Gender-based inter-personal violence against women has been articulated as an issue within a very wide range of projects – for example as an issue of gender equality within gendered social democratic projects, or as a human rights issue. The EU was founded with a mission to prevent war and the holocaust from ever happening again in Europe; only more recently has its mission been seen as primarily one of engage-ment in political economy. The methods used by the EU to prevent war and the holocaust involved the redefinition of nations and states through a manipulation of the process of economic integration, while the Council of Europe became the guardian of human rights in Europe. Contemporary feminism in Europe is pragmatic in its adop-tion of legitimating frameworks to push for change in public policy and in its use of whichever is available to hand, while at the level of the UN human rights are more usually adopted. The conclusion drawn here is that a project to reduce violence can creatively utilise and hybridise multiple frameworks, including social democratic and human rights, in pursuit of its goal, and that feminism needs to be an integral part of this agenda.

Civil society has traditionally been seen as an arena in which human rights, with the promotion of individual autonomy, constitute the dominant justice framework. Yet, in relation to the feminist agenda concerning a woman's control over her own body in issues such as contraception, abortion and divorce, the human rights discourse has led to only a partial mobilisation and success, in spite of its powerful rhetorical resources. In the current debates about unequal and commercialised sexual practices, such as prostitution and pornography, the social democratic approach, which prioritises mutualism over individualism and commercialism, has constituted an important intervention. In practice, feminist projects utilise multiple frameworks and hybridise them whenever this appears to be more effective.

Conclusions

Feminist projects intersect with other projects in complex ways, at multiple levels, from theory to practice, within civil society and the state. There is a multiplicity of ways of framing and shaping feminism as a consequence of the various allies and enemies that coexist in the same political environment; hence these ways vary between countries and over time.

In practice, feminist projects have made use of multiple frameworks, have formed alliances and coalitions and have forged new hybrid projects in order to take forward their goals. These projects include alliances with environmentalism, social democracy and human rights projects.

Feminist projects are thriving, both separately and in alliance with others. But the key to their future lies not only in the way they address their allies, but also in the way they address the increasingly hostile context. This will be the subject of the next and final chapter.

8

Alternative Futures

Promising start, but major challenges ahead

Feminism is not dead, dissipated or surpassed. It is alive and well (as was shown in chapter 3). But, while feminism is growing, so too are the challenges to the achievement of its goals.

Feminism is taking a wide range of organisational forms, from grassroots to NGOs to governmental. It engages with and shapes other projects, from mainstream to radical. It exists even within the government, both in specialised equality bodies and in mainstream ministries, including those involved in economic growth and crime reduction. It can be found in local, national, transnational and global locations. The nature of the intersection of feminist projects with others, from mainstream to radical ones, has implications for the future of feminism and for societies around the world. This intersection can take a variety of forms. There is a possibility that feminism would be made invisible within these new alliances, coalitions and merged projects, and the consequences of its loss of visibility might be a lower priority accorded to feminist goals and a loss of feminist mobilisation. A very different set of relations at the same intersection might be the embedding of feminist goals in projects that have the power to carry these goals into the heart of government. Feminist goals could be integrated at the centre of projects for economic growth, crime reduction, sustainability, human rights and social democracy. Or they could be marginalised in small corners of relative purity of feminist goals. These alternative prospects for feminism have implications for the future of global society.

Feminist projects have been successful in improving the lives of women, in reducing gender inequality and in transforming the nature of gender relations. Many feminist goals have been accepted as part of consensus politics in numerous, though far from all, countries. For example, goals of equal pay for equal work, of equal access to education, of reducing male violence against women, and of equal rights to vote and participate in government are now widely accepted. Too commonly, it is not noticed just how recent this incorporation of feminist goals into mainstream aspirations is. However, many feminist goals are far from being fully achieved. While there is an increased presence of women in the public sphere, there are still major inequalities. Despite higher rates of employment, gender pay gaps and occupational segregation remain; while the presence of women in parliament is greater, it is not yet proportionate with that of men; while male violence against women is increasingly criminalised, gender-based violence remains rampant; while women are active in civil society, their sexual and reproductive rights are not yet fully achieved. And there are major differences between countries around the world in all these areas.

The ongoing transformation of the form of the gender regime from domestic to public, especially in the global North, constitutes a context in which feminism continues to develop. The more active presence of women in the public sphere has increased the interest in, and the opportunities for the articulation of, feminist projects. These feminist projects have implications for the further transformation and forms of the gender regime, as well as for the capitalist system with which the gender regime coevolves.

But feminism faces major challenges. These are partly due to the success of feminism and partly due to an increasingly hostile neoliberal context. Feminism is less visible because it has been institutionalised, mainstreamed, and hidden within intersecting projects. These new forms of engagement have the potential to increase the influence of feminism, but also pose the danger of submerging it under larger forces. In addition, the intensification of neoliberalism and the crises that are its consequence constitute major threats to the success of feminism. There are new forms of projects opposing feminism, in a climate that is increasingly hostile to human well-being. Crises of finance, of the environment and of war pose major critical threats to the achievement of feminist goals and to those of its allies. Processes of de-democratisation, as the governance of major services moves from a democratic state to capital and markets, and civil liberties are diminished as war is prioritised over peace, create a difficult context for the forms of feminism that have come to rely on access to democratic processes. The cessation of the rise in women's employment and the increase in economic inequalities potentially diminishes the prospects for reducing gender gaps in care and employment.

The way in which these opportunities and threats are addressed by feminist projects is central not only to the future of feminism, but to everyone.

Mainstreaming Feminism: Both Distinct and Integrated

Feminism has developed and institutionalised organisational forms in addition to grassroots mobilisation and has entered the mainstream, as well as globalising and engaging with intersecting projects.

Institutional forms of feminism have developed that go beyond the traditional types of grassroots and NGO mobilisation (as was shown in chapter 4). Feminist projects have built their own institutions, and at the same time they have become embedded within institutions initially built by others. Feminism takes not only the fluid innovative form of a movement or a wave, but is also institutionalised in civil society and the state. In its institutionalised forms, especially those within the state, it is usually less visible to the media. So, while the process of institutionalisation increases the resilience of feminist organisations and their impact on some types of issues, the loss of visibility can have some negative implications for feminist mobilisation. At the same time, the fluid coming and going of grassroots and NGO activities has not ceased; rather, there is a much wider spectrum of feminist modes of organisation.

Some feminist projects have joined the mainstream, becoming integral parts of governmental programmes and institutions, or sedimented into social formations (as was shown in chapter 5). There is a tension in mainstreaming between the potentially increased influence of feminism in powerful institutions and the potential loss of more radical parts of the feminist agenda. Feminist goals are to be found institutionalised in specialised state agencies for equality (sometimes gender only, sometimes together with other inequalities), for instance policy units in government ministries or commissions for the implementation of equality laws and policies. In addition, feminist goals have been mainstreamed into some government departments, from ministries responsible for economic growth (including the provision of childcare) to ministries responsible for reducing crime (including violence against women). These changes have increased feminist influence within some powerful institutions, but only some parts of the feminist agenda are engaged in this way.

Mainstreaming is most effective in securing change when there is simultaneous engagement with powerful central bodies and the maintenance of specialised feminist-based organisations. The combination, achieved through alliances and coalitions, between grassroots, NGOs and governmental bodies produces more substantial change than an exclusive development of activities either in specialised organisations or in the mainstream.

Globalising Feminism: Local, National and Transnational

While feminism is often a local and a national practice, many feminist projects are transnational, drawing ideas and strength from alliances that cross national boundaries. The various institutional spaces around the UN have facilitated the increasingly global rather than transnational-only direction of this development. But feminist projects remain unevenly embedded in different states and social formations. Their priorities vary for several reasons, including the differences in the forms of the gender regimes in their places of origin and activity. Alliances between projects are important, even if sometimes asymmetric, depending on the different levels of the resources (economic, organisational and rhetorical) on which they can draw.

The re-framing of feminist politics in the context of global processes has increased the opportunities for its creative and innovative adaptation and expansion. As part of its legitimation strategy, this new framing elides the distinction between the global and the universal. The attempted reference group for this politics is that of a common humanity. This opens up a new round of political struggles in the construction of human rights, even as they are held up as timeless and universal. The global is becoming the defining horizon for many political projects. Globalisation today re-frames the notion of the universal. Yet the global is not the same as the abstract universal. Rather, the global constitutes a practical, special and time-specific realm, even as it can be purported to encompass the totality of contemporary human life. The global and the universal have an uneasy and ambiguous relationship in many contemporary analyses. This is because many political projects today make claims to justice on the basis of an ambiguously defined conception of the global or universal.

Although there is a certain amount of globalising of aspects of feminist projects, considerable differences remain in the extent to which these are embedded in governmental programmes and in social formations. There are major differences between countries, and they are linked to the latter's level of economic development and to their political histories. Within the global North and within the 'West' there are considerable differences between the global hegemons of the neoliberal US and the more social democratic EU. The relative balance between the US and the EU is important for global politics and for the gender projects of international bodies, including the UN.

Intersecting Feminism with Other Projects

Feminism rarely acts alone, but often in conjunction with other projects, either mainstream or progressive. The concept of intersectionality is usefully applied to the intersection of projects, and not only in its more conventional sense, which relates to sets of social relations. At points of intersection projects co-operate or contest, work in alliance or coalition, merge or hybridise, in symmetrical or asymmetrical ways (as was shown in chapter 7). As feminism intersects with other political and civil societal projects, there is a process of mutual adjustment between them. The intersection of these projects may take the form of an alliance or coalition in which each one retains its separate identity, or they may change each other so greatly that they hybridise or get synthesised into a new project, different from those that went before. The extent to which feminism is able to prioritise its own agenda as it engages and combines with these other agendas is determined by struggles over it.

Intersections with other projects thus produce a duality: potential opportunity as well as potential threat. On the one hand, there is the potential of feminist goals becoming embedded in a wide range of powerful projects, which carry the feminist project forward as part of their own. Not only is feminist success greater when it acts in combination with other projects, but these other projects are also more successful when they build alliances with feminism; they need feminism in order to be effective. This is due not only to the large size of the potential feminist constituency, since women make up half the world, but also to the emergence of employed and educated women as a political force. On the other hand, there is the threat of making feminist projects invisible, and thus of facilitating their fading away as they become absorbed in these other projects. While intersections potentially increase the forces supporting feminist goals, this may come at the expense of a loss of visibility for the feminist component. As these various forms of intersection develop, the noticeability of the feminist component may diminish even to a vanishing point.

This does not mean that feminist goals are not present, but merely that they are not immediately or directly recognisable in the summary description of the overall project. Nor does it necessarily mean that the feminist element of the project fades away, although such an outcome is possible.

The range of projects with which feminism intersects includes both those that are mainstream and those that are progressive – for instance economic growth, crime reduction, environmentalism, human development, human rights and social democracy. Many objections have been raised on theoretical grounds, in the social science literature, as to the possibility and sustainability of such alliances; they were discussed in earlier chapters. Yet, in practice, feminist projects have achieved all manner of alliances, coalitions and merged projects with a wide variety of other projects, many of which (though not all) have successfully advanced feminist goals. Theory needs to take account of these successful innovations by the practitioners.

Economic growth is a powerfully institutionalised mainstream project and governmental programme, which can take very different forms. A positive intersection with feminist projects takes place if both (1) adopt the goal of full employment of women and elimination of the discrimination against women that creates inefficient distortions in the labour market and (2) support the development of women's human capital – which might be diminished as a result of unnecessarily long interruptions of women's employment – through the provisions of childcare, eldercare, maternal, paternal and parental leaves, and flexibility in employment practices. Such an approach to economic growth requires intervention by a democratic state to reduce discrimination, to regulate working time and to provide care services. This is consistent with parallel interventions to regulate finance, to eliminate bubbles, tax dodging crises and the looting of treasuries, and to ensure the sustainability of growth through regulation, for example for a low carbon society. There is a gender project that may not be consistent with this alignment: maternalism and the protection of motherhood. But, even here, maternalist support for the development of the welfare state may bring these projects into alignment. Opposition to this alignment of the economic growth and feminism projects is often associated with fundamentalist opposition to state intervention, as in the neoliberal project.

The human development and well-being project, which is linked to the early work of Amartya Sen, offers a nuanced approach to development. This approach embraces economic development insofar as the latter also supports human development and human well-being. The

project is deeply involved in the campaign for the UN Millennium
Development Goals (MDG), which was supported by many governments and international financial institutions as well as by feminist
and other justice projects. The MDG included the goal of gender
equality; indeed the World Bank promotes the policy of educating
women, on the grounds that its result is good for economic growth.

The reduction of violent crime is another example of a mainstream
political agenda with which feminism is engaging. A significant part
of violent crime is directed by men towards women and has become
the focus of feminist projects. Violence against women has been
framed as the subject of progressive feminist projects, for example
as constitutive of gender inequality and as a violation of women's
human rights. It can also be addressed within a traditional 'law and
order' agenda that aims to reduce violent crime. Feminist responses
within the crime field more often adopt a penal welfare than a punitive approach to its remedy – that is, a social democratic rather than
an authoritarian one. In this way feminism can assist in shaping the
crime agenda.

The green agenda places its focus on the environment and includes
sustainability or the limiting of economic growth and the prevention
of global warming through the development of a low carbon society.
It is aligned with feminist projects especially in their shared approach
to governance. This extends to their concern for open democratic
governance, which would be necessary to achieve their goals, and
to their willingness to utilise the democratic state in order to regulate the excesses of markets and capital, which could destabilise the
environment of the planet for all. While specific goals might appear
to differ, they are not in tension with each other. The 'green' political
parties that have developed, for example in Germany and in the EU,
have been particularly hospitable to feminists. Green and feminist
projects have often found practical alignment and shared personnel.

The human rights agenda was originally formulated as the rights
of man, but has proved amenable to an extension that includes
the rights of women. The relative abstraction of the formulation
of human rights lends flexibility to the project, making it relatively
easy to synthesise it with many other projects. The UN Universal
Declaration of Human Rights, which is the current foundation for
many rights-based claims around the world, has been reinterpreted
so as to provide specifically for women's protection from the violence
of men. The flexibility of the framework is demonstrated in the contestation over the inclusion of sexual and reproductive rights (such
as same sex partnerships and abortion) under the umbrella. By itself,

the agenda of 'human rights' offers more rhetorical than practical support, since it is relatively weakly institutionalised, with the possible exception of some international laws.

In like manner, the social democratic agenda was originally more focused on the interests of men than on those of women, and it has similarly shown itself open to the inclusion of new perceptions of women's interests. The demands for a deepening democracy and for regulating the economy in the interests of workers and citizens have been extended to the regulation of violence. Social democracy is more deeply institutionalised than human rights, but in the current era perhaps has less rhetorical sway. Recent attempts by social democratic institutions to use the rhetoric of human rights to support their claims offer interesting examples of hybridisation between these two projects, which in social theory are so often seen as opposed.

There has been a number of recent attempts to create a synthesis between these various mainstream and progressive projects and feminism, in such a way as to strengthen both the feminist project and the others. When the projects have been successfully hybridised, each one is more powerful.

Changes in the Gender Regime

Gendered and feminist projects are dynamically constructed and reconstructed in the context of gender relations, which are constituted simultaneously by the institutional domains of economy, polity, violence and civil society (as discussed in chapter 6). Women's interests cannot be read off from the single dimension of their gender positions; rather, women's (and men's) perceptions of their interests are constructed in complex ways, through all institutional domains of the gender regime. Nevertheless, the ongoing transformation of the gender regime in many countries offers new resources and opportunities for the development of feminist projects. Further, changes in the type of the gender regime – domestic or public – and in the variety of its public form – neoliberal or social democratic – affect the constitution of gender relations and have implications for feminist projects.

In the global North especially, there is a series of changes with important implications for feminist projects. The extension of market/capitalist relations to women's work, especially to previously domesticated care work, but also to subsistence labour, means that the majority of the population, and not only a minority (namely able-bodied men of working age), is becoming subject to marketised relations of production. The incomplete nature and the varied forms of this transition, with only partial socialisation of domestic care work by the state and market, lead to tensions in the performance of this work between the state, the market, and unpaid domestic labour. Another change in this category is the changing gender composition of professional jobs: there has been an increase in the proportion of women in medicine and law and among university professors, especially those in the public sector. Yet another example is that of the gendering of the private sector/public sector divide: women are employed in, and consumers of, the public sector to a greater extent than men; hence cutting back the public sector through cuts in state expenditure is a gendered cut. Another important change consists in the increased political mobilisation of women as they join the paid workforce, and their greater presence in trade unions, civil society organisations and parliament. The changing gender composition of these political organisations and institutions also has important effects on the feminist project – for example trade unions rooted in men's skilled and semi-skilled working in private manufacturing have declined, and at the same time there has been an increase in unions rooted in professional working in public services, which includes many more women.

Understanding the distinction between the domestic and the public gender regime is important for analysing the differences between those gender projects that embrace maternalism as something positive for women and those that seek to advance the interests of women by embracing equality between women and men through the development of the same standard for both, even though this process requires transformation. The distinction between neoliberal and social democratic public gender regimes is important for understanding that there may be resistance to a shift from the domestic to the public gender regime, if it is thought that the form of the latter will be harsh and unequal because it lacks the vision of a social democratic form.

The Emergence of Employed Women as the New Champions of Social Democracy

The most important emergent political force is that of employed women, who are becoming the new champions of social democracy. In the global North, especially in Europe, there has been an ongoing gendered transformation of the social democratic project – a transformation linked to changes in the structure of the economy. The traditional base of social democracy – the trade union membership of male manual workers in the manufacturing industry – has declined. There is a new constituency for social democracy among employed women, especially those in the public sector, who had been a growing section of the workforce in the North until the financial crisis of 2008. This increase in the proportion of women in paid employment and the parallel decrease in the proportion of women deriving their livelihood from domestic care work is linked to the transformation of the gender regime from a domestic to a public form. Women have shortened the period of time they used to spend in intensive childcare and out of the labour market, returning to employment earlier than in previous decades.

The transformation of the gender regime from domestic to public form changes the context in which the goals of projects pursued by women develop. Employed women will often perceive their interests in ways that are different from those of women who are not employed, but are committed instead to a domestic route to their livelihood. This can be seen in the political preferences and voting patterns and in the increasing trade union membership of women. Analysis of political preferences and of voting patterns has found that employed women are more likely to vote in a social democratic direction and to support the public provision of services than others are. Such services include health, education and childcare, which in some way are related to the socialisation of domestic labour. The gender gap in political preferences is further compounded by the gendered division between public and private sectors of employment, workers in the public sector being now more likely to be both female and supportive of public services.

The political preferences of employed women are more likely to have practical effects when these women are organised and when they have allies. Women have been increasing their presence in civil societal, political and governmental institutions. This is linked, sometimes directly and sometimes indirectly, to the rise in women's paid employment. Women have increased their presence in trade unions, typically making up around half of the membership in the countries of the global north. This higher proportion is a result partly of the stronger presence of women in trade unions and partly of the decline in the membership of men. Women in trade unions are more likely to be in the public sector (especially in education and health) than in the private sector. As discussed in chapter 3, trade unions play an important part in feminist projects. While there are several types of potential allies, an important set is to be found in labour and social democratic movements. Such allies have been more often found in Europe, and especially in the Nordic countries, than in the US.

Social democracy has often been understood as if it were a working-class-led project of justice, based in trade union and labour organisation, with political ambitions to democratise the state so that it could become an instrument of this project. Social democracy in Europe is often perceived to be in decline as a result of the reduction in the strength of trade unions, which was in turn a joint consequence of the shrinking of the industrial base of traditional trade unionism in mining and heavy manufacturing and of the neoliberal assault.

The shape of the social democratic project is changing as a result of the increasing engagement of women and feminist projects. Linked to the changes in the gender composition of social democracy are changes in the priority policies. The public provision of support for public care services has been rising up its agenda, as has been the better regulation of employment, which aims to promote equality between women and men and the re-balancing of work and care. Policies to address violence against women are increasingly becoming part of the political agenda. The gendering of social democracy is changing – both the composition of its constituency and its priority goals.

However, the structural changes that have facilitated the rise of this new political constituency for social democracy are potentially jeopardised by the financial and economic crisis produced by neoliberalism, which limits women's employment and may limit their political opportunities.

Hostile Context

While feminism is increasing in strength, the wider context is becoming increasingly hostile to the practical achievement of feminist goals (as shown in chapter 6). There are new as well as old threats to feminism from hostile forces. The neoliberal turn, with its concomitant features of increasing inequality, de-democratisation, financialisation, securitisation and environmental crisis, poses a challenge to feminism and to the achievement of gender equality.

The financial crisis, a consequence of the excesses of neoliberalism, produces a hostile context too, because the recession blocks economic expansion and rapid reductions in government budget deficits lead to cuts in jobs and public services disproportionately used by women. These changes increase gender inequality directly, through their disproportionate impact on women's jobs and welfare, as well as by creating a less hospitable political context for women's effective engagement in the public sphere and for innovative gender policies. The reduction in employment for women has potentially serious consequences, directly for the well-being of women, and also for their developing political engagement in democratic institutions in civil society and the state. Budget reductions may lead to cuts in the new public programmes designed to tackle gender-based violence against women.

Neoliberal processes de-democratise countries in the global North, as public services previously under the democratic control of the state are privatised and the heightening of security measures in the context of war and terror reduces civil liberties. This whole process reduces the political opportunities for feminism, which thrives in conditions of democratisation.

There is a resurgent neoliberalism and an opposition to the social democratic project, both in practice and in rhetoric. Discursively, this is expressed in terms of giving priority to 'choice' and 'economic growth', which are understood to be delivered better by the market than by the state. Within this perspective, the state is interpreted as a primarily 'bureaucratic' rather than 'democratic' entity.

The environmental crisis of peak oil and peak ambient temperature is likely to lead to lowered living standards and eventually to stem the rise in longevity. Global warming will cause a reduction in food production and an increase in extreme weather events. Contestation over scarce energy supply will increase the likelihood of resource wars. Women are disproportionately the losers from the environmental crisis, even though all are affected.

However, there are alternative futures (George 2004); neither the intensification of neoliberalism nor its replacement by xenophobic protectionism or by state capitalism is inevitable. There are other possibilities, one of them being social democracy (Walby 2009).

Hegemons and Tipping Points

The financial crisis of 2008 and the ensuing economic recession, which were followed by stimulus packages and then by deficit reduction, constitute a potential tipping point between different varieties of modernity. Sudden increases in inequality and polarisation between the rich and the poor have often been seen as provoking movements for radical progressive alternatives. The waves of protest, throughout Europe, against the cuts in spending made after the 2008 financial crisis, recession and sovereign debt problems may be seen to illustrate such a view. Within such a perspective, the financial crisis could constitute a tipping point into a radical trajectory of development, which leads to social democracy. However, increases in unemployment in Europe have been at least as much associated with the demobilisation of the labour movement and with the weakening of the social democratic projects. Indeed right-wing groups can take advantage of disasters and economic crises, treating them as contexts that might enable them both to achieve and to justify the radical restructuring of political economies in a neoliberal direction.

Different forms of modernity can be promoted through projects and governmental programmes, but they are also embedded in diverse social formations. For global futures, the form of modernity carried by the global hegemons is especially significant, since the latter have important implications for the landscape within which other social formations develop. Currently the leading global hegemon, the US, adopts a neoliberal form in both gender and class regimes, while the EU, an emergent global hegemon, still adopts a relatively more social democratic form. While there are other potential hegemons, such as China, which has its own, distinctive form of state capitalism, these are not yet of the same power and influence, although the situation is changing, because of China's rapid economic growth.

One significant factor in the shaping of global futures is that of the balance between the US and EU. This is a gendered balance of power because of the different forms of gender regimes carried by these polities and social formations. It is also a balance between neoliberal and relatively social democratic forces. If the EU were to have primary influence, becoming the leading hegemon, then global policies on gender issues might also be different.

There is a possibility of the EU overtaking the US as the leading global hegemon. The EU has a larger population and, through the GDP of all its member states, a larger economy than the US; but it does not have the same military might, and it has significantly less internal political cohesion. However, the EU is set to increase in size, as countries queuing up to join it do so. At the same time, the misuse of resources in aggressive militarised actions might weaken the US. Hence, if the EU were to gain internal cohesion, it could well overtake the US in global influence. The balancing of forces in favour of the EU over the US, and hence in favour of social democratic over neoliberal influences in the world, would create quite a different context, much more benign and open to the further development of feminist projects.

The consequences of the 2008 financial crisis, in the form of deep recessions and unsustainable sovereign debt in some member states of the European Union, have destabilised the Eurozone and consequently threaten the EU itself. As member states (beginning with Greece, Ireland and Portugal in 2010) struggle to avoid bankruptcy in the face of challenges from aggressive and mobile finance capital, the EU confronts two courses of action: either the disintegration of the political project of unifying Europe, which rests on economic integration, or the rapid deepening of that project, so that it may encompass the financial system that has suddenly revealed itself to be so fragile. The forces for disintegration include the rise of nationalist, racist and xenophobic projects, which is indicated for example in there being sufficient far right MEPs to form a new party of their own in the European Parliament in 2009. The forces for further integration include those, such as Merkel and other German politicians, who continue to see the EU as important, not only for economic development, but also for preventing the recurrence of war in Europe. These forces for EU integration potentially include feminist projects, which have seen the benefits of EU governance for gender equality in those areas where it has legitimate power. This moment in 2011 is a potential tipping point in the nature of the EU and, ultimately, the world. There may be either disintegration of the EU or its transformation from a loose into a tightly integrated polity and economy. If the project to develop the EU were to fail, then there would be no hegemon powerful enough to address the intensifying neoliberalism projected by the US.

The Relevance of Feminism for Alternative Futures

In this context of potential instability of existing forms of social arrangements, what are the implications of the strengthening of feminism? Feminism has a key role to play in the formation of future societies. If it is weak and demobilised, then neoliberalism is the more likely future. If it is strong and well allied, then there is the possibility of a tip towards a social democratic social formation that incorporates the principles of human rights. These are, potentially, changes not only to the gender regime, but also to the form of capitalism and to the possibility of resolving the environmental crisis.

Feminist projects are important for changing the form of the gender regime. There is a historical precedent to this: first-wave feminism, at the turn of the nineteenth and twentieth centuries, helped to push forward the transition from domestic to public forms through its successes, which included not only the vote, but access to education, access to seats on juries, and many more. Contemporary feminism is important in the continuous transformation of the gender regime and in the reduction of gender inequality.

Feminism can in principle change not only the nature of the gender regime, but also the nature of capitalism. In particular, the newly gendered social democratic project has serious implications for the form of capitalism. This project demands state provision for care work, the regulation of working time, the deepening of democracy, the reduction of violence, and mutualism rather than the commercialisation of intimacy. Each of these measures is simultaneously relevant to capitalism and to the gender regime. If democracy and civil society/political mobilisations matter, then the feminist project has the potential to affect significantly the form of capitalism as well as the gender regime.

The environmental crisis, especially global warming, is unlikely to be contained or resolved without a deepening of democracy and a reduction in inequality, both of which occur more frequently in social democratic than in neoliberal forms of modernity. Green political projects are often (though not always) closely interrelated with feminist ones. This is not surprising, since both types of project demand the democratic regulation of capital in the interests of the many, not the few.

So what is the future? Changes in gender inequality have been moving in a different direction from that of class inequality for most of the last half century. Gender inequalities have been slightly declining, while those of class inequality have been increasing. This is, at least partly, a consequence of the strength of the feminist project and of changes in the structure of the gender regime, which have included the deepening of democracy. A social democratic project that is infused with feminism has significant implications for the form of capitalism. Such a project, hybridised from earlier feminist and labourist social democratic ones, constitutes a potential source of change for capitalism, with implications for the environment. However, the world is on a knife-edge, as the after-shocks of the financial crisis have the potential to tip either into an intensified version of neoliberalism or into an emergent gendered social democracy.

If social democracy is to realise its potential, then it must embrace its gender dimension. The social democratic project for economic growth needs to include the full employment of women – which itself requires regulating equalities and working time in the workplace and the provision of state support for the care of the young and elderly – and the governance of finance by, and in the interests of, users and potential losers, not merely bankers. The social democratic project for the polity means developing the mechanisms needed to deepen democracy, so that the presence of women in governing institutions may be equal to that of men and the democratic remit may broaden, not be narrowed through privatisation. The social democratic project needs to widen its range of priority concerns beyond those of political economy. This new range needs to include a properly articulated social democratic approach to violence and securitisation, both crime and war. It also needs to include mutualism rather than commercialism as the principle of organisation of civil society, involving the human right to bodily integrity, so that women's individual control over their bodies may be respected, and to address the problem of the commercialisation of sex in pornography and prostitution.

Only if the social democratic project were to embrace more fully its feminist partners would it have much likelihood of success in becoming powerful again. If there is an effective synthesis between social democracy and feminism, then the majority of the population would be engaged in a democratic project that stood some chance of success in reforming capitalism and in tackling the environmental crisis, as well as in reducing gender and other forms of inequality.

Feminism is important not only for gender inequality, but also for the shape of society as a whole. The form of gender relations is the cause of the form of the wider social formation as much as it is a consequence of it. Feminist projects have profound implications for many political and societal outcomes, in addition to gendered ones, if they are part of effective alliances. The world is at a tipping point between intensified neoliberalism and social democracy. Alternative futures hinge on the future of feminism.

References

Abortion Rights (2011) *Home Page*. Retrieved from http://www.abortion rights.org.uk/ (20 January 2011).

Acker, Joan (2000) 'Revisiting class: Thinking from gender, race and organizations', *Social Politics*, 7 (2): 192–214.

Amnesty International (2011) *Home Page*. Retrieved from http://www. amnesty.org.uk/ (20 January 2011).

Anderson, Benedict (1983) *Imagined Communities*. London: Verso.

Annan, Kofi (1999) 'Secretary-General says "Global People-Power" best thing for United Nations in long time'. Retrieved from http://www.unis. unvienna.org/unis/pressrels/1999/sg2465.html (20 January 2011).

Anthias, Floya and Nira Yuval-Davis (1992) *Racialized Boundaries: Race, Nation, Gender, Colour, and Class and the Anti-Racist Struggle*. London: Routledge.

Anti-Slavery (2011) *Campaigns: Human Trafficking Petition*. Retrieved from http://www.antislavery.org/english/campaigns/eu_trafficking_directive.aspx (20 January 2011).

Archer, Margaret S. (1995) *Realist Social Theory: The Morphogenetic Approach*. Cambridge: Cambridge University Press.

Arestis, Philip and Malcolm Sawyer (2005) 'Neoliberalism and the third way', in Alfredo Saad-Filho and Deborah Johnston (eds), *Neoliberalism*, pp. 177–83. London: Pluto Press.

Ariffin, Rohanna (ed.) (1997) *Shame, Secrecy and Silence: Study on Rape in Penang*. Penang, Malaysia: Women's Crisis Centre Penang.

Armstrong, Jo, Sylvia Walby and Sofia Strid (2009) 'The gendered division of labour: How can we assess the quality of employment and care policy from a gender equality perspective?' *Benefits: A Journal of Poverty and Social Justice*, 17 (3): 263–75.

Arrighi, Giovanni (1994) *The Long Twentieth Century: Money, Power and the Origins of Our Times*. London: Verso.

Association for Women's Rights in Development (AWID) (2011) *About*

AWID. Retrieved from http://www.awid.org/About-AWID/What-is-AWID (20 January 2011).

Bagguley, Paul (1991) *From Protest to Acquiescence? Political Movements of the Unemployed*. Basingstoke: Macmillan.

Bagguley, Paul (2002) 'Contemporary British feminism: A social movement in abeyance?', *Social Movement Studies*, 1 (2): 169–85.

Bakker, Isabella (1998) *Unpaid Work and Macroeconomics: New Discussions, New Tools for Action*. Ottawa, Canada: Status of Women Canada.

Banks, Olive (1981) *Faces of Feminism: A Study of Feminism as a Social Movement*. Oxford: Martin Robertson.

Banyard, Kat (2010) *The Equality Illusion: The Truth about Women and Men Today*. London: Faber and Faber.

Barmes, Lizzie, with Sue Ashtiany (2003) 'The diversity approach to achieving equality: Potential and pitfalls', *Industrial Law Journal*, 32 (4): 274–96.

Bauman, Zygmunt (1989) *Modernity and the Holocaust*. Cambridge: Polity.

Bauman, Zygmunt (1991) *Modernity and Ambivalence*. Cambridge: Polity.

Bauman, Zygmunt (1996) 'On communitarians and human freedom: Or, how to square the circle', *Theory, Culture and Society*, 13 (2): 79–90.

Baumgardner, Jennifer and Amy Richards (2001) *Manifesta: Young Women, Feminism and the Future*. New York: Saint Martin's Press.

B-eat (2011) *Home Page*. Retrieved from www.b-eat.co.uk (20 January 2011).

Beck, Ulrich (1992) *Risk Society*. London: Sage.

Beck, Ulrich (2002) *Individualization: Institutionalized Individualization and its Social and Political Consequences*. London: Sage.

Beck, Ulrich, Anthony Giddens and Scott Lash (1994) *Reflexive Modernization: Politics, Tradition and Aesthetics in the Modern Social Order*. Cambridge: Polity.

Behning, Ute and Amparo Serrano Pascual (eds) (2001) *Gender Mainstreaming in the European Employment Strategy*. Brussels: European Trade Union Institute.

Bell, Diane and Renate Klein (eds) (1996) *Radically Speaking: Feminism Reclaimed*. London: Zed Books.

Bell, Mark (2004) *Critical Review of Academic Literature Relating to the EU Directives to Combat Discrimination*. Brussels: European Commission.

Ben-Galim, Dalia, Mary Campbell and Jane Lewis (2007) 'Equality and diversity: A new approach to gender equality policy in the UK', *International Journal of Law in Context*, 3: 19–33.

Benhabib, Seyla (1992) *Situating the Self: Gender, Community and Postmodernism in Contemporary Ethics*. Cambridge: Polity.

Benhabib, Seyla (1999) 'Sexual difference and collective identities: The new global constellation', *Signs*, 24 (2): 335–61.

Bergmann, Barbara (1986) *The Economic Emergence of Women*. New York: Basic Books.

Berkovitch, Nitza (1999) *From Motherhood to Citizenship: Women's Rights and International Organizations*. Baltimore: John Hopkins University Press.

Berman, Sheri (2006) *The Primacy of Politics: Social Democracy and the Making of Europe's Twentieth Century*. Cambridge: Cambridge University Press.

Beveridge, Fiona, Sue Nott and Kylie Stephen (2000) 'Mainstreaming and the engendering of policy-making: A means to an end?' *Journal of European Public Policy*, 7 (3): 385–405.

Bock, Gisela and Pat Thane (eds) (1991) *Maternity and Gender Policies: Women and the Rise of the European Welfare States, 1880s–1950s*. London: Routledge.

Booth, Christine and Cinnamon Bennett (2002) 'Gender mainstreaming in the European Union', *European Journal of Women's Studies*, 9 (4): 430–46.

Bornschier, Volker and Patrick Ziltener (1999) 'The revitalization of Western Europe and the politics of the "social dimension"', in Thomas Boje, Bart van Steenbergen and Sylvia Walby (eds), *European Societies: Fusion or Fission?*, pp. 33–52. London: Routledge.

Boswell, Terry and Christopher Chase-Dunn (2000) *The Spiral of Capitalism and Socialism: Toward Global Democracy*. Boulder: Lynne Reiner Publishers.

Braidotti, Rosi (1994) *Nomadic Subjects: Embodiment and Sexual Difference in Contemporary Feminist Theory*. Columbia: Columbia University Press.

Braithwaite, Mary (1999) *Mainstreaming Equal Opportunities in the Structural Funds. Report for the European Commission DG XVI*. Brussels: European Commission.

Briskin, Linda (2006) *Equity Bargaining/Bargaining for Equity*. York, Canada: York University. Retrieved from http://www.yorku.ca/lbriskin/pdf/bar gainingpaperFINAL3secure.pdf (20 January 2011).

Brooks, Ann (1997) *Postfeminisms: Feminism, Cultural Theory and Cultural Forms*. London: Routledge.

Brown, Wendy (1995) *States of Injury: Power and Freedom in Late Modernity*. Princeton: Princeton University Press.

Brownmiller, Susan (1976) *Against Our Will: Men, Women and Rape*. London: Penguin.

Budlender, Debbie, Diane Elson, Guy Hewitt and Tanni Mukhopadhyay (eds) (2002) *Gender Budgets Make Cents: Understanding Gender Responsive Budgets*. London: Commonwealth Secretariat.

Bumiller, Kristin (2008) *In an Abusive State: How Neoliberalism Appropriated the Feminist Movement against Sexual Violence*. Durham: Duke University Press.

Bunch, Charlotte (1995) 'Transforming human rights from a feminist perspective', in Julie Peters and Andrea Wolper (eds), *Women's Rights, Human Rights: International Feminist Perspectives*, pp. 11–17. London: Routledge.

Burawoy, Michael (1979) *Manufacturing Consent*. Chicago: University of Chicago Press.

Burman, Sheri (2006) *The Primacy of Politics: Social Democracy and the Making of Europe's Twentieth Century*. Cambridge: Cambridge University Press.

Burstein, Paul, R. Marie Bricher and Rachel L. Einwohner (1995) 'Policy alternatives and political change: Work, family and gender on the congressional agenda, 1945–1990', *American Sociological Review*, 60: 67–83.

Butler, Judith (1990) *Gender Trouble: Feminism and the Subversion of Identity*. New York: Routledge.

Calhoun, Craig (1995) *Critical Social Theory*. Oxford: Blackwell.

Campbell, J. C. (1992) 'Wife-battering: Cultural contexts versus western social sciences', in D. A. Counts, J. K. Brown and J. C. Campbell (eds.), *Sanctions and Sanctuary: Cultural Perspectives on the Beating of Wives*, pp. 229–49. Boulder: Westview Press.

Carnival of Feminists (2011) *Home Page*. Retrieved from www.feminist carnival.blogspot.com (20 January 2011).

Castells, Manuel (1996) *The Information Age: Economy, Society and Culture*, vol. 1: *The Rise of the Network Society*. Oxford: Blackwell.

Castells, Manuel (1997) *The Information Age: Economy, Society and Culture*, vol. 2: *The Power of Identity*. Oxford: Blackwell.

Castells, Manuel (1998) *The Information Age: Economy, Society and Culture*, vol. 3: *End of Millennium*. Oxford: Blackwell.

Cerny, Philip G. (1997) 'Globalization and the erosion of democracy', *European Journal of Political Research*, 36 (1): 1–26.

Chabot, Sean and Jan Willem Duyvendak (2002) 'Globalization and transnational diffusion between social movements: Reconceptualizing the dissemination of the Gandhian repertoire and the "coming out" routine', *Theory and Society*, 31 (6): 697–740.

Chafetz, Janet Saltzman and Anthony Gary Dworkin (1986) *Female Revolt: Women's Movements in World and Historical Perspective*. Totowa, NJ: Rowman and Allanheld.

Charles, Nickie (2000) *Feminism, the State and Social Policy*. Basingstoke: Macmillan.

Chase-Dunn, Christopher (1998) *Global Formation: Structures of the World-Economy*, 2nd edn. Oxford: Blackwell.

Chase-Dunn, Christopher, Yukio Kawano and Benjamin D. Brewer (2000) 'Trade globalization since 1795: Waves of integration in the world-system', *American Sociological Review*, 65: 77–95.

Child Poverty Action Group (2011) *Home Page*. Retrieved from http://www.cpag.org.uk/ (20 January 2011).

Childs, Sarah (2002) 'Hitting the target: Are Labour women MPs "acting for" women?' *Parliamentary Affairs*, 55 (1): 143–53.

Childs, Sarah, Paul Webb and Sally Marthaler (2010) 'Constituting and substantively representing women: Applying new approaches to the UK case study', *Politics and Gender*, 6: 199–223.

Christians for Biblical Equality (2011) 'Mission and history'. Rerieved from http://www.cbeinternational.org/?q=content/our-mission-and-history (20 January 2011).

Cockburn, Cynthia (2000) 'The anti-essentialist choice: Nationalism and feminism in the interaction between two women's projects', *Nations and Nationalism*, 6 (4): 611–29.

Colgan, Fiona and Sue Ledwith (eds) (2002) *Gender, Diversity and Trade Unions: International Perspectives*. London: Routledge.

Collins, Patricia Hill (1998) 'It's all in the family: Intersections of gender, race, and nation', *Hypatia*, 13 (3): 62–82.

Commission for Racial Equality (2005) *40 Years of Law Against Racial Discrimination*. Birmingham: Commission for Racial Equality.

Communities and Local Government (2007) *Discrimination Law Review*. London: Department of Communities and Local Government.

Communities and Local Government (2009) 'Race cohesion and faith'. Retrieved from http://www.communities.gov.uk/communities/racecohesionfaith/ (24 June 2009).

Conaghan, Joanne (2000) 'Reassessing the feminist theoretical project in law', *Journal of Law and Society*, 27 (3): 351–85.

Conaghan, Joanne (2009) 'Intersectionality and the feminist project in law', in Emily Grabhan, Davina Cooper, Jane Krishnada and Didi Herman (eds), *Intersectionality and Beyond*, pp. 21–48. London: Routledge.

Confederation of British Industry (2003) '"Equality and diversity: Making it happen": The CBI response'. London: CBI.

Connell, R. W. (2002) *Gender*. Cambridge: Polity.

Council of Europe (1998) *Gender Mainstreaming: Conceptual Framework, Methodology and Presentation of Good Practices*. Strasbourg: Council of Europe. EG-S-MS (98) 2 rev.

Counts, D. A., J. K. Brown and J. C. Campbell (eds) (1992) *Sanctions and Sanctuary: Cultural Perspectives on the Beating of Wives*. Boulder: Westview Press.

Crawley, Heaven (2001) *Refugees and Gender: Law and Process*. Bristol: Jordan.

Crenshaw, Kimberlé Williams (1991) 'Mapping the margins: Intersectionality, identity politics, and violence against women of color', *Stanford Law Review*, 43 (6): 1241–99.

Crouch, Colin and Wolfgang Streeck (eds) (1997) *Political Economy of Modern Capitalism: Mapping Convergence and Diversity*. London: Sage.

Cudworth, Erika (2005) *Developing Ecofeminist Theory: The Complexity of Difference*. London: Palgrave.

Dahlerup, Drude (2006) 'The story of the theory of critical mass', *Politics and Gender*, 2 (4): 511–22.

Daly, Mary (1978) *Gyn/Ecology: The Metaethics of Radical Feminism*. London: Women's Press.

Daly, Mary (2005) 'Gender mainstreaming in theory and practice', *Social Politics*, 12 (3): 433–50.

Davies, Miranda (ed.) (1993) *Women and Violence: Realities and Responses Worldwide*. London: Zed Books.

Davis, Angela (1981) *Women, Race and Class*. London: The Women's Press.

Davis, Kathy (2007) *The Making of "Our Bodies Ourselves": How Feminism Travels across Borders*. Durham: Duke University Press.

Daycare Trust (2011) *Home Page*. Retrieved from http://www.daycaretrust. org.uk/ (20 January 2011).

Dean, Jonathan (2010) *Rethinking Contemporary Feminist Politics*. London: Palgrave Macmillan.

Delanty, Gerard and Krishna Kumar (eds) (2006) *Handbook of Nations and Nationalism*. London: Sage.

Della Porta, Donatella and Mario Diani (1999) *Social Movements: An Introduction*. Oxford: Blackwell.

Department of Trade and Industry (DTI) (2004) *Fairness for All: A New Commission for Equality and Human Rights*. Cmd 6185. Retrieved from http://www.dti.gov.uk/access/equalitywhitepaper.pdf (14 May 2004).

Development Alternatives with Women for a New Era (DAWN) (2011) *Home Page*. Retrieved from http://www.dawnnet.org/index.php (20 January 2011).

Dex, Shirley and Colin Smith (2002) *The Nature and Pattern of Family Friendly Employment Policies in Britain*. Bristol: Policy Press.

Diani, Mario (1996) 'Linking mobilization frames and political opportunities: Insights from regional populism in Italy', *American Sociological Review*, 61: 1053–69.

Dines, Gail (2010) *PORNLAND: How Porn Has Hijacked our Sexuality*. Uckfield: Beacon Press.

Dobash, R. Emerson and Russell P. Dobash (1992) *Women, Violence and Social Change*. London: Routledge.

Drake, Barbara (1984) *Women in Trade Unions* [1920]. London: Virago.

Duluth (2011) *Domestic Abuse Intervention Programme*. Retrieved from http://www.theduluthmodel.org/duluthmodel.php (20 January 2011).

Edwards, Susan (1996) *Sex and Gender in the Legal Process*. London: Blackstone.

Ehrenreich, Barbara and Arlie Hochschild (eds) (2003) *Global Woman: Nannies, Maids, and Sex Workers in the New Economy*. London: Granta.

Eisenstein, Hester (2009) *Feminism Seduced: How Global Elites Use Women's Labor and Ideas to Exploit the World*. Boulder: Paradigm.

Eisinger, Peter (1973) 'The conditions of protest behaviour in American cities', *American Political Science Review*, 67: 11–28.

Elgström, Ole (2000) 'Norm negotiations. The construction of new norms regarding gender and development in EU foreign aid policy', *Journal of European Public Policy*, 7 (3): 457–76.

Elson, Diane (1998) 'The economic, the political and the domestic: Businesses, states and households in the organization of production', *New Political Economy*, 3 (2): 189–208.

End Violence against Women (EVAW) (2011) *Homepage*. Retrieved from http://www.endviolenceagainstwomen.org.uk/ (20 January 2011).

Enloe, Cynthia (1989) *Bananas, Beaches and Bases: Making Feminist Sense of International Relations*. London: Pandora.

Enloe, Cynthia (2007) *Globalization and Militarism: Feminists Make the Link*. Plymouth: Rowman and Littlefield.

Equalities Review (2007) *Fairness and Freedom: The Final Report of the Equalities Review*. London: Cabinet Office.

Equality and Diversity Forum (2011) *Home Page*. Retrieved from http://www.edf.org.uk/ (20 January 2011).

Equality and Human Rights Commission (2011) *Home Page*. Retrieved from http://www.equalityhumanrights.com/ (20 January 2011).

Eriksson, Maria and Marianne Hester (2001) 'Violent men as good-enough fathers: A look at England and Sweden', *Violence against Women*, 7 (7): 779–98.

Esping-Andersen, Gøsta (1990) *The Three Worlds of Welfare Capitalism*. Cambridge: Polity.

Esping-Andersen, Gøsta (1997) 'Hybrid or unique? The Japanese welfare state between Europe and America', *Journal of European Social Policy*, 7 (3): 179–89.

Esping-Andersen, Gøsta (1999) *Social Foundations of Postindustrial Economies*. Oxford: Oxford University Press.

Esping-Andersen, Gøsta (2002) *Why We Need a New Welfare State*. Oxford: Oxford University Press.

European Commission (1999) 'Gender mainstreaming in the European employment strategy'. Doc EQOP 61-99 DG EMPL/D/5 1 October 1999. Brussels: European Commission.

European Commission (2000) *Communication from the Commission to the Council, the European Parliament, the Economic and Social Committee and the Committee of the Regions: Towards a Community Framework Strategy on Gender Equality (2001–2005)*. Brussels, 7.6.2000, COM (2000) 335 final, 2000/0143 (CNS).

European Commission (2003) 'Council Decision of 22 July 2003 (2003/578/EC) on Guidelines for the Employment Policies of the Member States', *Official Journal of the European Union* L 197/13, 05.08.2003.

European Commission (2004) *Equality and Non-Discrimination in an Enlarged European Union*. Green Paper. Brussels: European Commission.

European Commission (2006) *A Roadmap for Equality between Women and Men 2006–2010*. Brussels. Retrieved from http://eur-lex.europa.eu/LexUriServ/LexUriServ.do?uri=COM:2006:0092:FIN:EN:PDF (24 May 2010).

European Commission (2007) *Equal Opportunities and Equal Treatment for Women and Men in Employment and Occupation*. Retrieved from http://europa.eu/legislation_summaries/employment_and_social_policy/equality_between_men_and_women/c10940_en.htm (20 January 2011).

European Commission (2010a) *Gender Mainstreaming.* Retrieved from http://ec.europa.eu/social/main.jsp?catId=421&langId=en (20 May 2010).

European Commission (2010b) *New Strategy on Gender Equality.* COM (2010) 491 final. Brussels: European Commission. Retrieved from http://ec.europa.eu/social/main.jsp?langId=en&catId=89&newsId=890&furtherNews=yes (20 January 2011).

European Commission (2010c) *A Strengthened Commitment to Equality between Women and Men: A Women's Charter.* Retrieved from http://ec.europa.eu/commission_2010-2014/president/news/documents/pdf/20100305_1_en.pdf (20January 2011).

European Commission (2010d) *Europe 2020: A European Strategy for Smart, Sustainable and Inclusive Growth.* Brussels: European Commission.

European Commission (2010e) *The European Commission Appoints an Anti-Trafficking Coordinator.* Retrieved from http://ec.europa.eu/anti-trafficking/entity.action;jsessionid=dSmSNbrJP335TyXDM17Jktl5yVBqMvHqn2FynLtlGfT1JR2y8GSV!1145937442?id=e72b38b6-2724-40c5-810a-f444fdc8849a (20 January 2011).

European Commission (2011a) *Daphne Programme to Prevent and Combat Violence against Children, Young People and Women.* Retrieved from http://ec.europa.eu/justice/funding/daphne3/funding_daphne3_en.htm (20 January 2011).

European Commission (2011b) *Directorate-General on Employment, Social Affairs and Social Affairs Home Page.* Retrieved from http://ec.europa.eu/social/main.jsp?langId=en&catId=656. (20 January 2011).

European Gender Budget Network (2007) *Manifesto.* Retrieved from http://www.infopolis.es/web/GenderBudgets/manifesto.html (20 January 2011).

European Green Party (2011) *Home Page.* Retrieved from http://european-greens.eu/ (20 January 2011).

European Institute for Gender Equality (EIGE) (2011) *Home Page.* Retrieved from http://www.eige.europa.eu/ (20 January 2011).

European Parliament (2011) *Women's Rights and Gender Equality Committee: Home Page.* Retrieved from http://www.europarl.europa.eu/activities/committees/homeCom.do;jsessionid=74192B1293183F3F5FA8127C55E71BE9.node1?language=EN&body=FEMM (20 January 2011).

European Trade Union Confederation (ETUC) (2011) *About Us.* Retrieved from http://www.etuc.org/r/5 (20 January 2011).

European Union Fundamental Rights Agency (2011) *Violence against Women: An EU-wide Survey.* Retrieved from http://www.fra.europa.eu/fraWebsite/research/projects/proj_eu_survey_vaw_en.htm (20 January 2011).

European United Left/Nordic Green Left, European Parliamentary Group (GUE/NGL) (2011) *Homepage.* Retrieved from http://www.guengl.org/showPage.jsp?ID=1 (20 January 2011).

European Women's Lobby (EWL) (2005) *Position Paper of the European*

Women's Lobby on the setting up of a European Gender Institute. Brussels. European Women's Lobby.

European Women's Lobby (2011) *Home Page.* Retrieved from http://www. womenlobby.org/ (20 January 2011).

Evans, Sara M. and Barbara J. Nelson (eds) (1989) *Wage Justice: Comparable Worth and the Paradox of Technocratic Reform.* Chicago: University of Chicago Press.

Eveline, Joan and Carol Bacchi (2005) 'What are we mainstreaming when we mainstream gender?' *International Feminist Journal of Politics*, 7 (4): 496–512.

Eyerman, Ron and Andrew Jamieson (1991) *Social Movements: A Cognitive Approach.* Cambridge: Polity.

The f word: contemporary UK feminism (2011) *Home Page.* Retrieved from http://www.thefword.org.uk/ (20 January 2011).

Faderman, Lillian (1981) *Surpassing the Love of Men: Romantic Friendship and Love between Women from the Renaissance to the Present.* London: Junction Books.

Fairbairns, Zoë, Helen Graham, Ali Neilson, Emma Robertson and Ann Kaloski (eds) (2002) *Saying What We Want: Women's Demands in the Feminist Seventies and Now.* York: Raw Nerve Books Limited, Centre for Women's Studies, University of York. Retrieved from http://www.zoe fairbairns.co.uk/Saying_What_We_Want.pdf (20 May 2010).

Faludi, Susan (1991) *Backlash: The Undeclared War against American Women.* New York: Crown.

Faludi, Susan (1992) *Backlash: The Undeclared War against Women.* London: Chatto and Windus.

Fawcett Society (2000) *The Gender/Generation Gap.* London: Fawcett Society.

Fawcett Society (2011) *Home Page.* Retrieved from http://www.fawcett society.org.uk/index.asp?Pageid=1 (20 January 2011).

Felski, Rita (1997) 'The doxa of difference', *Signs*, 23 (1): 1–22.

Feminism in London (2011) *Home Page.* Retrieved from http://www. feminisminlondon.org.uk/home.ikml (20 January 2011).

Feminist and Women's Studies Association (2011) *About Us.* Retrieved from http://fwsa.wordpress.com/about/ (20 January 2011).

Feminist Library, The (2011) *Home Page.* Retrieved from http://feminist library.co.uk/ (20 January 2011).

Ferree, Myra Marx (1980) 'Working class feminism: A consideration of the consequences of employment', *Sociological Quarterly*, 21: 173–84.

Ferree, Myra Marx and Beth B. Hess (1995) *Controversy and Coalition: The New Feminist Movement across Three Decades of Change*, 2nd edn. New York: Simon and Schuster Macmillan.

Ferree, Myra Marx, William A. Gamson, Jürgen Gerhards and Dieter Rucht (2002a) 'Four models of the public sphere in modern democracies', *Theory and Society*, 31: 289–324.

Ferree, Myra Marx, William A. Gamson, Jürgen Gerhards and Dieter Rucht (2002b) *Shaping Abortion Discourse: Democracy and the Public Sphere in Germany and the United States.* Cambridge: Cambridge University Press.

Ferree, Myra Marx and William A. Gamson (2003) 'The gendering of governance and the governance of gender', in Barbara Hobson (ed.), *Recognition Struggles and Social Movements: Contested Identities, Agency and Power*, pp. 35–63. Cambridge: Cambridge University Press.

Ferree, Myra Marx (2009) 'Inequality, intersectionality and the politics of discourse: Framing feminist alliances', in Emanuela Lombardo, Petra Meier and Mieke Verloo (eds) (2009) *The Discursive Politics of Gender Equality: Stretching, Bending and Policymaking*, pp. 86–104. London: Routledge.

Firestone, Shulamith (1974) *The Dialectic of Sex: The Case for Feminist Revolution.* New York: Morrow.

Folbre, Nancy (2001) *The Invisible Heart: Economics and Family Values.* New York: New Press.

Franzway, Suzanne and Mary Margaret Fonow (2008) 'An Australian feminist twist on transnational labor activism', *Signs*, 33 (3): 537–43.

Fraser, Nancy (1989) *Unruly Practices: Power, Discourse and Gender in Contemporary Social Theory.* Cambridge: Polity.

Fraser, Nancy (1997) *Justice Interruptus: Critical Reflections on the "Postsocialist" Condition.* London: Routledge.

Fraser, Nancy (2009) 'Feminism, capitalism and the cunning of history', *New Left Review*, 56: 97–117.

Freedman, Jane (2001) *Feminism.* Buckingham: Open University Press.

Friedman, Elisabeth (1995) 'Women's human rights: The emergence of a movement', in Julie Peters and Andrea Wolper (eds), *Women's Rights, Human Rights: International Feminist Perspectives*, pp. 18–35. London: Routledge.

Fung, Archon and Erik Olin Wright (2001) 'Deepening democracy: Innovations in empowered participatory governance', *Politics and Society*, 29 (1): 5–41.

Gagnon, Suzanne and Sue Ledwith (eds) (2000) *Women, Diversity and Democracy in Trade Unions.* Oxford: Oxford Brookes University.

Galbraith, John Kenneth (1975) *The Great Crash 1929* [1954]. London: Penguin.

Gamson, William A. (1975) The *Strategy of Social Protest.* Homewood, IL: The Dorsey Press.

Garland, David (2001) *The Culture of Control: Crime and Social Order in Contemporary Society.* Oxford: Oxford University Press.

Garrison, Ednie Kaeh (2000) 'U.S. Feminism – Grrrl style! Youth (sub) cultures and the technologies of the third wave', *Feminist Studies*, 26 (1): 141–70.

Gelb, Joyce (1989) *Feminism and Politics: A Comparative Perspective.* Berkeley: University of California Press.

Gellner, Ernest (1983) *Nations and Nationalism*. Oxford: Blackwell.

GenderCC (2011) *Gender and Climate Change Home Page*. Retrieved from http://www.gendercc.net/ (20 January 2011).

Gender Equality Architecture Reform (GEAR) Campaign (2009) 'Gear up: building a United Nations that really works for all women'. Retrieved from http://gear.groupsite.com/ (25 June 2009).

Gender Equality Architecture Reform (GEAR) Campaign (2011) *Home Page*. Retrieved from http://www.gearcampaign.org/ (20 January 2011).

George, Susan (2004) *Another World is Possible If . . .* London: Verso.

Giddens, Anthony (1992) *The Transformation of Intimacy: Sexuality, Love and Eroticism in Modern Societies*. Cambridge: Polity.

Giddens, Anthony (1994) *Beyond Left and Right: The Future of Radical Politics*. Cambridge: Polity.

Giddens, Anthony (1998) *The Third Way: The Renewal of Social Democracy*. Cambridge: Polity.

Giddens, Anthony (2009) *Politics of Climate Change*. Cambridge: Polity.

Gill, Rosalind (2006) *Gender and the Media*. Cambridge: Polity.

Gilligan, Carol (1982) *In a Different Voice*. Cambridge, MA: Harvard University Press.

Gillis, Stacy, Gillian Howe and Rebecca Munford (eds) (2007) *Third Wave Feminism: A Critical Exploration*, 2nd edn. London: Palgrave Macmillan.

Gilroy, Paul (1993) *The Black Atlantic: Modernity and Double Consciousness*. London: Verso.

Githens, Marianne, Pippa Norris and Joni Lovenduski (eds) (1995) *Different Roles, Different Voices: Women and Politics in the United States and Europe*. New York: HarperCollins.

Global Media Monitoring Project (2010) *Who Makes the News*. Retrieved from http://www.whomakesthenews.org/images/stories/website/gmmp_reports/2010/global/gmmp_global_report_en.pdf (20 January 2011).

Goss, David, Fiona Goss and Derek Adam-Smith (2000) 'Disability and employment: A comparative critique of UK legislation', *International Journal of Human Resource Management*, 11 (4): 807–21.

Gottfried, Heidi and Laura Reese (2003) 'Gender, policy, politics and work: Feminist comparative and transnational research', *Review of Policy Research*, 20 (1): 3–20.

Gottschall, Karin and Katherine Bird (2003) 'Family leave policies and labor market segregation in Germany: Reinvention or reform of the male breadwinner model?', *Review of Policy Research*, 20 (1): 115–34.

Gottschall, Karin and Daniela Kroos (2007) 'Self-employment in comparative perspective: General trends and the case of new media', in Sylvia Walby, Heidi Gottfried, Karin Gottschall and Mari Osawa (eds), *Gendering the Knowledge Economy*, pp. 163–87. London: Palgrave.

Government Equalities Office (GEO) (2009) *Business Plan 2009–2010*. London: Government Equalities Office. Retrieved from http://www.

equalities.gov.uk/PDF/295311_GEO_BusinessPlan_acc.pdf (24 June 2009).

Government Equalities Office (GEO) (2011) *Home Page*. Retrieved from http://www.equalities.gov.uk/ (20 January 2011).

Grace, S. (1995) *Policing Domestic Violence in the 1990s*. Home Office Research Study No. 139. London: Home Office.

Grainger, Heidi and Martin Crowther (2007) *Trade Union Membership 2006*. London: DTI and ONS. Retrieved from http://www.bis.gov.uk/files/file39006.pdf (20 January 2011).

Gramsci, Antonio (1971) *Selections from the Prison Notebooks of Antonio Gramsci*. London: Lawrence and Wishart.

Greenspan, Alan (2008) *The Age of Turbulence*. London: Penguin.

Gregory, Jeanne (1987) *Sex, Race and the Law: Legislating for Equality*. London: Sage.

Gregory, Jeanne (1999) 'Re-visiting the sex equality laws', in Sylvia Walby (ed.), *New Agendas for Women*, pp. 98–118. Basingstoke: Macmillan.

Grey, Sandra and Marian Sawer (eds) (2008) *Women's Movements: Flourishing or in Abeyance?* London: Routledge.

Grosser, Kate and Jeremy Moon (2005) 'Gender mainstreaming and corporate social responsibility', *International Feminist Journal of Politics*, 7 (4): 532–54.

Guerrina, Roberta (2002) 'Mothering in Europe: Feminist critique of European policies on motherhood and employment', *European Journal of Women's Studies*, 9 (1): 49–68.

Haas, Peter M. (1992) 'Introduction: Epistemic communities and international policy coordination', *International Organization*, 46 (1): 1–35.

Haavio-Manila, Elina (ed.) (1985) *Unfinished Democracy: Women in Nordic Politics*. Oxford: Pergamon.

Habermas, Jürgen (1987) *The Theory of Communicative Action*, vol. 1: *The Critique of Functionalist Reason* [1981]. Cambridge: Polity.

Habermas, Jürgen (1991) *The Theory of Communicative Action*, vol. 2: *Reason and the Rationalization of Society* [1981]. Cambridge: Polity.

Hague, Gill and Ellen Malos (1993) *Domestic Violence: Action for Change*. Cheltenham: New Clarion Press.

Hall, Peter A. and David Soskice (eds) (2001) *Varieties of Capitalism: The Institutional Foundations of Comparative Advantage*. Oxford: Oxford University Press.

Halsaa, Beatrice (1998) 'A strategic partnership for women's policies in Norway', in Geertje Lycklama à Nijeholt, Virginia Vargas and Saskia Wieringa (eds), *Women's Movements and Public Policy in Europe, Latin America and the Caribbean*, pp. 167–89. New York: Garland.

Hancock, Ange-Marie (2007) 'When multiplication doesn't equal quick addition: Examining intersectionality as a research paradigm', *Perspectives on Politics*, 5 (1): 63–79.

Haney, Lynne (1996) 'Homeboys, babies, men in suits: The state and the reproduction of male dominance', *American Sociological Review*, 61 (5): 759–78.

Hankivsky, Olena (2005) 'Gender mainstreaming vs. diversity mainstreaming: A preliminary examination of the role and transformative potential of feminist theory', *Canadian Journal of Political Science*, 38 (4): 977–1001.

Hanmer, Jalna (1978) 'Violence and the social control of women', in Gary Littlejohn, Barry Smart, John Wakeford and Nira Yuval-Davis (eds), *Power and the State*, pp. 217–38. London: Croom Helm.

Hanmer, Jalna, Jill Radford and Elizabeth Stanko (eds) (1989) *Women, Policing and Male Violence: International Perspectives*. London: Routledge.

Haraway, Donna (1988) 'Situated knowledges: The science question in feminism and the privilege of partial perspective', *Feminist Studies*, 14 (3): 575–99.

Harding, Sandra (1986) *The Science Question in Feminism*. Ithaca: Cornell University Press.

Hardt, Michael and Antonio Negri (2000) *Empire*. Cambridge, MA: Harvard University Press.

Hardt, Michael and Antonio Negri (2006) *Multitude: War and Democracy in the Age of Empire*. London: Penguin Books.

Harkness, Susan (1996) 'The gender earnings gap: Evidence from the UK', *Fiscal Studies*, 17: 1–36.

Hartmann, Heidi (1976) 'Capitalism, patriarchy and job segregation by sex', *Signs*, 1: 137–70.

Harvey, David (2005) *A Brief History of Neoliberalism*. Oxford: Oxford University Press.

Harwin, Nicola (1997) 'The role of Women's Aid and refuge support services for women and children', in Susan Bewley, John Friend and Gillian Mezey (eds), *Violence against Women*, pp. 59–75. London: Royal College of Obstetricians and Gynaecologists.

Hawkesworth, Mary (1997) 'Confounding gender', *Signs*, 22 (3): 649–85.

Haxton, Eva and Claes Olsson (eds) (1999) *Gender Focus on the WTO*. Uppsala, Sweden: Global Publications Foundation.

Hedlund, Gun (1998) 'Gender, power and organizational changes in Swedish local politics.' Unpublished paper, Mimeo, Centre for Women's Studies, Orebro University, Sweden.

Heelas, Paul, Linda Woodhead, Benjamin Seel, Bronislaw Szerszynski and Karin Tusting (2004) *The Spiritual Revolution: Why Religion Is Giving Way to Spirituality*. London: Blackwell.

Heise, Lori L. (1996) 'Violence against women: Global organizing for change', in Jeffrey L. Edleson and Zvi C. Eisikovits (eds), *Future Interventions with Battered Women and their Families*. London: Sage.

Held, David (1995) *Democracy and the Global Order: From the Modern State to Cosmopolitan Governance*. Cambridge: Polity.

Held, David (1996) *Models of Democracy*, 2nd edn. Cambridge: Polity.

Held, David (2004) *Global Covenant: The Social Democratic Alternative to the Washington Consensus*. Cambridge: Polity.

Held, David, Anthony McGrew, David Goldblatt and Jonathan Perraton (1999) *Global Transformations: Politics, Economics and Culture*. Cambridge: Polity.

Henry, Astrid (2004) *Not My Mother's Sister: Generational Conflict and Third-Wave Feminism*. Bloomington: Indiana University Press.

Hepple, Bob, Mary Coussey and Tufyal Choudhury (2000) *Equality: A New Framework. Report of the Independent Review of the Enforcement of UK Anti-Discrimination Legislation*. London: Hart Publishing.

Hester, Marianne and Lorraine Radford (1996) *Domestic Violence and Child Contact Arrangements in England and Denmark*. Bristol: Policy Press.

Hester, Marianne, Liz Kelly and Jill Radford (eds) (1996) *Women, Violence and Male Power*. Buckingham: Open University Press.

Hettne, Bjorn, Andras Inotai and Osvaldo Sunkel (eds) (1999) *Globalism and the New Regionalism*, vol. 1. Basingstoke: Macmillan.

Heywood, Leslie L. (2005) *The Women's Movement Today: An Encyclopedia of Third-Wave Feminism*. Burnham: Greenwood Press.

Hicks, Alexander and Lane Kenworthy (2003) 'Varieties of welfare capitalism', *Socio-Economic Review*, 1: 27–61.

Himmelweit, Susan (2000) 'The work of the UK Women's Budget Group'. Paper presented to the Inter-Agency Workshop on Improving the Effectiveness of Integrating Gender into Government Budgets, Marlborough House, London, 26–7 April 2000.

Himmelweit, Susan (2002) 'Making visible the hidden economy: The case for gender-impact analysis of economic policy', *Feminist Economics*, 8 (1): 49–70.

Hindin, Michelle J., Sunita Kishor, Donna L. Ansara and Macro International (2008) *Intimate Partner Violence among Couples in 10 DHS Countries: Predictors and Health Outcomes*. USAid. DHS Analytical Studies 18. Retrieved from http://www.measuredhs.com/pubs/pdf/AS18/AS18.pdf (20 January 2011).

Hirst, Paul and Grahame Thompson (1996) *Globalization in Question: The International Economy and the Possibilities of Governance*. Cambridge: Polity.

Hirst, Paul and Grahame Thompson (2000) 'Globalization in one country? The peculiarities of the British', *Economy and Society*, 29 (3): 335–56.

Hobsbawm, Eric and Terence Ranger (eds) (1983) *The Invention of Tradition*. Cambridge: Cambridge University Press.

HM Government (2010) *Call to End Violence against Women and Girls*. Retrieved from http://www.homeoffice.gov.uk/publications/crime/call-end-violence-women-girls/vawg-paper?view=Binary (20 January 2011).

HM Treasury (2010) *Business Plan 2010–2015*. London: HM Treasury.

Hobson, Barbara (ed.) (2000) *Gender and Citizenship in Transition*. London: Macmillan.

Hobson, Barbara (ed.) (2003) *Recognition Struggles and Social Movements:*

Contested Identities, Agency and Power. Cambridge: Cambridge University Press.

Holland, John, H. (2000) *Emergence: From Chaos to Order*. Oxford: Oxford University Press.

Holli, Anne Maria (1997) 'On equality and Trojan horses: The challenges of the Finnish experience to feminist theory', *European Journal of Women's Studies*, 4 (2): 133–64.

Holmes, Rebecca, Nicola Jones and Hannah Marsden (2009) *Gender Vulnerabilities, Food Price Shocks and Social Protection Responses*. London: Overseas Development Institute.

Holmwood, John (2001) 'Gender and critical realism: A critique of Sayer', *Sociology*, 35 (4): 947–65.

Hoskyns, Catherine (1996) *Integrating Gender: Women, Law and Politics in the European Union*. London: Verso.

Huber, Evelyne and John D. Stephens (2000) 'Partisan governance, women's employment, and the social democratic service state', *American Sociological Review*, 65: 323–42.

Hutchings, Kimberly (1997) 'Moral deliberation and political judgement: Reflections on Benhabib's interactive universalism', *Theory, Culture & Society*, 14 (1): 131–42.

Inglehart, Ronald (1997) *Modernization and Postmodernization: Cultural, Economic, and Political Change in 43 Societies*. Princeton: Princeton University Press.

Inglehart, Ronald and Pippa Norris (2000) 'The developmental theory of the gender gap: Women's and men's voting behavior in global perspective', *International Political Science Review*, 21 (4): 441–63.

Inglehart, Ronald and Pippa Norris (2003) *Rising Tide: Gender Equality and Cultural Change around the World*. Cambridge: Cambridge University Press.

Intergovernmental Panel on Climate Change (2011) *Homepage*. Retrieved from http://www.ipcc.ch/ (20 January 2011).

International Development Research Centre (IDRC) (2005) *Gender Responsive Budgeting*. Retrieved from http://www.gender-budgets.org/en/ ev-64152-201-1-DO_TOPIC.html (26 May 2005).

International Labour Organisation (ILO) (2005) *A Global Alliance against Forced Labour*. Geneva: ILO.

International Labour Organisation (2011) *About the ILO*. Retrieved from http://www.ilo.org/global/About_the_ILO/lang--en/index.htm (20 January 2011).

Inter-Parliamentary Union (1995) *Women in Parliaments: 1945–1995: A World Statistical Survey*. Geneva: Inter-Parliamentary Union.

Inter-Parliamentary Union (2010) *Women in National Parliaments*. Retrieved from http://www.ipu.org/wmn-e/world.htm (20 January 2011).

Jackson, Tim (2009) *Prosperity without Growth? The Transition to a Sustainable Economy*. London: Sustainable Development Commission.

Jahan, Rounaq (1995) *The Elusive Agenda: Mainstreaming Women in Development*. London: Zed Books.

Jakobsen, Janet R. (1998) *Working Alliances and the Politics of Difference: Diversity and Feminist Ethics*. Bloomington: Indiana University Press.

Jayawardena, Kumari (ed.) (1986) *Feminism and Nationalism in the Third World*. London: Zed Books.

Jenson, Jane (1989) 'Paradigms and political discourse: Protective legislation in France and the United States before 1914', *Canadian Journal of Political Science/Revue Canadienne de Science Politique*, 22 (2): 235–58.

Jenson, Jane (1997) 'Who cares? Gender and welfare regimes', *Social Politics*, 4 (2): 182–7.

Jessop, Bob (2002) *The Future of the Capitalist State*. Cambridge: Polity.

Joannou, Maroula and June Purvis (eds) (2009) *The Women's Suffrage Movement: New Feminist Perspectives*. Manchester: Manchester University Press.

Johnson, Holly (1996) *Dangerous Domains: Violence against Women in Canada*. Canada: Nelson Canada.

Joshi, Heather and Pierella Paci (1998) *Unequal Pay for Women and Men: Evidence from the British Birth Cohort Studies*. Cambridge, MA: MIT Press.

Kabeer, Naila (2003) *Gender Mainstreaming in Poverty Eradication and the Millennium Development Goals*. London: Commonwealth Secretariat.

Kandiyoti, Deniz (ed.) (1991) *Women, Islam and the State*. Basingstoke: Macmillan.

Kanter, Rosabeth Moss (1977) 'Some effects of proportions of group life: Skewed sex ratios and response to token women', *American Journal of Sociology*, 82: 965–90.

Kantola, Johanna and Kevät Nousiainen (2009) 'Institutionalizing intersectionality in Europe', *International Feminist Journal of Politics*, 11 (4): 459–77.

Karlsson, Gunnel (1998) 'Social democratic women's coup in the Swedish parliament', in Drude von der Fehr, Anna G. Jónasdóttir and Bente Rosenbeck (eds), *Is There a Nordic Feminism? Nordic Feminist Thought on Culture and Society*, pp. 44–68. London: UCL Press.

Kauffman, Stuart A. (1995) *At Home in the Universe: The Search for Laws of Self-Organization and Complexity*. London: Viking.

Keane, John (2003) *Global Civil Society?* Cambridge: Cambridge University Press.

Keck, Margaret E. and Kathryn Sikkink (1998) *Activists beyond Borders: Advocacy Networks in International Politics*. Ithaca: Cornell University Press.

Kelly, Erin and Frank Dobbin (1999) 'Civil rights law at work: Sex discrimination and the rise of maternity leave policies', *American Journal of Sociology*, 105 (2): 455–92.

Kelly, Liz (1999) 'Violence against women: A policy of neglect or a neglect of policy', in Sylvia Walby (ed.), *New Agendas for Women*, pp. 119–47. Basingstoke: Macmillan.

Kelly, Liz (2005) 'Inside outsiders: Mainstreaming gender into human rights discourse and practice', *International Feminist Journal of Politics*, 7 (4): 471–95.

Kelly, Liz (2007) 'Should violence be a priority for the Commission for Equality and Human Rights?', Key note speech for the Equality and Diversity Forum, London, June 2007.

Kelly, Liz, Julie Bindel, Sheila Burton, Dianne Butterworth, Kate Cook and Linda Regan (1999) *Domestic Violence Matters: An Evaluation of a Development Project*. London: Home Office.

Kelly, Liz and Linda Regan (2000) *Stopping Traffic: Exploring the Extent of, and Responses to, Trafficking in Women for Sexual Exploitation in the UK*. Police Research Series Paper 125. London: Home Office.

Kelly, Liz, Jo Lovett and Linda Regan (2005) *A Gap or a Chasm? Attrition in Reported Rape Cases*. Home Office Research Study 293. London: Home Office.

Kenworthy, Ken (2004) *Egalitarian Capitalism: Jobs, Incomes, and Growth in Affluent Countries*. New York: Russell Sage Foundation.

Keynes, John Maynard (1936) *The General Theory of Employment, Interest and Money*. London: Macmillan.

Kimmel, Michael S. (1987) 'Men's responses to feminism at the turn of the century', *Gender and Society*, 1 (3): 261–83.

Kinser, Amber E. (2004) 'Negotiating spaces for/through third wave feminism', *National Women's Studies Association Journal [NWSA]* 16 (3): 124–53.

Klasen, Stephan (2002) 'Low schooling for girls, slower growth for all? Cross-country evidence on the effect of gender inequality in education on economic development', *The World Bank Economic Review*, 16 (3): 345–73.

Klein, Naomi (2007) *The Shock Doctrine: The Rise of Disaster Capitalism*. London: Allen Lane.

Knutsen, Oddbjørn (2001) 'Social class, sector employment, and gender as party cleavages in the Scandinavian countries: A comparative longitudinal study, 1970–95', *Scandinavian Political Studies*, 24 (4): 311–50.

Korpi, Walter (1983) *The Democratic Class Struggle*. London: Routledge and Kegan Paul.

Korpi, Walter (2002) 'The great trough in unemployment: A long-term view of unemployment, inflation, strikes and the profit/wage ratio', *Politics and Society*, 30: 365–426.

Korpi, Walter (2003) 'Welfare-state regress in western Europe: Politics, institutions, globalization, and Europeanization', *Annual Review of Sociology*, 29: 589–609.

Koven, Seth and Sonya Michel (1990) 'Womanly duties: Maternalist politics and the origins of welfare states in France, Germany, Great Britain, and the United States, 1880–1920', *The American Historical Review*, 95 (4): 1076–1108.

Krizsán, Andrea, Marjolein Paantjens and Ilse van Lamoen (2005) 'Domestic violence', *The Greek Review of Social Research*, 117 (B): 63–92.

Krug, Etienne G., Linda L. Dahlberg, James A. Mercy, Anthony B. Zwi and Rafael Lozano (2002) *World Report on Violence and Health*. Geneva: World Health Organization.

Krugman, Paul (2008) *The Return of Depression Economics and the Crisis of 2008*. London: Penguin.

Kuhn, Thomas (1979) *The Structure of Scientific Revolutions*. Chicago: University of Chicago Press.

Kymlicka, Will (1991) *Liberalism, Community and Culture*. Oxford: Clarendon Press.

Kymlicka, Will (1995) *Multicultural Citizenship: A Liberal Theory of Minority Rights*. Oxford: Clarendon Press.

Kyoto Protocol (1997) *Kyoto Protocol to the United Nations Framework Convention on Climate Change*. Retrieved from http://unfccc.int/resource/docs/convkp/kpeng.html (20 January 2011).

Labour Party (1995) *Peace at Home: A Labour Party Consultation on the Elimination of Domestic and Sexual Violence against Women*. London: Labour Party.

Laclau, Ernesto and Chantal Mouffe (1985) *Hegemony and Socialist Strategy*. London: Verso.

Lash, Scott (1996) 'Postmodern ethics: The missing ground', *Theory, Culture and Society*, 13 (2): 91–104.

Ledwith, Sue and Fiona Colgan (eds) (1996) *Women in Organizations: Challenging Gender Politics*. Basingstoke: Macmillan.

Lees, Sue (1996) *Carnal Knowledge: Rape on Trial*. London: Hamish Hamilton.

Le Grand, Julian (2007) *The Other Invisible Hand: Delivering Public Services through Choice and Competition*. Princeton: Princeton University Press.

Leibfried, Stephan and Paul Pierson (eds) (1995) *European Social Policy: Between Fragmentation and Integration*. Washington, DC: Brookings.

Levy, Ariel (2006) *Female Chauvinist Pigs: Women and the Rise of Raunch Culture*. London: Pocket Books.

Lewenhak, Sheila (1977) *Women and Trade Unions: An Outline History of Women in the British Trade Union Movement*. London: Ernest Benn.

Lewis, Jane (1992) 'Gender and the development of welfare regimes', *Journal of European Social Policy*, 3: 159–73.

Lewis, Ruth, Rebecca E. Dobash, Russell Dobash and Kate Cavanagh (2001) 'Law's progressive potential: The value of engagement with the law for domestic violence', *Social and Legal Studies*, 10 (1): 105–30.

Liddington, Jill and Jill Norris (1978) *One Hand Tied behind Us: The Rise of the Women's Suffrage Movement*. London: Virago.

Lombardo, Emanuela (2005) 'Integrating or setting the agenda? Gender mainstreaming in the European Constitution-making process', *Social Politics*, 12 (3): 412–32.

Lombardo, Emanuela and Mieke Verloo (2009) 'Institutionalizing intersectionality in the European Union? Policy developments and contestations', *International Feminist Journal of Politics*, 11 (4): 478–95.

Lombardo, Emanuela, Petra Meier and Mieke Verloo (eds) (2009) *The Discursive Politics of Gender Equality: Stretching, Bending and Policymaking*. London: Routledge.

London Feminist Network (2011) *Home Page*. Retrieved from http://londonfeministnetwork.org.uk/ (20 January 2011).

Lorber, Judith (2000) 'Using gender to undo gender: A feminist degendering movement', *Feminist Theory*, 1 (1): 79–95.

Lovenduski, Joni (2005) *Feminizing Politics*. Cambridge: Polity.

Lovenduski, Joni (ed.) (2005) *State Feminism and Political Representation*. Cambridge: Cambridge University Press.

Lovenduski, Joni and Pippa Norris (ed.) (1993) *Gender and Party Politics*. London: Sage.

Lovenduski, Joni and Vicky Randall (1993) *Contemporary Feminist Politics: Women and Power in Britain*. Oxford: Oxford University Press.

Lovett, Jo, Linda Regan and Liz Kelly (2004) *Sexual Assault Referral Centres: Developing Good Practice and Maximising Potentials*. Home Office Research Study 285. London: Home Office.

Low Pay Commission (2011) Retrieved from http://www.lowpay.gov.uk/ (20 January 2011).

MacKinnon, Catharine (1989) *Toward a Feminist Theory of the State*. Cambridge, MA: Harvard University Press.

Maddison, Angus (2003) *The World Economy: Historical Statistics*. Paris: OECD.

Maffesoli, Michel (1996) *The Time of Tribes: The Decline of Individualism in Mass Society*. London: Sage.

Mann, Michael (2003) *Incoherent Empire*. London: Verso.

Mansbridge, Jane (2005) 'Quota problems: Combating the dangers of essentialism', *Politics and Gender*, 1 (4): 622–37.

Manza, Jeff and Clem Brooks (1998) 'The gender gap in US Presidential elections: When? Why? Implications?', *American Journal of Sociology*, 103 (5): 1235–66.

Marchand, Marianne H. (1996) 'Reconceptualising "gender and development" in an era of "globalization"', *Millennium: Journal of International Studies*, 25 (3): 577–603.

Marshall, Thomas Humphrey (1950) *Citizenship and Social Class*. Cambridge: Cambridge University Press.

Marty, Martin and Appleby R. Scott (eds) (1993) *Fundamentalisms and Society*. Chicago: University of Chicago Press.

Matthews, Nancy (1994) *Confronting Rape: The Feminist Anti-Rape Movement and the State*. London: Routledge.

Mayer, Ann Elizabeth (1995) 'Cultural particularism as a bar to women's human rights: Reflections on the Middle Eastern experience', in Julie Peters and Andrea Wolper (eds), *Women's Rights, Human Rights: International Feminist Perspectives*, pp. 176–88. London: Routledge.

Mazey, Sonia (2000) 'Introduction: Integrating gender – Intellectual and "real world" mainstreaming', *Journal of European Public Policy*, 7 (3): 333–45.

Mazur, Amy (2002) *Theorizing Feminist Policy*. Oxford: Oxford University Press.

McAdam, Doug, Sidney Tarrow and Charles Tilly (2001) *Dynamics of Contention*. Cambridge: Cambridge University Press.

McCall, Leslie (2005) 'The complexity of intersectionality', *Signs*, 30 (3): 1771–800.

McCarthy, John D. and Mayer N. Zald (1977) 'Resource mobilization and social movements: A partial theory', *American Journal of Sociology*, 82: 1212–41.

McRobbie, Angela (2008) *The Aftermath of Feminism: Gender, Culture and Social Change*. London: Sage.

Medaglia, Azadeh (2000) *Patriarchal Structures and Ethnicity*. Aldershot: Ashgate.

Meehan, Elizabeth and Sevenhuijsen, Selma (eds) (1991) *Equality Politics and Gender*. London: Sage.

Melucci, Alberto (1989) *Nomads of the Present: Social Movements and Individual Needs in Contemporary Society*. London: Hutchinson.

Menon, Nivedita (2002) 'Universalism without foundations?', *Economy and Society*, 31 (1): 152–69.

Meyer, John W., John Boli, George, M. Thomas and Francisco O. Ramirez (1997) 'World society and the nation–state', *American Journal of Sociology*, 103 (1): 144–81.

Meyer, Mary K. and Elisabeth Prügl (eds) (1999) *Gender Politics in Global Governance*. Lanham, MD: Rowman and Littlefield.

Middleton, Lucy (ed.) (1977) *Women in the Labour Movement: The British Experience*. London: Croom Helm.

Mies, Maria (1986) *Patriarchy and Accumulation on a World Scale: Women in the International Division of Labour*. London: Zed Books.

Mies, Maria and Vandana Shiva (1993) *Ecofeminism*. London: Zed Books.

Miller, Peter and Nikolas Rose (1990) 'Governing economic life', *Economy and Society*, 19 (1): 1–31.

Millett, Kate (1977) *Sexual Politics*. London: Virago.

Million Women Rise (2011) *Home Page*. Retrieved from http://www.million womenrise.com/ (20 January 2011).

Mirza, Heidi Safia (ed.) (1997) *Black British Feminism: A Reader*. London: Routledge.

Mitleton-Kelly, Eve (2003) *Complex Systems and Evolutionary Perspectives* on *Organisations: The Application of Complexity Theory to Organisations.* Oxford: Elsevier.

Mitter, Swasti (1986) *Common Fate, Common Bond: Women in the Global Economy.* London: Pluto.

Moghadam, Valentine M. (ed.) (1994) *Identity Politics and Women: Cultural Reassertions and Feminisms in International Perspective.* Boulder, CO: Westview Press.

Moghadam, Valentine M. (1996a) 'The fourth world conference on women: dissension and consensus', *Indian Journal of Gender Studies*, 3 (1): 93–102.

Moghadam, Valentine M. (ed.) (1996b) *Patriarchy and Development.* Oxford: Clarendon Press.

Moghadam, Valentine M. (1998) 'Feminisms and development', *Gender and History*, 10 (3): 590–7.

Moghadam, Valentine M. (2000) 'Transnational feminist networks: Collective action in an era of globalization', *International Sociology*, 15 (1): 57–85.

Moghadam, Valentine M. (2005) *Globalizing Women: Transnational Feminist Networks.* Baltimore: John Hopkins University Press.

Mohanty, Chandra Talpade (1991) 'Under western eyes: Feminist scholarship and colonial discourses', in Chandra Talpade Mohanty, Ann Russo and Lourdes Torres (eds), *Third World Women and the Politics of Feminism*, pp. 51–80. Bloomington: Indiana University Press.

Monbiot, George (2006) *Heat: How to Stop the Planet Burning.* London: Allen Lane.

Moore, Barrington, Jr. (1966) *Social Origins of Dictatorship and Democracy.* Harmondsworth: Penguin.

Morgan, Robin (ed.) (1970) *Sisterhood Is Powerful: An Anthology of Writings from the Women's Liberation Movement.* New York: Vintage Books.

Morrell, Caroline (1981) *"Black Friday" and Violence against Women in the Suffragette Movement.* London: Women's Research and Resources Centre.

Moser, Caroline (1993) *Gender Planning and Development: Theory, Practice and Training.* London: Routledge.

Moser, Caroline (2005) 'Has gender mainstreaming failed?' *International Feminist Journal of Politics*, 7 (4): 576–90.

Mósesdóttir, Lilja and Rósa G. Erlingsdóttir (2005) 'Spreading the word across Europe: Gender mainstreaming as a political and policy project', *International Feminist Journal of Politics*, 7 (4): 513–31.

Mósesdóttir, Lilja (2011) 'Gender inequalities in the knowledge society', *Gender, Work and Organization*, 18 (1): 30–47.

National Alliance of Women's Organizations (NAWO) (2011) *Home Page.* Retrieved from http://www.nawo.org.uk/ (20 January 2011).

National Organization for Women (2011) *About Now.* Retrieved from http://www.now.org/organization/info.html (20 January 2011).

National Union of Students (NUS) Women's Campaign (2011) *Home Page.* Retrieved from www.officeronline.co.uk/women (20 January 2011).

Nelson, Barbara J. and Nalma Chowdhury (eds) (1994) *Women and Politics Worldwide*. New Haven: Yale University Press.

Norris, Pippa (1996a) 'Women politicians: Transforming Westminster?', *Parliamentary Affairs*, 49 (1): 89–102.

Norris, Pippa (1996b) 'Mobilising the "Women's Vote": The gender-generation gap in voting behaviour', *Parliamentary Affairs*, 49 (2): 333–42.

Norris, Pippa and Joni Lovenduski (1995) *Political Recruitment: Gender, Race and Class in the British Parliament*. Cambridge: Cambridge University Press.

Nussbaum, Martha C. (2000a) *Sex and Justice*. New York: Oxford University Press.

Nussbaum, Martha C. (2000b) *Women and Human Development: The Capabilities Approach*. Cambridge: Cambridge University Press.

Oakley, Ann (1974) *The Sociology of Housework*. Oxford: Martin Robertson.

Object (2011a) *Home Page*. Retrieved from http://www.object.org.uk/index.php/home (20 January 2011).

Object (2011b) *Criminal Records for Punters*. Retrieved from http://www.object.org.uk/index.php/component/content/article/3-news/98-press-release-criminal-records-for-punters-from-april-1st (20 January 2011).

O'Cinneide, Colm (2002) *A Single Equality Body: Lessons from Abroad*. Manchester: Equal Opportunities Commission, Commission for Racial Equality and Disability Rights Commission.

O'Cinneide, Colm (2007) 'The Commission for Equality and Human Rights: A new institution for new and uncertain times', *Industrial Law Journal*, 36 (2): 141–62.

O'Connor, Julia S., Ann Shola Orloff and Sheila Shaver (1999) *States, Markets, Families: Gender, Liberalism and Social Policy in Australia, Canada, Great Britain and the United States*. Cambridge: Cambridge University Press.

Office for National Statistics (ONS) (2007) *Report from the Review of Equality Data*. London: ONS.

Ohlander, Ann-Sofie (1991) 'The invisible child? The struggle for a Social Democratic family policy', in Gisela Bock and Pat Thane (eds), *Maternity and Gender Policies: Women and the Rise of the European Welfare States 1880s–1950s*, pp. 60–72. London: Routledge.

Ohmae, Kenichi (1995) *The End of the Nation State: The Rise of Regional Economics*. London: HarperCollins.

Okin, Susan Moller (1999) *Is Multiculturalism Bad for Women?* Princeton: Princeton University Press.

Orloff, Ann Shola (1993) 'Gender and the social rights of citizenship: The comparative analysis of state policies and gender relations', *American Sociological Review*, 58 (3): 308–28.

Outshoorn, Joyce and Kantola, Johanna (eds) (2007) *Changing State Feminism*. Basingstoke: Palgrave Macmillan.

Pahl, Jan (ed.) (1985) *Private Violence and Public Policy: The Needs of Battered Women and the Response of the Public Services*. London: Routledge.

Paine, Thomas (1984) *The Rights of Man*. Harmondsworth: Penguin.

Pascual Serrano, Amparo and Ute Behning (eds) (2001) *Gender Mainstreaming in the European Employment Strategy*. Brussels: European Trade Union Institute.

Penna Sue and Martin O'Brien (2006) 'What price social and health care? Commodities, competition and consumers', *Social Work and Society*, 4 (2): 217–31.

Perez, Carlota (2009) 'The double bubble at the turn of the century: Technological roots and structural implications', *Cambridge Journal of Economics*, 33, 779–805.

Perrons, Diane (2005) 'Gender mainstreaming in European Union policy: Why now?', *Social Politics*, 12 (3): 389–411.

Peters, Julie and Andrea Wolper (eds) (1995) *Women's Rights, Human Rights: International Feminist Perspectives*. London: Routledge.

Peterson, V. Spike (1996) 'The politics of identification in the context of globalization', *Women's Studies International Forum*, 19 (1/2): 5–15.

Peterson, V. Spike and Anne Sisson Runyan (1999) *Global Gender Issues*. Boulder, Colorado: Westview Press.

Phillips, Anne (1995) *The Politics of Presence: The Political Representation of Gender, Ethnicity, and Race*. Oxford: Clarendon Press.

Phillips, Anne (1999) *Which Equalities Matter?* Cambridge: Polity.

Phillips, Trevor (2008) 'An undeclared war on women', *New Statesman*, 24 March. Retrieved from http://www.newstatesman.com/life-and-society/2008/03/rape-women-violence-equality (20 January 2011).

Phizacklea, Annie (1990) *Unpacking the Fashion Industry*. London: Routledge.

Phoenix, A. and P. Pattynama (2006) 'Editorial: Intersectionality', *European Journal of Women's Studies*, 13(3): 187–92.

Pietilä, Hilkka (1996) *Making Women Matter: The Role of the United Nations*. London: Zed Books.

Pillinger, Jane (1992) *Feminising the Market: Women's Pay and Employment in the European Community*. Basingstoke: Macmillan.

Pillinger, Jane (2005) 'Pay equity now! International gender mainstreaming and gender pay equity in the public services', *International Feminist Journal of Politics*, 7 (4): 591–9.

Piven, Frances Fox and Richard A. Cloward (2000) 'Power repertoires and globalization', *Politics and Society*, 28 (3): 413–30.

PLS Ramboll Management (2002) *Specialised Bodies to Promote Equality and/ or Combat Discrimination*. Copenhagen: PLS Ramboll.

Plumwood, Val (1993) *Feminism and the Mastery of Nature*. London: Routledge.

Polanyi, Karl (1957) *The Great Transformation: The Political and Economic Origins of Our Time*. Boston: Beacon Press.

Pollack, Mark A. and Emilie Hafner-Burton (2000) 'Mainstreaming gender in the European Union', *Journal of European Public Policy*, 7 (3): 432–56.

Pollert, Anna (1996) 'Gender and class revisited', *Sociology*, 30 (4): 639–59.

Potter, David, David Goldblatt, Margaret Kiloh and Paul Lewis (eds) (1997) *Democratization*. Cambridge: Polity.

Press for Change (2010) *Home Page*. Retrieved from http://www.pfc.org.uk/.

Qvist, Gunnar (1980) 'Policy towards women and the women's struggle in Sweden', *Scandinavian Journal of History*, 5: 51–74.

Rai, Shirin M. (ed.) (2000) *International Perspectives on Gender and Democratization*. Basingstoke: Macmillan.

Rai, Shirin M. (ed.) (2003) *Mainstreaming Gender, Democratising the State? Institutional Mechanisms for the Advancement of Women*. Manchester: Manchester University Press.

Ramirez, Francisco O., Yasemin Soysal and Suzanne Shanahan (1997) 'The changing logic of political citizenship: Cross-national acquisition of women's suffrage rights, 1890–1990', *American Sociological Review*, 62: 735–45.

Randall, Vicky (2000) 'Childcare policy in the European states: Limits to convergence', *Journal of European Public Policy*, 7 (3): 346–68.

Rankin, Katharine N. (2001) 'Governing development: Neoliberalism, microcredit, and rational economic woman', *Economy and Society*, 30 (1): 18–37.

Rao, Arati (1995) 'The politics of gender and culture in international human rights discourse', in Julie Peters and Andrea Wolper (eds), *Women's Rights, Human Rights: International Feminist Perspectives*, pp. 167–75. London: Routledge.

Rape Crisis, England and Wales (2011) *Home Page*. Retrieved from http://www.rapecrisis.org.uk/ (20 January 2011).

Rawls, John (1978) *A Theory of Justice*. Oxford: Oxford University Press.

Redfern, Catherine and Kristin Aune (2010) *Reclaiming the f Word: The New Feminist Movement*. London: Zed Books.

Rees, Teresa (1998) *Mainstreaming Equality in the European Union: Education, Training and Labour Market Policies*. London: Routledge.

Rees, Teresa (2005) 'Reflections on the uneven development of gender mainstreaming', *International Feminist Journal of Politics*, 7 (4): 555–74.

Rights of Women (2011) *Home Page*. Retrieved from www.rightsofwomen.org.uk (20 January 2011).

Risman, Barbara J. (2004) 'Gender as a social structure: Theory wrestling with activism', *Gender and Society*, 18 (4): 429–50.

Risse, Thomas (1999) 'International norms and domestic change: Arguing and communicative behaviour in the human rights area', *Politics and Society*, 27 (4): 529–59.

Roberts, J. Timmons and Bradley C. Parks (2007) *A Climate of Injustice: Global Inequality, North–South Politics, and Climate Policy*. Cambridge, MA: MIT Press.

Robinson, William I. (2004) *A Theory of Global Capitalism*. Baltimore: John Hopkins University Press.

Roggeband, Conny and Mieke Verloo (2006) 'Evaluating gender impact assessment in the Netherlands (1994–2004): A political process approach', *Policy and Politics*, 34 (4): 615–32.

Roseneil, Sasha (1995) *Disarming Patriarchy: Feminism and Political Action at Greenham Common*. Buckingham: Open University Press.

Rossilli, Mariagrazia (1997) 'The European Community's policy on the equality of women: From the Treaty of Rome to the present', *The European Journal of Women's Studies*, 4 (1): 63–82.

Rowbotham, Sheila (1997) *A Century of Women: The History of Women in Britain and the United States*. London: Penguin.

Rowbotham, Sheila and Stephanie Linkogle (eds) (2000) *Women Resist Globalization: Mobilizing for Livelihood and Rights*. London: Zed Books.

Rubery, Jill, Mark Smith and Colette Fagan (1999) *Women's Employment in Europe: Trends and Prospects*. London: Routledge.

Sainsbury, Diane (1996) *Gender, Equality and Welfare States*. Cambridge: Cambridge University Press.

Sandel, Michael J. (1998) *Liberalism and the Limits of Justice*, 2nd edn. Cambridge: Cambridge University Press.

Sassen, Saskia (2001) *The Global City: New York, London, Tokyo*, 2nd edn. Princeton, NJ: Princeton University Press.

Sassen, Saskia (2006) *Territory. Authority. Rights. From Medieval to Global Assemblages*. Princeton: Princeton University Press.

Sawyers, Traci M. and David S. Meyer (1999) 'Missed opportunities: Social movement abeyance and public policy', *Social Problems*, 46 (2): 187–206.

Sayer, Andrew (1997) 'Essentialism, social constructionism and beyond', *Sociological Review*, 45 (3): 453–87.

Sayer, Andrew (2000) 'System, life-world and gender: Associational versus counterfactual thinking', *Sociology*, 34: 707–25.

Scottish Women's Aid (2011) *Home Page*. Retrieved from http://www.scottishwomensaid.org.uk/ (20 January 2011).

Scholte, Jan Aarte (2000) *Globalization: A Critical Introduction*. Basingstoke: Macmillan.

Scharpf, Fritz W. (1997) 'Economic integration, democracy and the welfare state', *Journal of European Public Policy*, 4 (1): 18–36.

Scott, Joan W. (1988) 'Deconstructing equality-versus-difference: Or, the uses of poststructuralist theory for feminism', *Feminist Studies*, 14 (1): 33–49.

Sen, Amartya (1999) *Development as Freedom*. Oxford: Oxford University Press.

Sen, Amartya (2009) *The Idea of Justice*. London: Allen Lane.

Sen, Gita (2000) 'Gender mainstreaming in finance ministries', *World Development*, 28 (7): 1370–90.

Sen, Purna (1998) 'A basket of resources: Women's resistance to domestic violence in Calcutta'. Unpublished PhD thesis, University of Bristol.

Sevenhuijsen, Selma (1998) *Citizenship and the Ethics of Care.* London: Routledge.

Shaheed, Farida (2010) *Report of the Independent Expert in the Field of Cultural Rights to the Human Rights Council.* Geneva: United Nations Human Rights Council. Retrieved from http://www2.ohchr.org/english/bodies/hrcouncil/docs/14session/A.HRC.14.36_en.pdf (18 June 2010).

Sharp, Rhonda and Ray Broomhill (2002) 'Budgeting for equality: The Australian experience', *Feminist Economics*, 8 (1): 25–47.

Shaw, Jenny and Diane Perrons (eds) (1995) *Making Gender Work: Managing Equal Opportunities.* Buckingham: Open University Press.

Shaw, Jo (2002) 'The European Union and gender mainstreaming: Constitutionally embedded or comprehensively marginalised?' *Feminist Legal Studies*, 10: 213–26.

Shaw, Jo (2005) 'Mainstreaming equality and diversity in European Union law and policy', *Current Legal Problems*, 58 (1): 255–312.

Shepherd, Laura J. (2008) *Gender, Violence and Security: Discourse as Practice.* London: Zed Books.

Shire, Karen (2007) 'Gender and the conceptualization of the knowledge economy in comparison', in Sylvia Walby, Heidi Gottfried, Karin Gottschall and Mari Osawa (eds), *Gendering the Knowledge Economy*, pp. 51–77. London: Palgrave.

Shiva, Vandana (2005) *Globalization's New Wars: Seed, Water and Life Forms.* New Delhi: Women Unlimited.

Showden, Carisa (2009) 'What's political about the new feminisms?' *Frontiers*, 30 (2): 166–98.

Shugart, Helene A., Catherine Egley Waggoner, and D. Lynn O'Brien Hallstein (2001) 'Mediating third-wave feminism: Appropriation as postmodern media practice', *Critical Studies in Media Communication*, 18 (2): 194–210.

Silliman, Jael (1999) 'Expanding civil society: Shrinking political spaces – The case of women's nongovernmental organizations', *Social Politics*, 6 (1): 23–53.

Skjeie, Hege (1991) 'The rhetoric of difference: On women's inclusion into political elites', *Politics and Society*, 2: 233–63.

Skocpol, Theda (1995) *Protecting Soldiers and Mothers: Political Origins of Social Policy in the United States.* Cambridge, MA: Harvard University Press.

Smart, Carol (1989) *Feminism and the Power of Law.* London: Routledge.

Smith, Anthony D. (1986) *The Ethnic Origins of Nations.* Oxford: Blackwell.

Smith, Mark and Paola Villa (2010) 'The ever-declining role of gender equality in the European Employment Strategy', *Industrial Relations Journal*, 41 (6): 526–43.

Snider, Laureen (2003) 'Constituting the punishable woman: Atavistic man incarcerates postmodern women', *British Journal of Criminology*, 43: 354–78.

Snow, David A., E. Burke Rochford, Steven K. Worden and Robert D. Benford (1986) 'Frame alignment processes, micromobilization, and movement participation', *American Sociological Review*, 51: 464–81.

Snyder, M. (2003) 'Women determine development: The unfinished revolution', *Signs*, 29 (2): 619–32.

Soros, George (2008) *The New Paradigm for Financial Markets: The Credit Crisis of 2008 and What It Means.* London: Public Affairs.

Southall Black Sisters (2011) *Home Page.* Retrieved from http://www.southallblacksisters.org.uk/ (20 January 2011).

Soysal, Nuhoglu Yasemin (1994) *The Limits of Citizenship: Migrants and Postnational Membership in Europe.* Chicago: University of Chicago Press.

Sparr, Pamela (ed.) (1994) *Mortgaging Women's Lives: Feminist Critiques of Structural Adjustment.* London: Zed Books.

Spellman, Elizabeth V. (1988) *Inessential Woman: Problems of Exclusion in Feminist Thought.* Boston: Beacon Press.

Spender, Dale (1983) *Women of Ideas and What Men Have Done to Them.* London: Ark.

Sperling, Valerie, Myra Marx Ferree and Barbara Risman (2001) 'Constructing global feminism: Transnational advocacy networks and Russian women's activism', *Signs*, 26 (4): 1155–86.

Springer, Kimberly (2002) 'Third wave black feminism?', *Signs*, 27 (4): 1059–82.

Squires, Judith (1999) *Gender in Political Theory.* Cambridge: Polity.

Squires, Judith (2005) 'Is mainstreaming transformative? Theorizing mainstreaming in the context of diversity and deliberation', *Social Politics*, 12 (3): 366–88.

Squires, Judith (2007) *The New Politics of Gender Equality.* London: Palgrave Macmillan.

Squires, Judith (2009) 'Intersecting inequalities: Britain's Equality Review', *International Feminist Journal of Politics*, 11 (4): 496–512.

Squires, Judith and Mark Wickham-Jones (2001) *Women in Parliament: A Comparative Analysis.* Manchester: Equal Opportunities Commission.

Squires, Judith and Mark Wickham-Jones (2004) 'New Labour, gender mainstreaming and the Women and Equality Unit', *British Journal of Politics and International Relations*, 6 (1): 81–98.

Stamatopolou, Elissavet (1995) 'Women's rights and the United Nations', in Julie Peters and Andrea Wolper (eds), *Women's Rights, Human Rights: International Feminist Perspectives*, pp. 36–48. London: Routledge.

Standing, Guy (1999) *Global Labour Flexibility: Seeking Distributive Justice.* Basingstoke: Macmillan.

Stanko, Elizabeth (1988) 'Keeping women in and out of line: Sexual harassment and occupational segregation', in Sylvia Walby (ed.), *Gender Segregation at Work*, pp. 91–9. Milton Keynes: Open University Press.

Stern, Nicholas (2007) *The Economics of Climate Change: The Stern Review*. Cambridge: Cambridge University Press.

Stetson, Dorothy McBride (ed.) (2002) *Abortion Movements, Women's Politics and the Democratic State: A Comparative Study of State Feminism*. Oxford: Oxford University Press.

Stetson, Dorothy McBride and Amy Mazur (eds) (1995) *Comparative State Feminism*. Oxford: Oxford University Press.

Stiglitz, Joseph E. (2002) *Globalization and Its Discontents*. London: Allen Lane.

Stiglitz, Joseph E. (2006) *Making Globalization Work*. London: Penguin.

Stonewall (2011) *Home Page*. Retrieved from http://www.stonewall.org.uk/ (20 January 2011).

Strachey, Ray (1979) *The Cause: A Short History of the Women's Movement in Great Britain* [1929]. London: Virago.

Stratigaki, Maria (2004) 'The cooption of gender concepts in EU policies: The case of the "reconciliation of work and family"', *Social Politics*, 11 (1): 30–56.

Strauss-Kahn, Dominique (2010) 'Europe's growth challenges'. Retrieved from http://www.imf.org/external/np/speeches/2010/111910.htm (20 January 2011).

Streeck, Wolfgang (1992) *Social Institutions and Economic Performance: Studies of Industrial Relations in Advanced Capitalist Economies*. London: Sage.

Sybylla, Roe (2001) 'Hearing whose voice? The ethics of care and the practices of liberty: A critique', *Economy and Society*, 30 (1): 66–84.

Tasker, Yvonne and Diane Negra (eds) (2007) *Interrogating Postfeminism: Gender and the Politics of Popular Culture*. Durham, NC: Duke University Press.

Taylor, Charles (ed.) (1994) *Multiculturalism: Examining the Politics of Recognition*. Princeton: Princeton University Press.

Taylor, Verta (1989) 'Social movement continuity: The women's movement in abeyance', *American Sociological Review*, 54: 761–75.

Taylor-Browne, Julie (ed.) (2001) *What Works in Reducing Domestic Violence? A Comprehensive Guide for Professionals*. London: Whiting and Birch.

Theisen, Ann-Marie, Nadine Spoden, Mieke Verloo and Sylvia Walby (2005) *Beijing+10: Progress Made within the European Union. Report of the Luxembourg Presidency of the Council of the European Union*. Luxembourg: Ministry of Equal Opportunities.

Thomas, Sue (1991) 'The impact of women on state legislative policies', *Journal of Politics*, 53 (4): 958–76.

Tilly, Charles (1978) *From Mobilization to Revolution*. Reading, MA: Addison-Wesley.

Tilly, Charles (1990) *Coercion, Capital and European State*s, *a.d. 990–1992*. Oxford: Blackwell.

Titmuss, Richard (1972) *The Gift Relationship: From Blood to Social Policy.* New York: Vintage.

Toro, Maria Suarez (1995) 'Popularizing women's human rights at the local level: A grassroots methodology for setting the international agenda', in Julie Peters and Andrea Wolper (eds), *Women's Rights, Human Rights: International Feminist Perspectives*, pp. 189–94. London: Routledge.

Trades Union Congress (TUC) (2011a) *Home Page.* Retrieved from http://www.tuc.org.uk/ (20 January 2011).

Trades Union Congress (TUC) (2011b) *Equality Issues.* Retrieved from http://www.tuc.org.uk/equality/index.cfm?mins=383&minors=383 (20 January 2011).

Tronto, Joan (1993) *Moral Boundaries: A Political Argument for an Ethic of Care.* New York: Routledge.

True, Jacqui (2003) 'Mainstreaming gender in global public policy', *International Feminist Journal of Politics*, 5 (3): 368–96.

True, Jacqui and M. Mintrom (2001) 'Transnational networks and policy diffusion: The case of gender mainstreaming', *International Studies Quarterly*, 45 (1): 27–57.

Turner, Jackie and Liz Kelly (2009) 'Trade secrets: Intersections between diasporas and crime groups in the constitution of the human trafficking chain', *British Journal of Criminology*, 49 (2): 184–201.

UK Feminista (2011) *Home Page.* Retrieved from www.ukfeminista.org.uk (20 January 2011).

United Green Parties of Europe (2009) *A Green New Deal for Europe.* Retrieved from http://europeangreens.eu/menu/egp-manifesto/ (20 January 2011).

United Nations (1995) *Platform for Action.* Fourth World Conference on Women, Beijing, China: UNDAW. Retrieved from http://www.un.org/womenwatch/daw/beijing/platform/ (20 January 2011).

United Nations (2011) *UN Millennium Development Goals.* Retrieved from http://www.un.org/millenniumgoals/ (20 January 2011).

United Nations Development Programme (UNDP) (2009) *Human Development Report 2009.* New York: Palgrave Macmillan.

United Nations, Division for the Advancement of Women (UNDAW) (2009) *Violence Against Women: Handbook and Supplement for Legislation.* New York: UN. Retrieved from http://www.un.org/womenwatch/daw/vaw/v-handbook.htm (20 January 2011).

UN General Assembly (1993) *Declaration on the Elimination of Violence Against Women* Retrieved from http://www.un.org/documents/ga/res/48/a48r104.htm (20 January 2011).

UNIFEM (2000) *Progress of the World's Women.* Retrieved from http://www.unwomen.org/resources/progress-of-the-worlds-women/ (20 January 2011).

UN Secretary-General (2006) *In-Depth Study on All Forms of Violence against Women. Report to the General Assembly of the United Nations.* New

York: UN. Retrieved from http://www.un.org/womenwatch/daw/vaw/
SGstudyvaw.htm (20 January 2011).

UN Women (2011) *Home Page*. Retrieved from http://www.unwomen.org/
(20 January 2011).

UNISON (2009) *A Guide to Equality in UNISON*. London: UNISON.
Retrieved from http://www.unison.org.uk/file/Guide%20to%20equality
%20in%20UNISON.pdf (20 January 2011).

UNiTE (2011a) *UNiTE to End Violence Against Women*. Retrieved from
http://www.un.org/en/women/endviolence/ (20 January 2011).

UNiTE (2011b) *Equalities*. Retrieved from http://www.unitetheunion.org/
resources/equalities.aspx (20 January 2011).

Urry, John (2003) *Global Complexity*. Cambridge: Polity.

Urry, John (2011) *Climate Change and Society*. Cambridge: Polity.

Valiente, Celia (2007) 'Developing countries and new democracies matter:
An overview of research on state feminism worldwide', *Politics and Gender*,
3 (4): 530–41.

Valticos, Nicolas (1969) 'Fifty years of standard-setting activities by the
International Labour Organization', *International Labour Review*, 100 (3):
201–37.

van der Vleuten, Anna (2005) 'Pincers and prestige: Explaining the implementation of EU gender equality legislation', *Comparative European
Politics* 3: 464–88.

van Staveren, Irene (2002) 'Global finance and gender', in Albrecht
Schnabel and Jan Aart Scholte (eds), *Civil Society and Global Finance*,
pp. 228–46. London: Routledge.

Vargas, Virginia and Saskia Wieringa (1998), 'The triangles of empowerment: Processes and actors in the making of public policy', in Geertje
Lycklama à Nijeholt, Virginia Vargas, and Saskia Wieringa (eds), *Women's
Movements and Public Policy in Europe, Latin America and the Caribbean*,
pp. 3–23. New York: Garland.

Veitch, Janet (2005) 'Gender mainstreaming in the UK government',
International Feminist Journal of Politics, 7 (4): 600–6.

Verloo, Mieke (2001) 'Another velvet revolution? Gender mainstreaming
and the politics of implementation'. IWM Working Paper No. 5/2001.
Institute for Human Sciences, Vienna.

Verloo, Mieke (2005a) 'Mainstreaming gender equality in Europe: A critical
frame analysis approach', *The Greek Review of Social Research*, 117 (B):
11–34.

Verloo, Mieke (2005b) 'Reflections on the concept and practice of the
Council of Europe approach to gender mainstreaming', *Social Politics*, 12
(3): 344–65.

Verloo, Mieke (2006) 'Multiple inequalities, intersectionality and
the European Union', *European Journal of Women's Studies*, 13 (3):
211–28.

Vinnicombe, Susan (2004) 'The business case for women directors'. Paper presented to ESRC Gender Mainstreaming Seminar, DTI, London 2004.

Visser, Jelle (2006) 'Union membership statistics in 24 countries', *Monthly Labor Review* (January): 38–49.

Wacquant, Loïc (2009) *Punishing the Poor: The Neoliberal Government of Social Insecurity*. Durham: Duke University Press.

Wängnerud, Lena (2000) 'Testing the politics of presence: Women's representation in the Swedish Riksdag', *Scandinavian Political Studies*, 23 (1): 67–91.

Walby, Sylvia (1986) *Patriarchy at Work*. Cambridge: Polity.

Walby, Sylvia (1988) 'Gender politics and social theory', *Sociology*, 22 (2): 215–32.

Walby, Sylvia (1990) *Theorizing Patriarchy*. Oxford: Blackwell.

Walby, Sylvia (1992) 'Woman and nation', *International Journal of Comparative Sociology*, 33(1/2): 81–100.

Walby, Sylvia (1993) '"Backlash" in historical context', in Mary Kennedy, Cathy Lubelska and Val Walsh (eds), *Making Connections: Women's Studies, Women's Movements, Women's Lives*, pp. 79–89. London: Taylor and Francis.

Walby, Sylvia (1994) 'Is citizenship gendered?' *Sociology*, 28 (2): 379–95.

Walby, Sylvia (1997) *Gender Transformations*. London: Routledge.

Walby, Sylvia (1999a) 'The new regulatory state: The social powers of the European Union', *British Journal of Sociology*, 50 (1): 118–40.

Walby, Sylvia (1999b) 'The European Union and equal opportunities policies', *European Societies*, 1 (1): 59–80.

Walby, Sylvia (ed.) (1999c) *New Agendas for Women*. Basingstoke: Macmillan.

Walby, Sylvia (2000) 'Gender, globalization and democracy', *Gender and Development*, 8 (1): 20–8.

Walby, Sylvia (2001a) 'From community to coalition: The politics of recognition as the handmaiden of the politics of redistribution', *Theory, Culture and Society*, 18 (2/3): 113–35.

Walby, Sylvia (2001b) 'Gender mainstreaming in the European employment strategy: The British case', in Ute Behning and Amparo Serrano Pascual (eds), *Gender Mainstreaming in the European Employment Strategy*. Brussels: European Trade Union Institute.

Walby, Sylvia (2002) 'Feminism in a global era', *Economy and Society*, 31 (4): 533–57.

Walby, Sylvia (2003) 'The myth of the nation-state: Theorizing society and polities in a global era', *Sociology*, 37(1): 531–48.

Walby, Sylvia (2004a) 'The European Union and gender equality: Emergent varieties of gender regime', *Social Politics*, 11 (1): 4–29.

Walby, Sylvia (2004b) *The Cost of Domestic Violence*. London: Department of Trade and Industry, Women and Equality Unit.

Walby, Sylvia (2005) 'Gender mainstreaming: Productive tensions in theory and practice', *Social Politics*, 12 (3): 321–43.

Walby, Sylvia (2006) 'Gender approaches to nations and nationalism', in Gerard Delanty and Krishan Kumar (eds), *Handbook of Nations and Nationalism*, pp. 118–28. London: Sage.

Walby, Sylvia (2007) 'Complexity theory, systems theory and multiple intersecting social inequalities', *The Philosophy of the Social Sciences*, 37 (4): 449–70.

Walby, Sylvia (2009) *Globalization and Inequalities: Complexity and Contested Modernities*. London: Sage.

Walby, Sylvia (2010) 'Sen and the measurement of justice: Capabilities or equality'. Unpublished manuscript. Lancaster University, Mimeo.

Walby, Sylvia and Wendy Olsen (2002) *The Impact of Women's Position in the Labour Market on Pay and Implications for UK Productivity*. London: Department for Trade and Industry, Women and Equality Unit.

Walby, Sylvia, Heidi Gottfried, Karin Gottschall and Mari Osawa (eds) (2007) *Gendering the Knowledge Economy: Comparative Perspectives*. London: Palgrave.

Walby, Sylvia, Jo Armstrong and Leslie Humphreys (2008) *Review of Equality Statistics*. Manchester: Equality and Human Rights Commission.

Walby, Sylvia, Jo Armstrong and Sofia Strid (2010a) 'Intersectionality: Multiple inequalities in social theory'. Unpublished manuscript. Lancaster University.

Walby, Sylvia, Jo Armstrong and Sofia Strid (2010b) 'Intersectionality and the quality of the gender equality architecture'. Unpublished manuscript. Lancaster University.

Wallerstein, Immanuel (1974) *The Modern World-System: Capitalist Agriculture and the Origins of the European World-Economy in the Sixteenth Century*. New York: Academic Press.

Wallerstein, Immanuel (2004) *World-Systems Analysis: An Introduction*. Durham: Duke University Press.

Walter, Natasha (1999) *The New Feminism*. London: Virago.

Walter, Natasha (2010) *Living Dolls: The Return of Sexism*. London: Virago.

Ward, Margaret (1989) *Unmanageable Revolutionaries: Women and Irish Nationalism*. London: Pluto Press.

Waylen, Georgina (1996) *Gender in Third World Politics*. Buckingham: Open University Press.

Weeks, Jeffrey (2007) *The World We Have Won: The Remaking of Erotic and Intimate Life*. London: Routledge.

Weiler, J. H. H. (1997) 'The reformation of European Constitutionalism', *Journal of Common Market Studies*, 35 (1): 97–129.

Weldon, S. Laurel (2002) *Protest, Policy, and the Problem of Violence against Women: A Cross-National Comparison*. Pittsburgh: University of Pittsburgh Press.

Wenger, Etienne (1998) *Communities of Practice: Learning, Meaning and Identity*. Cambridge: Cambridge University Press.

Westmarland, Nicole (2004) 'Rape law reform in England and Wales'. Working Paper 7. Bristol: School of Policy Studies.

Westwood, Sallie (1984) *All Day, Every Day: Factory and Family in the Making of Women's Lives.* London: Pluto Press.

White Ribbon Campaign (2011) *Home Page.* Retrieved from www.white ribboncampaign.co.uk (20 January 2011).

Whitley, Richard (1999) *Divergent Capitalisms: The Social Structuring and Change of Business Systems.* New York and Oxford: Oxford University Press.

Willborn, Steven L. (1989) *A Secretary and a Cook: Challenging Women's Wages in the Courts of the United States and Great Britain.* Ithaca, NY: ILR Press, Cornell University.

Wobbe, Theresa (2003) 'From protecting to promoting: Evolving EU sex equality norms in an organizational field', *European Law Journal,* 9 (1): 88–108.

Wöhl, Stefanie (2008) 'Global governance as neoliberal governmentality: Gender mainstreaming in the European Employment Strategy', in Georgina Waylen and Shirin Rai (eds), *Global Governance: Feminist Perspectives,* pp. 64–83. London: Palgrave Macmillan.

Wolf, Naomi (1991) *The Beauty Myth: How Images of Beauty are used against Women.* London: Vintage Books.

Wollstonecraft, Mary (1992) [1972] *A Vindication of the Rights of Women.* London: Penguin.

Womankind (2011) *Home Page.* Retrieved from www.Womankind.org.uk (20 January 2011).

Women against Fundamentalism (2011) *Home Page.* Retrieved from http://www.womenagainstfundamentalism.org.uk/index.html (20 January 2011).

Women and Manual Trades (2011) *Home Page.* Retrieved from http://www.wamt.org/ (20 January 2011).

Women Demand (2006) *Feminist Seventies.* Retrieved from http://www.feministseventies.net/demandsx.html0 (20 January 2011).

Women into Politics (2011) *Home Page.* Retrieved from http://www.women intopolitics.org/ (20 January 2011).

Women Living under Muslim Laws (2011) *Home Page.* Retrieved from http://www.wluml.org/ (20 January 2011).

Women of Europe Newsletter (1999) No. 86 (May/June): p. 2.

Women's Aid, England (2011) *Home Page.* Retrieved from http://www.womensaid.org.uk/ (20 January 2011).

Women's Budget Group (2000) *Commentary on the Pre-Budget Report.* London: Women's Budget Group.

Women's Budget Group (2004) *Women's Budget Group Response to the 2004 Budget.* London: Women's Budget Group.

Women's Budget Group (2011) *Home Page.* Retrieved from http://www.wbg.org.uk/ (20 January 2011).

Women's International League for Peace and Freedom (2011) *Home Page*. Retrieved from http://www.wilpfinternational.org/ (20 January 2011).

Women's National Commission (WNC) (2008) *WNC Partners*. Retrieved from http://www.thewnc.org.uk/publications/cat_view/88-partners.html). (20 January 2011).

Women's National Commission (WNC) (2011) *Home Page*. Retrieved from http://www.thewnc.org.uk/ (20 January 2011).

Women's Resource Centre (2011) *Home Page*. Retrieved from www.wrc.org.uk (20 January 2011).

Women's Sports Foundation (2011) *Home Page*. Retrieved from http://www.womenssportsfoundation.org/ (20 January 2011).

Women's United Nations Report Network (WUNRN) (2011) *Home Page*. Retrieved from http://www.wunrn.com/ (20 January 2011).

Woodhead, Linda (2007) 'Gender differences in religious practice and significance', in James A. Beckford and N. J. Demerath III (eds), *The Sage Handbook of the Sociology of Religion*, pp. 550–70. London: Sage.

Woodiwiss, Anthony (1998) *Globalization, Human Rights and Labour Law in Pacific Asia*. Cambridge: Cambridge University Press.

Woodward, Alison (2003) 'European gender mainstreaming: Promises and pitfalls of transformative policy', *Review of Policy Research*, 20 (1): 65–88.

Woodward, Alison (2004) 'Building velvet triangles: Gender and informal governance', in Thomas Christiansen and Simona Piattoni (eds), *Informal Governance in the European Union*, pp. 76–93. Cheltenham: Edward Elgar.

Woodward, Alison (2008) 'Too late for gender mainstreaming? Taking stock in Brussels', *Journal of European Social Policy*, 18 (3): 289–302.

Woolf, Virginia (1938) *Three Guineas*. London: Harcourt, Brace and Ward.

World Bank (2007) *World Development Indicators*. April 2007 edition. Accessed at ESDS International (Mimas), Manchester University.

World Bank (2008) *World Development Indicators*, April 2008 edn. Washington, DC: World Bank.

World Bank (2010) *World DataBank: World Development Indicators*. Retrieved from http://databank.worldbank.org/ddp/home.do (22 September 2010).

World Economic Forum (2010) *The Global Gender Gap Report 2010*. Retrieved from http://www3.weforum.org/docs/WEF_GenderGap_Report_2010.pdf (20 January 2011).

World Health Organization (2007) *What is the Scale of the Obesity Problem in your Country?* Geneva: World Health Organization.

World Social Forum (2011) *Home Page*. Retrieved from http://www.forum socialmundial.org.br/index.php?cd_language=2 (20 January 2011).

Wright, Erik Olin (2010) *Envisioning Real Utopias*. London: Verso.

Yoko, Nuita, Yamaguchi Mitsuko and Kubo Kimiko (1994) 'The UN Convention on Eliminating Discrimination against Women and the status of women in Japan', in Barbara J. Nelson and Nalma Chowdhury (eds), *Women and Politics Worldwide*, pp. 398–414. New Haven: Yale University Press.

Young, Brigette (2000) 'Disciplinary neoliberalism in the European Union and gender politics', *New Political Economy*, 5 (1): 77–98.

Young, Iris Marion (1990) *Justice and the Politics of Difference*. Princeton, NJ: Princeton University Press.

Young, Iris Marion (1997) *Intersecting Voices: Dilemmas of Gender, Political Philosophy, and Policy*. Princeton, NJ: Princeton University Press.

Yuval-Davis, Nira (1997) *Gender and Nation*. London: Sage.

Yuval-Davis, Nira and Floya Anthias (eds) (1989) *Woman–Nation–State*. Basingstoke: Macmillan.

Zabalza, A. and Z. Tzannatos (1985) *Women and Equal Pay: The Effects of Legislation on Female Employment and Wages in Britain*. Cambridge: Cambridge University Press.

Zakaria, Fareed (2008) *The Post-American World*. New York: W. W. Norton.

Zeitlin, Jonathan and D. M. Trubek (eds) (2003) *Governing Work and Welfare in a New Economy: European and American Experiments*. Oxford: Oxford University Press.

Zero Tolerance (2011) *Home Page*. Retrieved from http://www.zero tolerance.org.uk/ (20 January 2011).

Zippel, Kathrin (2004) 'Transnational advocacy networks and policy cycles in the European Union: The case of sexual harassment', *Social Politics*, 11 (1): 57–85.

Zippel, Kathrin (2006) *The Politics of Sexual Harassment: A Comparative Study of the United States, European Union and Germany*. Cambridge: Cambridge University Press.

Index

Lightning Source UK Ltd.
Milton Keynes UK
UKOW05f1651071116
287063UK00008B/514/P